American Trails Series
XVII

CHIMNEY ROCK, NEBRASKA
Author's photo

The Wagon Trains of '44

A Comparative View of
the Individual Caravans
in the
Emigration of 1844 to Oregon

by
THOMAS A. RUMER

with Foreword by
MERRILL J. MATTES

THE ARTHUR H. CLARK COMPANY
Spokane, Washington   1990

LIBRARY OF CONGRESS CARD NUMBER 89–62716
ISBN 0–87062–197–1

Library of Congress Cataloging-in Publication Data
Rumer, Thomas A. The wagon trains of '44: a comparative view of the
individual caravans in the emigration of 1844 to Oregon/by Thomas A.
Rumer; with foreword by Merrill J. Mattes. 273 p.   cm. — (American trails
series; 17) Includes bibliographical references. ISBN 0-87062-197-1 (alk.
paper)   1. Overland journeys to the Pacific.   2. West (U.S.)—Description and travel—To 1848.   3. Oregon Trail.   4. Frontier and pioneer
life—West (U.S.) I. Title.   II. Series: American trail series; 17.
F592.R94 1989
917.804'2—dc20   89-62716
                                                                    CIP

To my parents, Ruth and Andy Rumer,
who are comfortable in the out-of-doors

Contents

Illustrations

Maps

Maps prepared by Thomas A. Rumer

Acknowledgements

Essential original source materials were made available, and permission to quote from them, by Thomas Osborn (the Jacob Hammer Journal); Elizabeth P. Jacox, Librarian, Idaho State Historical Society (the Edward Evans Parrish journal); Dr. Bonnie Hardwick, Head, Manuscripts Department, The Bancroft Library, University of California, Berkeley (the narratives by Edmund Bray, Asa Lovejoy, John Burch McClane, John Minto and Martha Ann Morrison Minto, Sidney W. Moss, Willard Hall Rees); Peggy Haines, Manuscripts Librarian, Oregon Historical Society Library (Alva Compton Riggs Shaw and William D. Stillwell). Rick Harmon, Editor, *Oregon Historical Quarterly*, and David L. Nicandri, Director, Washington Historical Society, granted permission for select quotes from publications of their agencies.

Library reference and other services were provided by: Judy Sheldon, Reference Librarian, California Historical Society; John Gonzales, Librarian, California Section, California State Library; Ann Reinert, Librarian, Nebraska Historical Society; Gordon Manning, Research and Reference Librarian, Oregon Historical Society; Lotte Larsen, Western Oregon State University.

Photo and map credits include: Beverly Elizabeth Lowe (Mr. and Mrs. John Minto and son); The California Historical Society (James Clyman); The Walters Art Gallery (Moses "Black" Harris by A. G. Miller); A. D. Ricketts (Robert Wilson Morrison); Lawrence Eno (Barnette/Bryan gravesite); Cy Eid (Hood River Valley scene); and the Polk County, Oregon, Historical Society (Mr. and Mrs. Nathaniel Ford).

Special acknowledgement is due Norma J. Eid, Tualatin, Oregon, who readily shared the results of her long search for information about emigrants of 1844 including her forebears the Neals (see Epilogue), and to historians Aubrey Haines and Merrill J. Mattes for critical readings of the manuscript.

Foreword
by Merrill J. Mattes

While the theme of the westward migrations of the mid-nineteenth century has always gripped the popular imagination, until recent years scholarly attention to the subject has been somewhat lackadaisical, with bare bones generalizations in textbooks of western history, and the publication of isolated overland journals often edited by someone with limited knowledge of trail history and geography. The first effort to research not one but several hundred overland journals as the basis for writing a history of the primary route—the main Platte and north Platte as far as Fort Laramie—was my *Great Platte River Road* (Nebraska State Historical Society, 1969). The first comprehensive scholarly treatment of the entire migration to the West Coast via the Oregon-California Trails complex, utilizing an even greater number of journals, was that by John D. Unruh, *The Plains Across* (University of Illinois Press, 1979). The impact of these two works has been to stimulate more intensive and accurate scholarly treatment of broader phases of the subject, as well as to improve the quality of journal-editing.

A few scholars have undertaken to examine selected single migration years. Professor Archer Butler Hulbert in his *Forty-Niners: the Chronicles of the California Trail* (Boston, 1931) made a stab in this direction and got a prize for stimulating public interest in the famous gold rush but his use of data from numerous authentic diaries was nullified by his devise of combining all diarists into one fictional company.

Dale M. Morgan was the true pioneer in this approach, setting a lofty standard of scholarship in his *Overland in 1846* (2 vols., Georgetown, California, 1953). Herbert Eaton examined *The Overland Trail to California in 1852* (New York, 1974), and Donna M. Wojick took care of what she calls *The Brazen Overlanders of 1845* (Portland, 1976). Now Thomas Rumer's book addresses the entire migration year 1844 and he does it magnificently.

In his classic *California Trails* (New York, 1962) George R. Stewart first examined and analyzed with professional acumen the 1844 migration, but with his main focus on the minority heading for California. Rumer's book is the first full-length review of the coincident Oregon migration. With an intimate knowledge of all known authoritative source materials, including the Jacob Hammer diary which Rumer himself discovered, he examines every facet of that migration—geographical, genealogical, chronological, and psychological—so that we are entitled to use here the term "definitive."

It breaks a scholar's heart to learn here that Willard Rees's journal of 1844 has been lost to posterity—he made the mistake of loaning it to someone—and his late period recollections were devoured by mice. Yet despite this loss and similar ones of other migration years that have been documented, the survival today of a fairly large body of emigrant narratives—diaries, journals, letters, and recollections—seems like a sequence of miracles—first that so many were actually written to begin with, and secondly, that so many of these accounts managed to survive the ravages of time, including fire, flood, or the simple loss of ancestral records by later uprooted generations.

We are just beginning to get a clear idea of approximately how many first hand accounts of central overland travel were written during the covered wagon era, 1841–1866. In my

Platte River Road Narratives (University of Illinois Press, 1988) I have identified over 2,000 such eye-witness accounts, excluding many of dubious merit, and a few I somehow missed despite an intensive nationwide search of known repositories. Also, despite this effort to identity "all known" overland accounts it is disconcerting to realize that the grand total may never be known for, surprisingly, more priceless records of the Great Migration keep right on surfacing, usually revealed to have been in exclusive private possession for as much as 150 years or the lapse of six generations. For example, since the publication of my bibliography—and in fact frequently tipped off by readers of this publication—I have learned of the existence of several more original diaries, or copies thereof, previously unknown to anyone except the owners.

Understandably, most of those recently revealed relate to the highly populous California gold rush climax period, 1849–1853, five years which account for over half of all Platte River Road travelers of the quarter century, 1841–1866. Conversely, the only recent discovery of an original diary written during the primary Oregon migrations, 1842–1848, is that by Rumer of the Hammer journal; the odds against another such exciting discovery now seem astronomical, considering the comparatively small number of early "Oregonians."

In my *Great Platte River Road* I calculated a total of 350,000 people who followed the Platte westward to various destinations, based on the combined evidence of some 700 eye-witness accounts. In my new book, with a much broader data base, including some surprising annual totals given by intelligent observers, I have upgraded the total to around 500,000. Accordingly, having examined and tallied the evidence of some 2,000 authentic and significant narratives, I have concluded that the frequency of record-keeping among covered wagon emigrants is on the order of one out of 250 for the entire twenty-five year period. However, during the brief climactic period of the California gold rush, 1849–1853, I estimate a total of 220,000 emigrants, while accounting for around 1,100 recorders, making a ratio of one out of 200, confirming my impression that during the gold rush the incidence of record-keeping (and reminiscing) was higher than for the later 'fifties and early 'sixties.

Compare the above with 1844. John Unruh tabulates about 1,500 people reaching Oregon that year, yet Rumer identifies around twenty testimonials for that season, a ratio of one to seventy-five! To me it is another miracle of sorts that the pioneers of 1844 seem to have had an even higher proportion of emigrant eye-witness recorders than that during the later great gold rush, given the fact that the earlier "Oregonians" had to follow a more primitive trail and, on balance, suffered distracting hardships and privations in even greater degree than the later "Californians."

Hitherto the 1844 migration year has not been a stand-out one in trail literature. Sandwiched between the famous 1843 cavalcade led (at least figuratively) and dramatized by the prophet-like Marcus Whitman, and the larger migration of 1845 immortalized by Joel Palmer, the 1844 version has hitherto received slight attention, with the exception of Stewart's focus on the contingent led by Elisha Stephens. Rumer may be credited now with finally putting 1844 in its proper perspective in the fateful decade which fulfilled the promise of Manifest Destiny.

While the 1844 California-bound emigrants were the first to find a way over the central Sierra Nevada—which would become the primary route of the Forty-niners—the Oregon pioneers were equally triumphant, being the first contingent of over 1,000 souls to Oregon and the first to bring a significant number of wagons to their destination, thus giving better

'44 in perspective

definition and credibility to the more difficult western half of
the true "Oregon Trail." Thus the way was finally cleared for
future "Oregonians," not only those of 1845 to 1848 but also
the respectable numbers of the 1850's who ignored the siren
call of California gold and turned to the Northwest.

It is important to stress another important but hitherto
little appreciated "first" to the credit of the emigrants of '44,
which is recognized by Rumer. That is, the company led by
Stephens was the first one of record (as distinct from fur
traders and missionaries) to jump off from Council Bluffs,
Iowa, and thus put them in a position to follow the route
along the north side of the Platte that later came to be
known as the "Council Bluffs Road." This happened to
coincide, in part, with the 1847 Mormon Pioneer Trail to
Utah. Historians generally have over-simplified things by
just calling the northern route "the Mormon Trail," and now
this trail has been enshrined by Act of Congress as the
Mormon Pioneer National Historic Trail. This lopsided accla-
mation of the northside "Mormon Trail," combined with
the myopic fascination of these same historians with the
southside "Oregon Trail," has resulted in the near oblitera-
tion of the important non-Mormon Council Bluffs Road in
western history writing. Yet the expanded data base reflected
in my *Platte River Road Narratives* demonstrates conclusively
that along the northside route non-Mormons outnumbered
Mormons by a ratio of at least five to one! Furthermore, an
analysis of all central overland accounts through 1866 leads
to another surprising conclusion: Of all the emigrants who
jumped off from various points along the Missouri River
—the two hundred-mile stretch between Council Bluffs and
the Kansas City areas—fully one-third or around 166,000
jumped off from Council Bluffs or neighboring Omaha! This
multitude, both publicized Mormons and un-publicized non-

Mormons, followed in the footsteps of the Stephens company of 1844!

By an incredible quirk of fate, among members of the migration who followed the southside Oregon Trail in 1844 was one who had been an early fur trader and as such became the first man of record, following the Stephen H. Long exploring party of 1820, to traverse what would become the Council Bluffs Road. As Rumer recognizes, this was James Clyman, in 1824 an employee of the Rocky Mountain Fur Company, along with Tom Fitzpatrick one of four who separated from the main party led by Jed Smith somewhere in the Rocky Mountains. They were compelled to cache their furs near Independence Rock and, straggling and starving down the North Platte and the Platte, became separated from each other along the route. Clyman, barely conscious, lurched toward and then collapsed at the gate of Fort Atkinson at the original "Council Bluffs" of Lewis and Clark. (Fitzpatrick and the others evidently found their way back to St. Louis by the southern route.) The so-called Returning Astorians under Robert Stuart in 1812 have been credited with "the discovery of the Oregon Trail," rightfully so because they reached the Missouri River by following the south side of the Platte. But it was James Clyman, 1844 emigrant, who in 1824 had followed the north side of the Platte to Council Bluffs. Thus, in retrospect, it seems that a case can be made that this record-keeping 1844 emigrant, because of his feat twenty years earlier, is entitled to recognition as "the discoverer of the Council Bluffs Road"!

The emigrants of '44 were among the earliest to behold the celebrated trail landmarks, notably Ash Hollow, Chimney Rock, Scotts Bluffs, Laramie Peak, and South Pass—all but Laramie Peak preserved and interpreted today by state or federal governments. Beyond South Pass the Stephens company inaugurated the first of the famous trail cut-offs, later called Sublette's Cutoff, a somewhat hazardous but direct way west to Green River, thus saving a lengthy detour via Fort Bridger. Ironically, it appears that the name, belonging to one of the noted Sublette brothers, should rightfully have been instead one or the other of the two ex-trapper guides with the Stephens company—Caleb Greenwood or one "Hitchcock."

There is need for a realistic reappraisal of other, more important, misleading trail terminology. I refer to the common use today of the term "Oregon Trail" to refer to the main route along the south side of the Platte. It is, of course, the correct term to use with Rumer's treatment of 1844 emigrants as well as other emigrants heading for Oregon through 1848. Beginning in 1849, however, the heavy majority of emigrants, for obvious reasons, refer only to the California Trail or, more often, "the California Road." Accordingly, today it is more accurate, therefore, to use the term Oregon-California Trail (or Trails) up to the point where the true Oregon Trail and the true California Trail parted company—at the mouth of the Raft River, tributary of the Snake River for some, or in the vicinity of Soda Springs for others who preferred an alleged short-cut to the Upper Raft River, the City of Rocks, and the headwaters of Humboldt River.

It may take an act of Congress—at any rate much more influence than I have been able to exert in my writings—to change both deplorable stereotypes, converting "Oregon Trail" to Oregon-California Trail(s), and rejuvenating the authentic Council Bluffs Road, at the same time leaving "the Mormon Trail" for the bona fide use of Mormons bound for Utah.

Perhaps the most memorable experience of emigrants

invading the wilderness was their joyful arrival at isolated trading posts or military forts. In 1844 Fort Kearny did not exist and Fort Bridger was just one year old. Fort Laramie and Fort Hall, however, were both then ten year old fur company establishments, the first operated by the American Fur Company, the latter by the Hudson's Bay Company which championed the acquisition of Oregon by Great Britain. Today Fort Hall has crumbled to dust but Fort Laramie (taken over by the U. S. Army in 1849), the most important human habitation along the entire length of the Oregon-California Trails complex, is preserved as Fort Laramie National Historic Site. Ten buildings still standing were mere shells or ruins when taken over by the National Park Service in 1938, but have now been restored to their pristine glory. While these structures post-date the emigration of 1844, at the south end of the parade ground is the preserved site of the trading post of 1844. To me—and I believe to thousands of others who flock to this place on their vacations—restored Fort Laramie—onetime trading post, military post, and wilderness haven for several hundred thousand covered wagon emigrants—is the ultimate memorial to "the winning of the West."

In conclusion, it is gratifying to note that, while the level of scholarship about the westward migrations has risen perceptibly in recent years—witness also the Arthur H. Clark multi-volume *Covered Wagon Women* series edited by Kenneth L. Holmes—thousands of laymen have been given fresh opportunities to express their interest in great western trails by becoming "trail activists." I refer to the new trail preservation movement, inspired not only by the authorization of federally protected "national historic trails" by the Congress of the United States but also to the new phenomenon of private citizens organizing to help preserve and interpret western trails as vital links in our American heritage. The pioneer of this movement is the Oregon-California Trails Association (OCTA) founded in 1982. The author and publisher of this book, as well as the undersigned, are among its over 1,500 present active members.

MERRILL J. MATTES

Littleton, Colorado, December, 1988

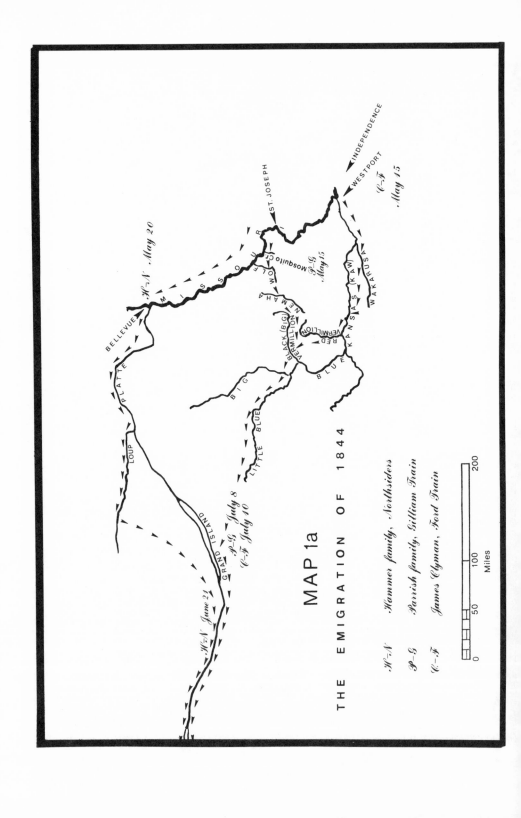

MAP 1a

THE EMIGRATION OF 1844

N.-N.   Hammer family, Northsiders

P.-G.   Parrish family, Gilliam Train

C.-F.   James Clyman, Ford Train

0   50   100   200
Miles

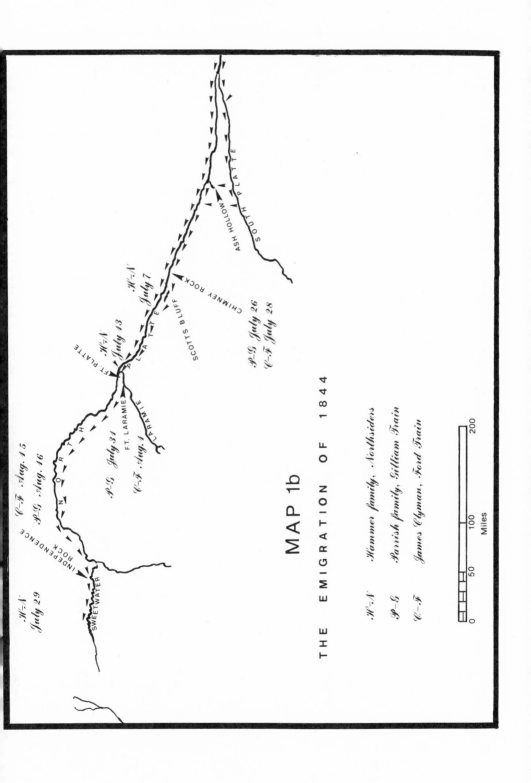

MAP 1b

THE EMIGRATION OF 1844

H–N   *Hammer family, Northsiders*

P–G   *Parrish family, Gilliam Train*

C–F   *James Clyman, Ford Train*

0   50   100   200

Miles

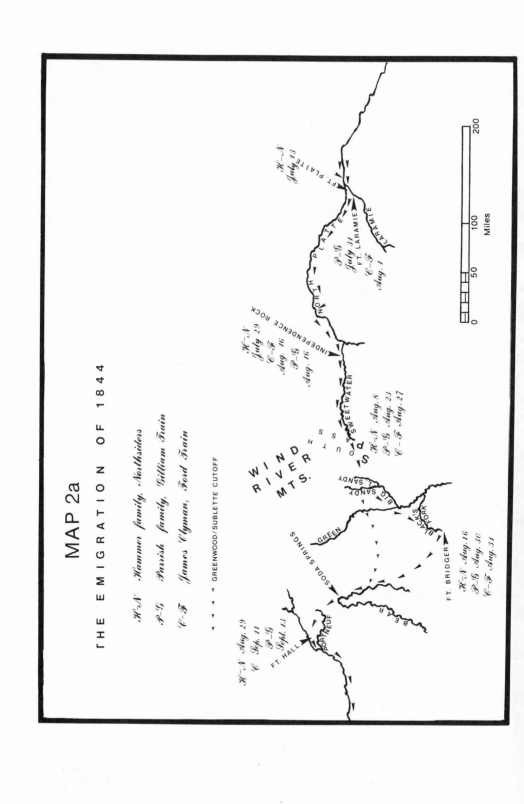

MAP 2a

THE EMIGRATION OF 1844

H–N   Hammer family, Northsiders

P–G   Parrish family, Gilliam Train

C–F   James Clyman, Ford Train

▾ ▾ ▾   GREENWOOD/SUBLETTE CUTOFF

FT. PLATTE

H–N
July 13

FT. LARAMIE

P–G
July 31
C–F
Aug. 1

NORTH PLATTE

INDEPENDENCE ROCK

H–N
July 29
C–F
Aug. 16
P–G
Aug. 16

SWEETWATER

SOUTH PASS

H–N Aug. 8
P–G Aug. 23
C–F Aug. 27

WIND
RIVER
MTS.

BIG SANDY

L. SANDY

GREEN

BLACKS
FORK

FT. BRIDGER

H–N Aug. 16
P–G Aug. 30
C–F Aug. 31

BEAR

SODA SPRINGS

PORTNEUF

FT. HALL

H–N Aug. 29
C Sept. 11
P–G Sept. 13

Miles

0   50   100   200

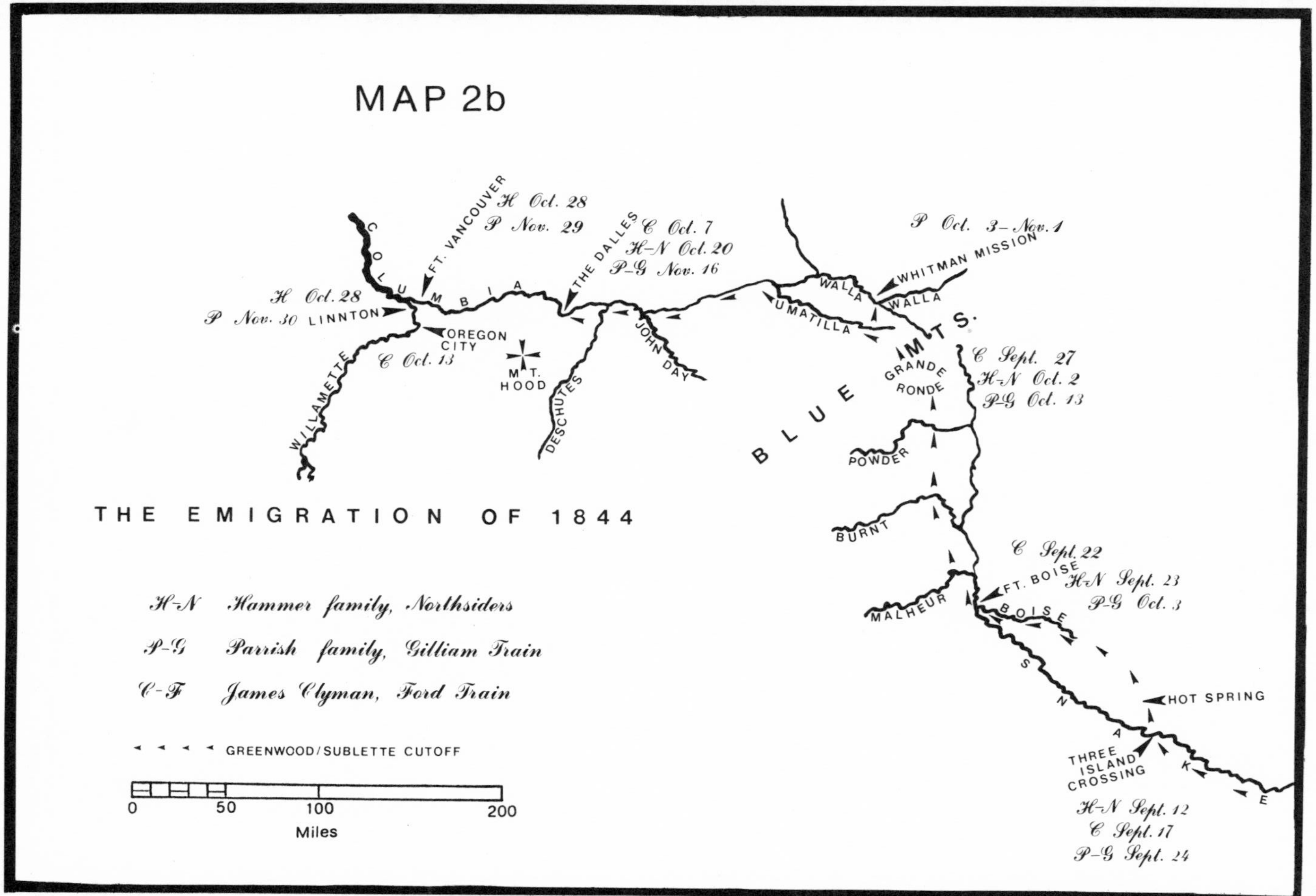
MAP 2b
THE EMIGRATION OF 1844
H-N Hammer family, Northsiders
P-G Parrish family, Gilliam Train
C-F James Clyman, Ford Train
GREENWOOD/SUBLETTE CUTOFF
0
50
100
200
Miles
COLUMBIA
FT. VANCOUVER
H Oct. 28
P Nov. 29
H Oct. 28
P Nov. 30 LINNTON
OREGON CITY
C Oct. 13
WILLAMETTE
MT. HOOD
THE DALLES
C Oct. 7
H-N Oct. 20
P-G Nov. 16
DESCHUTES
JOHN DAY
UMATILLA
WALLA
WALLA
WHITMAN MISSION
P Oct. 3 – Nov. 1
BLUE MTS.
GRANDE RONDE
C Sept. 27
H-N Oct. 2
P-G Oct. 13
POWDER
BURNT
MALHEUR
FT. BOISE
BOISE
C Sept. 22
H-N Sept. 23
P-G Oct. 3
SNAKE
HOT SPRING
THREE ISLAND CROSSING
H-N Sept. 12
C Sept. 17
P-G Sept. 24

Introduction

    Four wagon trains left the United States for the west coast of America in 1844, only the second year in which emigrations of appreciable size ventured to Oregon and California.

    The few published and unpublished overland journey narratives for that year offer diverse vantages from which to view the experience of the emigrants.

    Their route stretched for nearly two thousand miles: from jumping off points along the Missouri River, up through the northeast corner of present Kansas to the Platte River at Grand Island, thence west on the Great Platte River Road through Nebraska and well into Wyoming. The Oregon-California Trail as it is properly called continued from Independence Rock on the Sweetwater River, crossed the Rockies at the wide South Pass, branched southwest to Ft. Bridger (or proceeded due west along the Sublette Cutoff) continued into Idaho to the Bear River and the Snake River, from which the California Trail branched southwest not far west of Ft. Hall. Continuing along the Snake River, and then through the Blue Mountains, the Oregon Trail descended to the Columbia and followed that mighty river to The Dalles, the river itself being the thoroughfare thereafter to the Willamette River and south on its course through the valley of the same name.

    The first "northsider" train—that which crossed the Missouri River at Council Bluffs-Bellevue and followed the north bank of the Platte River—went west in 1844. This train, known generally as the Stephens-Murphy-Thorp party, was chronicled by Oregon-bound Quaker farmer Jacob Hammer who is the only one of record to have compiled a daily journal of the progress of one faction of that train. Moses Schallenberger's recollection narrative describes the journey of the California-bound group of that train. Later-life interviews with William M. Case also give a brief view of the journey of this train, as does a descriptive letter about the trip written by Edmund Bray.

Several narratives were contributed by "southsiders," those who crossed the Missouri River in the vicinity of St. Joseph or Independence before reaching the Platte River Road. Of this larger number (in two large trains and one small train), Edward Evans Parrish compiled a daily journal to which others later referred when compiling their reminiscences, John Minto most prominently among them. Like Parrish, young Minto was a member of the Cornelius Gilliam train which was likely the first to use the route from St. Joseph to intersect the "road" from Independence to the Grand Island in the Platte.

John Minto was an exuberant young Englishman, a former coal miner from Newcastle-on-Tyne, with ready good humor and an unbounded appreciation for the Trail experience. His wife, Martha Ann Morrison Minto, remembered the experience, as did Catherine Sager Pringle, through the eyes of her childhood. For her part, Sager-Pringle wrote as a member of a family upon whom were heaped extreme hardships. Also for the Gilliam train there is the brief and incomplete journal of Samuel Black Crockett, and the brief recollections of Washington Smith Gilliam and Martha Elizabeth Gilliam, son and daughter of the "General." Brief recollections were also contributed by William Shaw, T. M. Ramsdell, and Nancy Dickerson Welch. Journalist Fred Lockley years later took down the contents of a few remaining pages of Willard Hall Rees's ill-fated narrative (it had been reduced to shreds by mice). B. F. Nichols wrote a series of newspaper articles in 1906 and 1907 telling of the overland crossing that year as a youth. For the smaller entourage, that led by Andrew Sublette, brief references in other narratives, and a few pertinent comments by Sublette in letters, provide the chief source of information.

Former mountain man James Clyman's journal of 1844 provides a lengthy view from the train which began at Independence-Westport and which elected Nathaniel Ford leader. Clyman had been to the Wind River Mountains from 1822 to '24, was literate (though with self-taught spelling), keenly observant, at times genuinely humorous, and philosophical. His word pictures of many scenes along the Trail abound in effective imagery—he recreated the melancholy mood of the moment at some particularly desolate settings and in adverse weather conditions, and he celebrated other sights with a flare for descriptive expression. Considering the man's impressive store of Trail knowledge, it is indeed fortunate that James Clyman contributed to the record of '44.

Alanson Hinman's remarks published years later were of one who also traveled with the Ford train. He remained at the Whitman mission during the winter of 1844–45 as a school master before entering the Willamette Valley.

On the overland trails also in 1844 was a group on assignment for the federal government. Farther south and traveling east (though much of the trip out had been on the Oregon-California Trail) was John Charles Fremont, returning from his second expedition at the very time the emigrants of 1844 were but little more than two months into their long journey. Fremont would soon compile another of his detailed reports, the notes for which had been taken the year before at the many sites the emigrants of '44 would soon see. He had left the Missouri River in May of the year before, and, returning along the southern route from California, had arrived at Ft. Bent on the Arkansas River where in mid July he too witnessed the devastating work of the heavy rains in the region for which the spring and summer of 1844 would long be remembered.

On the night of July thirteenth, Fremont's camp was inundated and important items from his collection of botanical specimens were lost to the floodwaters. The Fremont party reached "the little town of Kansas" (later Kansas City, Missouri) on July thirty-first. Three weeks earlier, the wagon trains of the emigrants had reached the Platte River.

From these overland trail narratives and other select sources, a comparative study provides, figuratively, an aerial view of the year's emigration.

Chapter One
1844

. . .lose thyself in the continuous woods
Where rolls the Oregon and hears no sound
Save his own dashings . . .

"Thanatopsis" by William Cullen Bryant, 1817

In the early 1840's, John C. Fremont set out to map parts of the American West. Called "the pioneer of scientific exploration in the far west" by nineteenth century historian Hubert Howe Bancroft, Fremont had been directed by the Federal government to locate potential roads and sites for military posts in that vast expanse and to advise on areas which might accommodate settlement.

On his first expedition in 1842, guided by Kit Carson, Fremont ranged west as far as the Rocky Mountains, which, it had been popularly assumed, were impassable by wagons. But Fremont paid particular attention to South Pass, an accommodating breach in the mountains which would allow settlers' wagons (he envisioned thousands of these conveyances) to travel to the west coast of North America.

On his second expedition, begun in the spring of 1843 and completed in late summer of 1844, Fremont reached British Fort Vancouver on the Columbia River and on the return trip roamed south to California, crisscrossing the Great Basin in present Nevada and Utah. On both expeditions, in good weather and bad, he thrilled at the sights, recorded his observations of the country, and through feats of bravado, endurance and, to some, foolhardiness (as in portraying the aggressive American while a guest in Mexican California) he attracted an awaiting audience in government and elsewhere.

Fremont showed traits of both the pragmatist and the romantic, an official emissary of expansionism who wrote emotional descriptions of western sunsets. His close observations of the land he was traversing in the narrow corridors (albeit strategically chosen ones) of his lines of march provided the imagery by which thousands more pictured the regions through which they would have to pass to occupy the lands of the Pacific Northwest and California.

The qualities Americans perceived as characterizing Fremont's expeditions were those they liked to assume were common to them. Americans prided themselves as being among the most practical on the globe; and theirs was a hemisphere fairly teeming with adventure for those who dared to "jump off" from the few Missouri River settlements into the inestimable wilderness that stretched to the Pacific Ocean.

The "Texas Question" a few years earlier had already established the poles of opinion about westward expansion. (Texas would be annexed in March 1845; war with Mexico followed.) And while the Texas issue was heating up, many were looking even farther west, across the uncharted, windswept reaches of plains, plateaus, and mountains, to the fertile valleys of the Far West and the Pacific Northwest where, they assumed, agriculture and mercantile enterprises could be made to flourish. In the early 1840's, the presence in the Far West of the Mexican-Spanish, and in the Pacific Northwest of the Russians, and especially the British, piqued an amorphous sense of possessiveness among many in the States.

Fremont's *Reports*, the first published as a Senate Document (No. 243, 27th Congress, 3rd Session) in 1843 and reprinted several times by private publishers, became popular reading for many in high places and many more in workaday situations. For many, the first report read like romantic, alluring travel escapism. But they need not stare

off with vague imaginings. If before they had but pondered
the venture of emigrating to the Pacific Northwest, they
could now consider it seriously. And the number of those so
inclined was increasing.

To most of those actively caught up in the idea of transporting themselves and their family to the pristine settings in
the distant West, the word "Oregon" epitomized the quin-
tessential destination. Oregon! The pot of gold, it was said,
at the end of a 2,000-mile rainbow colored by the pigments of
geological wonders, numerous shining rivers, and months of
sunsets.

The name "Oregon" had first been used for "The River,"
or "the River of the West," the breathtaking expanse of
gun-barrel blue water flowing out of the Canadian Rockies to
the sea. For decades, travelers to the Pacific Northwest had
been telling about the grandeur and potential of the region.
In the late 1770's, adventurer and entrepreneur Captain
James Cook began a trade in sea otter furs that helped
publicize the region to British and American traders. The
River had been named the Columbia in 1792 by Bostonian
ship captain Robert Gray. Thomas Jefferson authorized the
expedition of Meriwether Lewis and William Clark to the
region in 1804–06. Five years later John Jacob Astor's fur
trading venture in the region established a settlement,
Astoria, near the mouth of the Columbia. Fur trade would
dominate the economy of the region for nearly three decades
to follow.

One could claim to have entered the "Oregon country"
when descending onto the Pacific slope of the Rocky Mountains. Oregon as a designation as well as a destination had
been bandied about in the halls of Congress several years
before Fremont's expeditions. Virginia Congressman John
Floyd introduced a bill in Congress in 1822 stating that "all
that portion of the territory of the United States north of the

forty-second degree of latitude, and west of the Rocky Mountains, shall constitute the Territory of Oregon," a region
including western portions of both present Wyoming and
Montana and all of Idaho, Oregon, Washington, and of
British Columbia.

Senator Floyd's bill had a much more serious intent, of
course, than a mere codifying of place-name nomenclature.
Four years earlier, in 1818, the United States and Great
Britain had agreed to joint occupancy of the territory, and to
restrain from forming any governmental entity there, in
short, any pretense to actual ownership or usurpation. By
1825, both Spain and Russia had relinquished their tenuous
self-proclaimed rights to land between the 42nd parallel
and 54°, 40 minutes north latitude. In 1827 Great Britain
and the United States renewed their agreement for joint
occupancy.

From the 1820's forward, the region had had a handful of
full-time white residents in addition to the native Indian
tribes. Former trappers, previously employed by the Pacific
Fur Company but who had not joined the Hudson's Bay
Company which came on the scene in 1821, settled in the
region. Next, American churchmen came to establish mission work: Jason Lee for the Methodists in 1834, and Marcus
Whitman for the American Board of Commissioners for
Foreign Missions in 1836. Jesuit Father Pierre Jean De Smet
came representing the Roman Catholics in 1838.

When Jason Lee returned to the states in 1838, he delivered
a petition, a "memorial" as such supplications were termed
at the time, signed by thirty-six persons, said to be a majority
of the residents there, stating their wish for the United
States to annex the region. U. S. Senator Lewis F. Linn of
Missouri, chairman of Congress's Committee on the Territories, became the champion of the petition early the next
year. Linn proposed military surveilance of the overland

routes to Oregon and land grants for settlers who braved the trip there.

News of the ventures of those who did go to Oregon in the earlier years, chiefly for furs, for mission work or as observers, was eagerly awaited. By the early 1840's, the myth-like aura of "The River" and the country it dominated was coming more into focus, particularly the Willamette Valley cradled by two mountain chains between which was the river which gave the Valley its name. Messages brought back from the region, and views of the countryside along the way, were quickly gathered in newspaper articles and were widely read with great interest. Especially in the Missouri River towns, such news was the stuff of which decisions and plans were made by those considering the trip. For from these select staging sites along the Missouri River, the jumping off points, actual emigrations, small in size and experimental in spirit, were already underway. And this even as Fremont "the Pathfinder" was in the field.

Beginning in 1841, emigrants had left the relative comforts of home to go west to a previously unsettled region which, it was widely assumed, was rightfully theirs. Never mind that native populations thought otherwise, and that at the time there was as yet no legal basis for acquiring the far western land which Midwestern farmers sought. In that year also, the Linn proposal was first introduced in Congress. And though this particular bill did not pass, the discussion that ensued served to fire debate in Congress and imaginations in local settings. Free land! Territorial expansion was public fare of the day, seasoned by residual discontent from the economic panic of 1837.

While there were those who counseled a less vigorous means for bolstering one's fortunes (and those of the nation), the rhetoric of expansionism was common. Typical of such speechifying was the "Petition of A Number of Citizens of Indiana Praying the occupation and settlement of the Oregon Territory [the latter term used generically] and the construction of a road thereto . . ." (U.S. Senate, 26th Congress, 1st Session, Doc. 244, March 4, 1840) which proclaimed that "Your memorialists . . . do fully concur . . . that the Oregon territory is ours of right, and ought to be occupied, protected, and settled by authority of the United States; and that a liberal grant of land therein ought to be made to citizen emigrants, to induce enterprising persons . . . to remove with their families thereto . . ." This should be done, the document stated, in a manner much like the "precedent set by Virginia" in offering land grants in Kentucky. To their credit, the memorialists suggested that the U. S. Government "purchase of the Indians of the Oregon territory the lands designed to be settled . . ."

The earliest emigrations (those for which the term could rightly be used), in 1841 and 1842 were tentative affairs. But much was learned, and, considering the conditions imposed on communications, the sporadic news and reports of those who had dared the trip comprised a body of knowledge about the route, the regions through which it passed, and the final destination.

The route to the Oregon country, whole or in part, was fairly well known to the exclusive fraternity of outdoorsmen such as Thomas Fitzpatrick, James Bridger, and their counterparts. Trappers and others had crossed the Rockies, followed the Snake River across present Idaho, traversed the Blue Mountains of present eastern Oregon and wended their way to the mighty Columbia.

Immediately preceding the emigration period of the early 1840's, a few in addition to the missionaries and others had gone for their own reasons. When Jason Lee returned with his "memorial" to foster support for U. S. acquisition of the Oregon country, his presentation in Peoria, Illinois, convinced a group of Peorians to go to Oregon. Thomas J. Farnham, formerly a Vermont lawyer, headed the group of eighteen or more young men—the "Oregon Dragoons"— who left from Independence, Missouri, on May 1, 1839. The "outfit" with which these adventurers equipped themselves, according to the period news journal of record, the *Niles National Register* of May 25, 1839, cost an average $161 and included "a good riding horse, a rifle (carrying ball from 13 to 42 lb.), brace of pistols, hunting knife, 8½ lbs. powder with lead in proportion, 2 wollen blankets, a pack poney to be purchased on frontier." $25 was also allowed for "contingencies."

The Peorians had a supply wagon, an essential characteristic of an emigration. But perhaps the only success to come out of the Peoria Party's endeavors was the writing career of Farnham (*Travels in the Great Western Prairies, the Anahuac and Rocky Mountains, and in the Oregon Territory*, 1841, and other titles). In a nutshell, the party, small as it was, dissolved into divisions, desertions and other disaffections. The wagon was left at Independence, outfitting was reorganized and supplanted, and not far into the Indian Territory west of the Missouri River the remaining travelers split into two smaller parties. Farnham and four others hired a guide at Bent's Fort on the Arkansas and headed for Brown's Hole on Green River. Once there, two turned back. Farnham and his two remaining companions arrived at The Dalles in 1839 on the first of October, and at Fort Vancouver on the eighteenth. Meanwhile, five others followed their own tack and arrived in the Valley in the summer of 1840. In that year also "the great reinforcement" (called that initially in hopeful expectation, and later, by some, in derision) of missionaries arrived by sea to aid Jason Lee's efforts.

It is generally agreed that the first "public" emigration—a party not made up solely of trappers, traders, missionaries,

aristocrat sightseers or some combination of these—was the
Bidwell-Bartleson party of 1841. This party of about seventy, including five women and one child, met in rendezvous
at Independence, Missouri, on May ninth and on the nineteenth set out on the journey with a small procession of
wagons and other vehicles. Following after mountain man
Thomas Fitzpatrick who was leading a group of Jesuits to Ft.
Hall, this party split nearly evenly at Soda Springs, half
going to Oregon and the others to California.

As with the Bidwell-Bartleson train, there would be those
who opted for California, the "road" to which was largely
imaginary. Each emigration bound for California, from 1841
to 1844, followed a different route, and each group could
consider itself fortunate to have made it at all. The California
contingent in 1841 abandoned their wagons while yet in the
northeast corner of present Nevada (few wheeled vehicles
previously had been taken farther west than Ft. Laramie)
and walked on with their livestock, arriving on November
fourth at the home of former Missourian John Marsh near
where the Sacramento and the Joaquin rivers joined. Though
footsore and somewhat dispirited by the disarray of their final
miles, they had traded on a store of luck that had served
them well. Marsh had sent letters to Missouri newspapers in
1840 inviting any who would come see and settle the part of
California in which he lived. He also suggested a route to
follow. Marsh's invitation had stirred the wanderlust in John
Bidwell. Early the next year, 1842, Bidwell's own account of
the trip to California was published in newspapers back East,
yet another reiteration of the prize to be won in the Far West.

And that year a party of one hundred and twenty five
persons (including "seventy men who could stand guard,"
according to participant Asa Lovejoy) left in mid May from
Independence for the trek west under the leadership of Dr.
Elijah White. Lansford W. Hastings (who later compiled an

emigrants' guidebook which contained some painfully mistaken information) was also in the party and before long assumed command in a contest of personalities and wills.

White, formerly a physician for the Indian mission work in the Willamette Valley, was in 1842 an estranged associate of missionary Jason Lee and was returning to the Valley as a semi-official Federal Indian "sub-agent", a questionable pretense to officialdom since the United States was not in legal possession of the region.

Sidney W. Moss, who also traveled in this party, recalled for H. H. Bancroft that the group was "western people strictly" who "left Independence May 16th, 1842." (Lovejoy said May twelfth, though he gave no place of departure.) Though Dr. White was supposedly in charge of the group, his leadership capabilities reportedly were not sufficient. Moss's comments about leadership in this instance are relevant since the topic would continue to be an important one for subsequent emigrations. Moss's opinion, actually a rather conclusive indictment, was that White, "lacked firmness of character . . . did not know anything about managing stock or teams . . . seemed to be totally ignorant of his duties . . . had no administrative ability . . . was not a practical man . . . loved to make little oratorical displays . . ." According to Lovejoy, White's waning authority collapsed when he acted on a hasty vote to kill all the dogs in the entourage, it being assumed by "a great many . . . that the dogs would get mad and bite." Mrs. Lovejoy added that, "The farmers were very much attached to their dogs."

Asa Lovejoy told historian Bancroft that the emigration of 1842 was nearly halted before it began by the warnings of those who should know—trappers and others, William Sublette among them—who told of recent hostilities of the Indians, and the potential for the same to befall emigrants who would attempt to beard the lion by entering the Indians' own home territory, particularly that of the Sioux.

In order to raise the number of persons they supposed advisable for security, Hastings and one or two others "exerted themselves" and "rode through . . . the Platte Purchase" promoting the trip, Lovejoy said, and thus a wagon train was gathered. From the beginning also, Lovejoy said, there was active vying for the leadership role.

A few days out of Independence, Lansford Hastings had insisted on taking over and thereafter "acted as captain." (Hastings, Moss recalled, "was a practical man, rather a talented man but very selfish.") Some, however, remained with Dr. White. And so, even with the initial concern about security, the group had split over internal differences before reaching the fur trading post at the mouth of Laramie Creek on the Platte River.

Joseph Bissonette who "was in charge of the lower fort [Ft. Platte] would not let them [the smaller faction yet following Dr. White] go" farther. But when the second, larger, group arrived the next day, the train reunited, with Hastings as head, and proceeded. Lovejoy noted that this second warning about the supposed danger ahead caused many of the women to want to go back; the men, however, "would not hear anything of that."

The imminence of danger was not the only dissuasion with which this group met on the Trail; even the exalted attributes of the final destination were disparaged at this point. The day the train left the fort, Lovejoy said, they met a party coming back to the States led by mountain man Thomas Fitzpatrick who told them that "there was not land enough in Oregon for our party." (Lovejoy questioned whether Fitzpatrick had ever been in the Valley.)

Perhaps it was the challenge of the thing (or the $300 or $500 which Lovejoy said was promised to Fitzpatrick, though

"I do not suppose it was ever paid") which caused the famous mountain man to agree to guide the White/Hastings train west to Ft. Bridger, through a region in which, it was reported, the Snakes (Shoshones) and Sioux were at war.

This party of emigrants, like the thousands who would follow in succeeding years, noted the Trail landmarks. Along the way, Fitzpatrick explained that the name "Independence Rock" derived from a "celebration" held there earlier by some mountain men on a Fourth of July. In remarking on the practice of scratching one's name on the Rock, Lovejoy assumed that he arrived there before Fremont, who, he supposed, was actually traveling behind the White/Hastings train in 1842. (According to Fremont's report of his 1842 expedition, he camped "one mile below Rock Independence" on August first.)

Hastings led the train as far as Green River west of South Pass where, Moss said, "Our company divided . . . and the [smaller] portion of which Hastings acted as Captain wanted to go across in wagons, while the remainder threw away their waggons and commenced packing."

At Ft. Hall they found the first official opposition to their entry into what Great Britain considered its own territory. "Major" Richard Grant, in command at Ft. Hall, was "pleasant for an Englishman," Moss said, but was "unwilling to have the country settled by the Americans." Grant suggested that California was a better place for the emigrants to go, though his stance "did not turn any of that emigration (1842) into California." (Hastings would later lead a group from Oregon into California.)

Also at Ft. Hall, according to Moss, the group "abandoned the [remaining] wagons" and traveled to The Dalles "with the Hudson Bay Company's annual brigade." Moss and the others "got here [in the Willamette Valley] on the twenty-sixth of September, about 10 oclock in the morning." The first person he met west of The Dalles was George Washington, a black man who had been a cook for the fur trappers at Astoria.

On October second, Moss was at Fort Vancouver and was "received a great deal better than I expected," an experience which many would have. For though Richard Grant at Ft. Hall expressed the official British stance on American emigration to the Oregon country, Dr. John McLoughlin, the eminently successful chief "factor" of the much larger British Fort Vancouver, was most hospitable. McLoughlin, who would later become an American citizen, was well known for the numerous times he provided food and transportation to Americans on their way to the Valley, careful, all the while, to direct them south of the Columbia, in that way maintaining temporarily for the British the region north of the river.

Though Moss reported that the 1842 emigration "brought no wagons in at all" (Lovejoy confirmed that, "We did not get our wagons through"), he stated that one wagon had made it into the Valley in 1841, having "rolled from Fort Hall as far as it would go to the Blue Mountains, . . . [where it was] packed on horses across the Blue Mountains until it got down to Whitman's Station and then was rolled on its own wheels to Walla Walla which was a trading post." This "common two horse lumber wagon" had been shown to him in 1842, Moss said, on the Tualatin Plains just west of present Portland. The wagon, it was said, had been brought in by Robert Newell, the former fur trapper with the American Fur Company who came to the Willamette Valley in 1840.

Unlike Sidney Moss, who gave his arrival in the Valley as September twenty-sixth, Asa Lovejoy was at the Whitman mission "in the later part of September" where he learned that Marcus Whitman had decided to return to the States to advertise the wonders of the Oregon country and to try to reverse a decision of the American Board of Foreign Missions to close his and Narcissa's mission at Waiilatpu and that of the Spaldings at Lapwai. In early October, Lovejoy, against his better judgement but apparently caught up in Whitman's convincing enthusiasm ("Dr. Whitman was a man of great energy") nevertheless started out with the doctor for the States. Remembering the trouble he and Hastings had had at Independence Rock when, having lingered behind the others, they had been surrounded by Indians who detained them in a threatening manner, Lovejoy and Whitman took the round-about way back east through Taos and Santa Fe.

Lovejoy and Whitman parted before reaching the Missouri River, with Whitman proceeding east and Lovejoy remaining at Bent's Fort on the Arkansas River. On Whitman's return trip along with hundreds of hopefuls of the "Great Migration" he found Lovejoy at Ft. Bridger and engaged him to help pilot the train to Ft. Hall. And so in that personal manner, the emigration of 1842 and that of the next year were interrelated.

The often mentioned Dr. Marcus Whitman, in addition to being a Presbyterian missionary to the Indians of the Northwest, was a boomer for Anglo-American occupation of the Oregon country. He was credited, by dint of example and inspiration, with being a guiding light to the 1,000 or more emigrants (263 men, 130 women and 610 children) who joined together as the often mentioned "Great Migration" which set out from their rendezvous twenty miles west of Independence, Missouri, on May 22, 1843. Initially, fur trader John Gantt was employed to pilot the train of 110 wagons to Ft. Hall, but beyond there, according to some, Whitman himself was the guide. One of the others of note handed a leadership role was Peter H. Burnett who would later write a detailed account of the trip in a series of letters to the *New York Herald*.

The relative "greatness" of the emigration that year was based, not surprisingly, on its size, which included some 5,000 head of cattle, the "Cow Column" of which Jesse Applegate later wrote eloquently. But the success of the "Migration" of '43 was due in large measure to the decisive accomplishment of arriving at Trail's end with wagons intact.

At Soda Springs, Whitman, "left the emigration . . . and went on to Fort Hall by way of a cutoff over the mountains," according to John Burch McClane who accompanied Whitman and who later provided historian Bancroft with information about that famous trek. McClane, as many others, referred to the attempts of Richard Grant at Ft. Hall to get all who came through to change their destination from Oregon to California. Grant urged the emigrants in 1843, as he had their predecessors, to leave their wagons at the fort. Whitman advised otherwise, even though, as McClane and the others knew, "wagons had not gone through before." But again, Whitman had provided the example, having taken a wagon (though cut down near Ft. Hall to a two wheeled contraption) as far as Ft. Boise on the trek he and Narcissa had made in 1836.

McClane also stated that, "At Fort Hall, Dr. Whitman had supplies brought by the Indians" since "A great many emigrations at Fort Hall were short of provisions." There also had to be a sharing of foodstuffs along the Trail as well, and again Whitman was remembered by McClane. "The old Dr. was one of those who would divide his last flour and there was not much left."

From Fort Hall, Whitman, his nephew Perrin B. Whitman, Richard and Nimrod Ford, Asa Lovejoy, and J. B. McClane went ahead to "make some explorations for the emigrants." McClane recalled that, "We left notes along the different parts of the road to direct those who followed us which way to go. They were just slips of paper fastened to the trees or stuck on stakes along the road. We went from Fort Hall to Fort Boise, via Salmon River Falls [Salmon Falls on the Snake River]." Beyond the Snake River country they followed the Burnt River where, "there was so much timber on that [river] that we did not take time to cut a road and we took the bed of the river. Where the brush was too thick on the edge we went to it someplaces swimming some places not."

"We managed to get through with a wagon to Grand Ronde. I drove that wagon myself. We hauled our provisions in that. We did not have much provisions to haul, to tell the truth." At one point this small party marking a route for the "Migration" was reduced to making soup by boiling "some beef bones." Whitman all the while seemed indestructible, gastronomic quirks notwithstanding: "The Dr. would eat about anything, but he was down on using salt." At Grande Ronde, some Christian Cayuse Indians treated the trail-blazers to a feast of "elk meat boiled with dried huckleberries and plenty of flour."

From Grande Ronde, Whitman rode on to the Spaldings' mission at Lapwai while McClane and the others proceeded to the Whitman mission where they stayed "several weeks . . . until the emigrants came up." Then Whitman and his small former route-marking party "went down on a boat from Walla Walla to The Dalles to meet the others," including Mrs. Whitman who in her husband's absence had gone to The Dalles after being threatened with harm at the mission, a foreboding hint of the trouble to come three years hence. From The Dalles and west on the Columbia, J. B. McClane rode in the canoe in which missionary Jason Lee, who had come to the Dalles to greet the emigrants of '43, was returning to the Methodist mission "about ten miles below Salem" on the Willamette River. And so those of the "Great Migration" entered the Valley.

For those who in 1843 opted for the Mexican held territory of California, Joseph B. Chiles had returned from the 1841 journey to help guide them to that destination. On May thirty-first, Fremont noted seeing the wagons of Chiles' group at Elm Grove, about thirty-five miles west of Independence. The much smaller California bound party (eight wagons, thirty people) followed in the rear of the much larger "Great Migration" train, though overtaking a few of its rear wagons at the Kansas River.

Chiles's group (officially led by guide Joseph Walker) abandoned their few wagons near Owens Lake in present California and in early December crossed the Sierra Nevada and came into the San Joaquin Valley.

By the end of 1843, then, there had been three emigrations. Anyone interested in the subject could imbibe heady drams of Trail lore at Independence, St. Joseph, and other points on the Missouri River. Many that year committed themselves to the journey and all that that implied for their immediate and future well-being. The idea of transplanting one's family in the Pacific Northwest or in California was now acceptable reasoning for the stalwart and otherwise respectable and not just for the adventurous by nature and the speculative by turn of mind.

There were in fact public meetings held to share what information was available about Oregon and the "road" there. The people in and around Bloomington, Iowa, for example, gathered as did many elsewhere in a series of meetings in 1843 to learn more about emigrating to Oregon. The *Bloomington Herald* of March 24, 1843, reported the recommendation of citizens there "to every person possessing the enterprise and patriotic spirit of the true American citizen to emigrate to Oregon Territory [not an official designation as yet] at as early a day as possible and thereby to secure to themselves a permanent and happy home, and to their country one of the fairest portions of her domain." Public meetings such as these would often be noted in newspapers in Missouri and elsewhere.

Those who could read the weather signs of future development foresaw annual emigrations becoming commonplace. Jesse Applegate, while yet at St. Louis early in April 1843, wrote to a relative saying that though the trip was "so wild an undertaking," one should hurry ahead. "If you are going to Oregon, by all means go this spring, for if Linn's Bill passes next year, every man and every man's neighbor and friends will moove[sic] in that direction."

The white population of the Oregon Country had grown to an estimated 1,000 by early 1843. The next year the number would be nearly half again as large, and double that in 1845 as hundreds and then thousands more traveled the route (1,932 map miles from Independence to Oregon City) which, though more in concept than construction, had become a popular public thoroughfare. (Later, in 1849 and the 1850's, there would be annual emigrations of twenty to fifty thousand! Most of these persons were going to California.)

Though by 1844 the Linn Bill had not become law, the mood for expansion was encouraged in large measure by the presidential electioneering that year. One candidate in particular, the Democrat James K. Polk, unequivocally promoted it in rhetoric designed to excite would-be emigrants to pack up and drive on to the Oregon country.

The Democratic party, decidedly expansionist in hue and cry, rallied around the alliterative campaign slogan "Fifty-Four Forty or Fight." The numerals were cartographers' designation for the parallel which, they said, should be the boundary between Canada and the U.S. (Polk and the Senate later agreed to the 49th parallel as the boundary.) The "fight" referred to the mood of an appreciable number in the states who brandished that means of territorial expansion if less emotional and grasping ones were not to be found. The Democrats' successful popular appeal that year, playing in part on the concept of a nearly unimaginable expanse of "free" land at the continent's western edge, brought about Mr. Polk's election as the eleventh President of the United States.

Thus, though a fight was boisterously threatened, for certain the possession of the Oregon region through actual occupation by settlers was well underway by 1844. The settlers' prize, of course, was land, and the year 1844 would be the first whole year in which settlers' ownership of land could be recognized even semi-officially and therefore in some manner guaranteed, even though a Congress-ordained territorial government was an eventuality another four years in the future.

The settlers' spontaneous system of property recognition had been developed by those who had arrived in the Valley in the emigrations of '41 and '42 and who had not been idle concerning their need for basic governmental services, particularly that relating to their land rights. On July 5, 1843, they had created the Organic Act which organized a provisional government, a primary function of which was to oversee the registration of the all-important land claims. And so, while Fremont was yet in the field, Americans in the Pacific Northwest were already producing public records documenting their claims to sections of land.

And in the spring of 1844, the fourth public emigration departed the Missouri River for the long haul west. More hopefuls in search of land were about to participate in one of the most notable overland journeys of the nineteenth century.

Fortunately, a few kept journals during the journey, and some would compose reminiscences years later. Among the southsider trains coming from Independence, Westport and St. Joseph through eastern Kansas, E. E. Parrish and Samuel Black Crockett kept daily accounts of their travels with the Cornelius Gilliam wagon train. John Minto would later write extensively of his experiences with the same train. The incomparable journal of James Clyman (a co-discoverer with Thomas Fitzpatrick in 1824 of the Platte River-Sweetwater River route that later became the key to the Oregon Trail) would evolve as one of the most important journals recorded. Former mountain man Clyman traveled with the Nathaniel Ford train in '44. Others of the southsider trains recorded their recollections some years later.

There was a third southsider train on the Trails that emigration season. Clyman, Parrish, Crockett and Minto all made references to the small group led by Andrew Sublette which included a few Catholic missionaries along with some men traveling to the mountains for their health. This small train set out from Westport Landing soon after the Ford train left that Missouri River jumping off point. Some made it to Brown's Hole in present Colorado.

For the northsiders who crossed the Missouri at Council Bluffs-Bellevue, fewer, and shorter, narratives survive. Moses Schallenberger eventually dictated his recollections of traveling with the Stephens-Murphy party. His narrative, until recently, has been the primary source of information about that party bound for California in '44.

The recollections of another northsider of '44, William M. Case, were published in the first volume (1900) of the Oregon Historical Society's *Quarterly*.

But in that train also was Indiana Quaker farmer Jacob Hammer, the only one of record who kept a journal of his daily progress and observations. (see *This Emigrating Company, the 1844 Oregon Trail Journal of Jacob Hammer.* Glendale, CA: The Arthur H. Clark Company, 1990.)

What follows is a view of the emigration of that early year—a look at specific aspects of the grand adventure of 1844: What were the circumstances of their setting out? What was the journey like? What did they find at the end of the Trail?

The story is told here in generalities and select specifics. It is a story of perseverance and human foibles on a trek of nearly 2,000 miles touching an amazing assortment of the continent's topographical features. It is a view near the beginning of the twenty-year wagon train era and thereby of the first stages of an evolving pattern of settlement of the nation's northwest coastal region. It is adventure, tragedy, comedy. It is public history.

Chapter Two

Preparations

The study of the narratives of 1844 is most effectively begun at the beginning—with the emigrants' preparations for the journey and their first days out from their former Missouri homesteads.

Although in reality the journey for all began officially with the westward crossing of the Missouri River—at the river landings near Independence-Westport Landing, Weston, St. Joseph, or Council Bluffs-Bellevue—for those of '44 (as with their few predecessors, and the thousands who would follow) the notion of the journey began in many different ways.

For William M. Case it began as early as a decade before. As a youth in Indiana he read the accounts of Lewis and Clark in a book loaned to his father by William Henry Harrison, former governor of the Old Northwest Territory and short-lived ninth U. S. President.

The Henry Sager family, representing numerous others, was seemingly always on the move. Catherine Sager described her father as "one of those restless men who are not content to remain long in one place." He moved his family to several sites in Ohio before coming to Missouri in 1838. After expressing an interest in Texas, he decided instead, with the help of his wife, for Oregon. News about Oregon was much talked about in her neighborhood, Ms. Sager remembered. Marcus Whitman had stopped at Westport in mid-February 1843, on his way to the East to publicize his vision of the potential of the Oregon country. He was back in Westport in mid-May, helping to organize the "Great Migration" that would go west that spring. By the next spring, the Sagers were packed and ready to go west.

It was less certain just where the trip began for James Clyman. By 1844, he had accumulated already a repertoire of wilderness experiences which included a cast of characters even then becoming legendary figures of far western history, among them, Jedediah Smith, Thomas Fitzpatrick, Jim Bridger and Moses Harris. Clyman was returning west after living for a few years in Illinois and Wisconsin where he had searched unsuccessfully, he wrote, for a healthy climate, which, it occurred to him, might have been in the western mountains all along.

For some, the journey indeed began well to the east of the Missouri River landings, and the topic of Oregon had been one of interest for some time. The Reverend E. E. Parrish, for example, "between . . . 1840 and 1843 . . . collected sundrie accounts of the climet, rivers, & its [Oregon Territory's] fertility & productive qualities." Favorably impressed with what he learned, he "finally concluded to make a start to that far off land of wheat and salmon & accordingly after making the best arangements our meanes would afford, we left our olde mantion house on, or in the spring of, A. D. 1843."

The Parrishes lived temporarily in a parsonage in Hoskinville, Ohio, and later a school house. Then at Marietta, Ohio, on October 12, 1843, they loaded "our new wagon which we named 'the great Western' " on board the steamboat *Mississippi* on the Ohio River to Cincinnati and then the *Importer* on the Mississippi River to St. Louis. For the total fare they paid $40. On October nineteenth they left St. Louis and traveled in their wagon "about 375 miles" to Platte City, Platte County, Missouri, on the Platte River (the tributary by that name east of the Missouri River).

In early December, the family moved to Andrew County

and Parrish used his ox team to haul farm produce for pay around Savannah, the county seat. There he met Cornelius Gilliam who, with his family, his brother Mitchell, and three brothers-in-law (William Shaw, John Nichols, and George Nelson) was going to Oregon. On April 15, 1844, the Parrishes "loaded once more our noble wagon, the great 'Western' . . . and roaled off for the Emigrant incampment on the West side of . . . Missouri River." They camped on the east bank that night and crossed the next day. Only now did Parrish (perhaps with tongue in cheek) consider himself committed to the journey: "So this 16th day of April settles the question: whether Edward is going to Oregon or not." The family joined several other families "in this bottom on the West side . . .; some have bean here for months." Others "are coming every day and crossing as fast as the boat can do it . . ."

John Minto announced his intentions for a journey west at a Christmas dinner at Pittsburgh, Pennsylvania. His family had come to the United States in 1840 from the coal mines of Newcastle-on-Tyne in Great Britain. At the time he made his plans known, the Pennsylvania mines where he worked had been shut down by labor unrest. As a young man of twenty-one in 1844, Minto was setting out with his double-barreled fowling piece, a gift from his father.

Minto's destination initially was Dubuque, Iowa, from whence he intended to seek work in the lead mines of the region. When he arrived in St. Louis, however, he heard that there was a wagon train gathering to go to the Oregon country and he opted instead for that more distant goal.

Parrish, Minto and Clyman notwithstanding, the majority of those heading west in '44, like other emigrations (except during the gold rushes), were farmers. There were also the customary craftsmen who were going west to practice their various trades. Some of the emigrants had lived in

Missouri from the mid to late 1830's. More often they had arrived in the early 1840's, coming to this westernmost state of the Union for similar reasons to those that now attracted them to Oregon and California: the ownership of productive land. William Shaw told historian Bancroft at the "pioneers camp meeting" in Salem, Oregon, in June 1878, that he had come to Missouri from Tennessee in 1819, earlier than most who went on to Oregon. When he came, Missouri "was principally woods . . . [with] some prairies . . . but it was generally timber covered with hickory, walnut and some hackberry, basswood, black oak and white oak."

Of those who farmed, "some had prairie farms," Shaw said, "but a good many had part of their farms to clear. The most of the emigration into that country was from Tennessee and Kentucky. They lived in log houses mostly hewn logs, some round. There were no saw mills. I sawed thousands of feet of lumber by hand for myself and other people. It was a long time before there were sawmills there; just a few years before I left [for Oregon]."

But on May 10, 1844, Shaw started for Oregon. "What started me this way was this: Linn's bill in Congress which was gotten up to settle this country [Oregon] was the first start that set me to thinking of coming here." Shaw also had heard P. L. Edwards (author of the *Sketch of the Oregon Territory, or Emigrants' Guide*) who "made several speeches" about his travels and "who had a book that [Benjamin L. E. de] Bonneville wrote [*The Adventures of Captain Bonneville*, 1837, by Washington Irving?]; I read that over, and Clark and Lewis' also. All these things induced me to come. I thought it was a good climate from what I could learn from the missionaries who were settled here. Their works I saw in the papers. Edwards had been here with them and then went back [to Missouri] and wrote an account and made several speeches and that started a great many men here."

Land, the ultimate goal for the majority, meant also a future for one's offspring. As Shaw explained, "Another inducement was to settle my family. My family was a family of boys, and they were getting to be men and I was not able to settle them in Missouri. Land began to get up, and it was hard to get, and I thought by moving to a new country my boys could shift for themselves. It was too cold in Missouri also. The climate was not good. I never was satisfied with Missouri in my life, although it was an easy country to make a living in. There was plenty to live on."

For many, the move to Missouri may have been but a springboard for travel farther west. Perhaps Jacob and Hannah Hammer had moved into Missouri's Platte Purchase for the purpose of establishing a farm which would later attract a buyer from among those farmers who, as members of a second wave of settlement, sought out such sites where a few acres had been "turned," where trees which stood in potential farm fields had been girdled, or even cut and the stumps pulled to allow long straight rows for plowing, and where a cabin had been built. One may well ask why Jacob Hammer as an Abolitionist, one committed to active protest against slavery, moved to a slave state at all if not to enter the fray in an active fashion, or, to prepare for the longer move to the west coast. With Texas being settled by slaveowners, his intent may have been to add his family to the numbers determined to keep Oregon from going the same way.

Some others who had intended to remain in Missouri, as had William Shaw, had found life there not to their liking. T. M. Ramsdell stated that, "Our emigration . . . from Missouri mostly became of periodical malarial sickness there . . . [and] . . . from financial troubles." As Ramsdell said, there were seasons when his neck of the woods was simply not a healthy place to live. As for "financial troubles," Ramsdell may have been referring to the poor market for farm products about which others complained in 1842 and '43. In an era when farms were relatively small, corn was selling in 1842 for ten cents a bushel, wheat for fifty cents, potatoes for six cents. Little relief was to be had in 1843; corn and oats were bringing six to ten cents a bushel, pork sold at a dollar a hundredweight and good horse stock brought but fifty to sixty dollars a head. Many farm homes were visited by sheriffs serving papers for indebtedness. To Ramsdell's family and others, the 320 acres (or 640 acres for married couples) in the Oregon country promised by the Linn Bill which for some time had been "before" Congress proved to be a prize worth pursuing.

The general notion, which evolved into the decision, to emigrate led to the actual preparation for the journey. The records of '44 contain a few detailed descriptions of that process by individual emigrants. First, as with the Sagers, those who owned land had to dispose of it (and, sadly, many belongings; the wagon box had little room for sentiment) before embarking on the combined business venture and adventure called the emigration. This capitalization (to invoke a grand term) for the romantic enterprise may have followed a few years' work on the farm to increase its value for sale, or it may have been an impulsive act suddenly promulgated by growing dissatisfaction with some facet of life in Missouri, some perplexing circumstance that served to emphasize what was seemingly promised in the Oregon country though it meant walking half a year to get there.

Willfully dispossessed, then, of their Missouri land, these seekers for land in Oregon had passed the first test of determination. Others, like young John Minto and Willard H. Rees, would work their way west by hiring on with families who needed help with their cattle or in driving a second wagon or taking a turn hunting game. The employment agreement could also include several weeks or months of work on the new claim in Oregon as well. There were several like Minto who went west with such an arrangement.

James Clyman represents yet another (though smaller) group of emigrants—the foot-loose few who enjoyed the adventure and whose destination and purpose was more a matter of recurrent impulses than the need to possess land like their more pragmatic companions whose families, wagons, and plowshares properly characterized the emigration.

Those who had liquidated their largest asset—their farm —"invested" the cash received in an outfit for the Trail. What hard cash was left, if any at all, was probably squirreled away in a leather drawstring pouch sequestered in the flour barrel or in one of the hidden compartments built into the floor of the wagon box. And so, with wagons packed and driving a few head of "loose" cattle, emigrant families began the journey.

The leave-taking of family and friends was illustrated in a few of the accounts. The Hammers left their home a few miles northeast of St. Joseph on April twenty-sixth, but stopped a few days at the home of Hannah's Aunt Mary Stokes near Savannah, county seat of Andrew County, Missouri. Jacob wrote also that a relative, Laban Hammer, accompanied them that far.

Before eventually joining the same train as the Parrishes (though as a member of a different company), John Minto had met Willard Rees at St. Louis who was going west and who told him about the wagon trains forming for the emigration. Minto's curiosity was aroused. The two of them booked passage to Weston and St. Joseph. Nine miles above St. Joseph they went across the river "to the emigrant camps" Minto said (Rees recalled that it was "on the Indians' side of the river opposite Caples Landing") where they met "Col." Michael T. Simmons, the eventual (but temporary) second in command of the Gilliam train. Rees stated that when he and Minto arrived, in mid April, there were "some thirty families encamped on the open timberland of the river bottom . . ."

From Michael Simmons, Minto first learned of the Linn Bill which promised free land in Oregon. He and Rees also learned that some emigrant families needed extra manpower for the trip. One family in particular, the Robert Wilson Morrisons, had been recommended to them and the two crossed the river to the east side and found that though Morrison already had engaged two men, one had married and decided to forego the trip to Oregon and the other was staying to care for an ailing father.

For their promise to help with the family's cattle and their two wagons, Minto and Rees were offered bed, board, and, Minto said, "washing and mending" by Mrs. Morrison. The two eager youths accepted. Rees was sent the approximate ten miles to St. Joseph with "some money and a bill of goods" to purchase the Morrison's "outfit". Minto stated specifically that the shopping list included "nine barrels of flour [and] three hundred pounds of corn meal." Minto himself meanwhile was told to fashion a "wagon pole" from a small oak tree felled just that day to "change a large four-horse wagon to be drawn by yokes of heavy oxen." Both Minto and Rees remembered that Mrs. Morrison had doubts about whether the family would ever see Rees, and their money, again. Rees' errand to St. Joseph took all day; he returned to the Morrison farm "late at night" along with his friend O. S. Thomas with whom he had set out earlier from Peoria, Illinois, for the West and for whom he had already accepted a position with Cornelius Gilliam when he and Minto had visited the emigrant camp on the west bank of the Missouri River.

Later in the day, the county sheriff and his family called to say good-by, as did Mrs. Morrison's brother and wife, and

(above) JOHN MINTO, ABOUT 1862
Courtesy of the Minto family,
by Beverly E. Lowe

(top right) ROBERT WILSON MORRISON
Courtesy of A. D. Ricketts

NANCY (MRS. ROBERT W.) MORRISON
AND GRANDSON, JOHN W. MINTO,
FIRST SON OF JOHN AND MARTHA
MORRISON MINTO
Courtesy of Beverly E. Lowe

several neighbors. Minto learned that the Morrisons had been busy of late hosting those who had come to bid farewell, and those who came "with articles to sell, which they considered specially fit for the trip to Oregon." On the last Sunday before the family left their home, "the tables were set four times for dinner" to accommodate the many visitors.

During this prolonged meal, and after a dispiriting discussion among those who were remaining in Missouri about the supposed dangers to be suffered at the hands of Indians on the way to Oregon, Mr. Morrison was asked pointedly why he was going. His answer, as Minto remembered it, was representative of the reasoning of many. "I allow," Morrison began, "the United States has the best right to that country, and I am going to help make that right good." And he added, "I am not satisfied here. There is little we raise that pays shipment to market; a little hemp and a little tobacco." Refusing to keep slaves, Morrison saw little chance to prosper in a region where he was forced to compete with those who did. Minto was so favorably impressed by his employer's words that, he wrote, "If I now had any definite purpose in being there with him, beyond the desire for action— the adventure natural to youth—it was for the freedom, the self-ownership, the self-reliant self-direction the words implied."

Mrs. Morrison, however, was not so favorably impressed with the idea. Though she was "bending all her energies in preparation," Minto wrote, the journey "was not in her judgement a wise business movement." She was no stranger to moving. Nancy Irwin and R. W. Morrison had been married on March 10, 1831, and two years later they moved from Montgomery County, Missouri, to Clay County on the Missouri River. Shortly thereafter, they moved to Clinton County, and when three years later Platte Purchase was opened for settlement, the Morrisons moved again, to a spot ten miles north of St. Joseph and two miles east of the river. She was apparently not enthusiastic about moving again, especially to far-off Oregon.

Nevertheless, the Morrisons and their two hired hands set to the task of packing. Many years later, Minto wrote to Bancroft that (as of ca. 1878) he had not seen "any statement of what was deemed a good 'fit out' for crossing the Plains and mountains to the Pacific coast," and so he listed the few essentials (though not always the quantities) that the Morrisons took. The food included was intended to last six months for the father and mother and six children (ages one to thirteen) and for Minto and Rees: 1,000 pounds of flour, a large box of corn meal, "as much bacon as was deemed a liberal proportion to the breadstuffs on the basis of a soldier's rations," coffee, sugar, dried apples, peaches, and beans, and a keg of strained wild honey. "It was expected," Minto continued, "that we would get fresh meat from the wild game of the country . . . but it was not relied upon." Martha Ann Morrison Minto, twelve years old in 1844, recalled that on the long trip her father gave away much of their own provisions to those who ran short.

Other supplies which the Morrisons took included clothing and bedding "chiefly of homespun manufacture," a "roomy" tent, cooking utensils "of the solid old fashion style before stoves came into general use." Morrison also took the "iron portions" of a plow and "several varieties of grass and vegetable seed." Mrs. Morrison had packed a spinning wheel "suitable for spinning flax, with a supply of lint, [and] two sleighs used for weaving on hand looms." The family arsenal included "four good rifles." Though Mrs. Morrison reportedly did not use her rifle on the trip, Minto was convinced that she could if the need arose.

Minto stated that five yokes of "heavy work oxen" were used to pull the family's two wagons (Rees said "one team of three yoke oxen"). The "loose" stock which was brought along included three mares "of good blood, an excellent gelding, [and] three milch cows." All the live stock was "the very best of their kind."

There is at least one instance in the narratives of '44 of a family making a second start that year. A brief memoir published in the Oregon Pioneer Association's *Transactions* of 1897 explains how James Welch and Nancy Dickerson Welch had set 'out in the spring of 1843 "with a number of families" from near "Bloomington, (now Muscatine), Iowa . . . traveling over the old Landers[sic] emigrant wagon road." But "after traveling for some time [we] were compelled to turn back on account of Indian depredations, so [we] temporarily stopped at 'Rubadeau's [Robidoux] landing,' now . . . St. Joseph, Mo. during the winter of 1843 . . . In the spring of 1844 [we] again resumed [our] journey [this time] with the Gilliam party of emigrants." (The Welches may have been among those of Bloomington who had benefited from the public meetings in that town in 1843 organized for the dissemination of information about Oregon and for planning the trip west.)

However they came to the notion or the decision, the emigrants of '44 were busy in April and May of that year with the final preparations for the long journey.

Chapter Three

Rendezvous

After selling their farms and packing their few remaining belongings, the emigrant families moved to camps near the Missouri River or, if starting later, on to the actual rendezvous site about both of which they had learned previously by newspaper, handbill, or the official agreement which some groups may have prepared, such as that credited to northsider A. C. R. Shaw (see Appendix B, volume XVI of The American Trails Series, *This Emigrating Company. The 1844 Oregon Trail Journal of Jacob Hammer.*) There the early arrivals awaited the others. The official beginning of the journey was estimated to correspond with a sufficient supply of grass on which the cattle could graze in the evenings after each day's travel. That time was usually in mid May.

Before proceeding to their rendezvous site, the Hammers spent several days at the home of Hannah Hammer's aunt Mary Stokes near Savannah, Missouri, "waiting for the company to get ready." Hannah, Jacob and their two children continued on May third to the Council Bluffs vicinity where (according to Edmund Bray) the northsiders that year were to meet. On their way, they stopped twice for others to make final preparations for the trip, and were joined by families northwest of Oregon City (Holt County, Missouri) at the Nishnabotna River. The Hammers arrived at the meeting place on May twentieth; the next day their train was organized. (Bray recalled that "we started on the 18th of May;" Hammer's journal entry for the thirteenth noted "some . . . going to . . . California.")

The Nishnabotna River site was also a place of rendezvous

for some of the California-bound families, according to the biographical sketch of Moses Schallenberger which appeared in 1888 in *Pen Pictures . . .,* a county history of Santa Clara County. Young Schallenberger was said to have arrived there "about the first of March" along with his sister Elizabeth Louise Schallenberger and her husband Dr. John Townsend, where they were joined by the Murphy family members for whom the Stephens-Murphy party of northsiders has generally been named.

For one southsider train, a meeting place was designated on the west bank of the Missouri River about nine miles above St. Joseph (where Minto and Rees first stopped).

The site of the emigrant camp was advertised in regional newspapers in the summer of 1843 by Cornelius Gilliam, who invited all interested parties to join him and his relatives at the site across the Missouri River at a point five miles west of Savannah. The meeting place was in the "Indian Territory" (as period maps affirmed) specifically the Sac and Fox reserve, so he may have had to arrange with the Indians and their agent for use of the site.

Gilliam set May tenth as a date when those who would follow him should meet in the river bottom in present Burr Oak Township, Doniphan County, Kansas. According to Washington Smith Gilliam, the "General's" son, the Gilliam family crossed the river on March second, well ahead of the date recommended for the others. B. F. Nichols wrote that "On the 10th of May, 1844, my father [Benjamin Nichols] and family, with a number of others, left the Missouri River at a point seven miles above St. Joe . . ." (Nichols thereby implied perhaps that his family crossed the river here on the appointed day for meeting and moved to the rendezvous site.)

Willard Rees remembered that in mid April, when he and

Minto first stopped at the site of the river crossing, some thirty families were present. "Some had been sojourning for two months grazing their stock on the rushes that grew in great abundance." The site for an actual rendezvous, however, had been planned for near the government's Indian agency twenty miles west of the river.

E. E. Parrish and family, who crossed the Missouri River on the ferry boat on April sixteenth to the "Emigrant incampment," were among those who crossed the river well ahead of the meeting date set by Gilliam. On May ninth they headed for the Indian agency apparently in the company of "General" Cornelius Gilliam and his family. They reached the Indian agency on May eleventh, remained there for five days awaiting new arrivals, then moved on with the train on May seventeenth.

The Morrison family, with hired hands John Minto and Willard Rees, ferried the Missouri on the day after the farewell dinner in their honor at the Morrison's home. According to Minto, they camped on the west bank of the Missouri and the next morning drove to the "Indian agency on Wolf River." At the Agency they were "detained for some days . . . by the almost constant rains," Minto stated.

Willard Rees recalled these specific events a bit differently, stating that it was near the first of May when "the old camp [on the west side of the Missouri] was broken up and the trains began to move west in the direction of the Iowa Indian Agency some twenty miles distant and appointed as the place of general rendezvous . . ." He remembered the crossing of Wolf Creek, which "was found to be too deep to ford." A bridge was constructed, the wagons were driven across and, near the Agency, the emigrants "went into camp where we remained several days" (Rees put it as early as May seventh). Though Parrish wrote on May sixteenth that

"We . . . crossed [Wolf Creek] on the Bridge," he had written on May thirteenth that a bridge across Wolf Creek had already been "swept away before the flood." A raft was used but failed to work, then "two canews" were used more successfully.

It was probably Rees, soon to be made "adjutant" (or company clerk) of the Gilliam train, who collected the data that was credited to Gilliam and printed in area newspapers in mid May listing among those "assembled at Ft. Leavenworth" the following occupations: "1 minister, 1 lawyer, 1 millwright, 3 millers, 1 tailor, 2 cabinet makers, 5 carpenters, 1 ship carpenter, 3 blacksmiths, 1 cooper, 1 tailoress, 1 wheelwright, 2 shoemakers, 1 weaver, 1 gunsmith, 1 wagonmaker, 1 merchant, and the rest farmers." The latter group was in a majority of course, being eighty-one in number of the 108 said to be in the "independent Oregon Colony at this date."

Another such list, varying somewhat, appeared in the Independence paper the *Western Expositor* of May eighteenth, included in a letter addressed to Nathaniel Ford and signed by "Captain Cornelius Gilliam, Oregon Camps, St. Joseph, May 15, 1844." This list subtracted one blacksmith, and added three wheelwrights. In addition, there were said to be "48 families, 108 men (of whom 60 are young men), 323 persons, 410 oxen, 160 cows (11 of which are team cows), 143 young cattle, 54 horses, 41 mules and 72 wagons."

William Shaw, Gilliam's brother-in-law (he was married to Sarah "Sally" Gilliam) crossed the Missouri River, as had others of the Gilliam train, at "what is called Capels Ferry," he told Bancroft. This Shaw family "left Missouri for Oregon on May tenth," possibly the date when they crossed the Missouri River. Though he did not give a reason, Shaw said that "I started later than the others." On his way to Wolf

Creek, Shaw was asked to take charge of the property left by
"a Mr. Bishop", who had just died. Here the Shaws too were
delayed further by the high water of the Wolf.

According to the recollections of Catherine Sager Pringle,
her family was among the last to arrive at the rendezvous of
the Gilliam train. Their preparations for the journey were
similar to that of others. They had sold their farm in Platte
County in late 1843 and "wintered" near the Missouri River
before setting out on what would prove for this beleaguered
family to be a particularly grief-stricken journey. At St.
Joseph the family met, as pre-arranged, with the Aaron
Chamberlain family and drove a few miles north of the town
and camped. The next day they continued to "Capler's
Landing" where they found other emigrants waiting to cross
the Missouri River and as yet accompanied by the friends and
relatives who had come to see them off.

After crossing the river, the Sagers camped for the night.
But the next morning, before they could proceed toward the
rendezvous, they were detained while Mr. Sager crossed back
to the east side to find his cattle that the night before had
followed a homing instinct back to the eastern bank. Meanwhile, the others had moved westward, leaving the Sagers to
catch up. And so, with cattle once again in tow, the family
set out alone. That day several in the family became ill,
Catherine indicated, from something akin to sea sickness
since they were not accustomed to the hours-long pitching
and yawing of the wagon (also, Mrs. Sager would soon give
birth). Still alone after traveling all day and into the night,
the family stopped in the road, unhitched their oxen (two
yoke of which, Catherine recalled, were "steady and well-
broken" while "the rest were young and unbroken") and
remained until the next morning when they advanced to the
rendezvous. Here they found the train in the process of being

organized and they were assigned to William Shaw's company.

For Samuel Black Crockett and the small party with whom he traveled, just getting to the rendezvous of the Gilliam train was an ordeal. In his brief day to day journal of the first few weeks of his emigration, Crockett recorded his labored progress, possibly from Putnam County, Missouri, it has been assumed. On April twenty-fifth, his party lost two oxen drowned in a swollen creek the exact location of which he did not record. On the thirtieth he was probably in the southwestern corner of Linn County, Missouri, after a trek of twenty-six miles.

On May first, Crockett and the others passed through Chillicothe, in Livingston County, and reached Gallatin, county seat of Davies County, on the third. By the ninth, they were at Savannah in Andrew County. But unlike the Hammers who had come through Savannah on April twenty-sixth, and who left that vicinity on May third traveling north, Crockett and his few companions traveled five miles to the Missouri River, where they found "a bad boat and difficult crossing." The next day—Saturday—they took the wagons across but their cattle scattered to the woods on the east bank. It took until Tuesday to gather the cattle. Once across the river again, they "crossed a desparate slough and encamped." On Thursday, May sixteenth, Crockett's party started for Wolf River and on the way the wagons "were mired in a quag; by unloading and doubling teams we got out." Upon reaching Wolf River they "found plenty of indians and part of the oregon company crossing the river on two canoes made for that purpose. [It] rained nearly all day." Parrish had crossed the Wolf on the fifteenth; those who Crockett observed crossing the Wolf on the sixteenth may have been the two wagons Parrish noted on the eighteenth which were "not far behind."

NATHANIEL FORD AND HIS WIFE
Courtesy of Polk County Historical Society, Oregon

On Friday, the seventeenth, Crockett wrote that, "All of the company crossed wolf river today and part of them left for the old encampment of the maim[sic] company and part of them encamped on the bank for the night." On Saturday they "traveled hard all day and overtook General Gillum's main company . . ."

Many of the narrators of '44 referred to the difficult crossing of the Wolf River. The route taken out from the St. Joseph vicinity later to be known as the St. Joseph road, a much-used feeder route, was possibly first used by the emigrants of '44. It was not easy going; the route wound often in 'S' configurations (if one kept to the ridges between the Missouri and the Kansas rivers) through "broken" country marked by numerous limestone outcrops. Eventually the country became rolling and the prairie began.

There is little news available in James Clyman's journal about events prior to the rendezvous of the train called by the name of its soon-to-be-elected leader, Nathaniel Ford. Clyman began his journal at Independence on May fourteenth, on which day he also passed through Westport and "came to camp at Elm Brook" (Elm Grove?). Independence, it should be noted, was on the south bank of the Missouri (on a portion of the river which meandered sometimes east and west) and had been the staging point for previous emigrations.

Another of the Ford train, twenty two year old Alanson Hinman, had come to Booneville, Missouri, from Pennsylvania to seek employment and had met "Col." Nathaniel Ford, "a local politician of some considerable reputation in that locality and a man who was very much interested in Oregon." A young man such as himself, Hinman stated, was "a valuable addition to the party" of emigrants Ford was assembling and was therefore invited to join the train. About the degree to which the emigrants were informed on the

subject of Oregon, Hinman said that they "knew considerable about the country, principally from the letters which
Peter Burnett [1843 emigrant] had written to the local papers
of Missouri." They had also followed the Congressional
debate about the territory to the west. "No one in the party
seems to have doubted that the United States possessed a
good title to the [Oregon] country," Hinman said of those he
met.

Chapter Four

Organizing for the Journey

Each of the trains of '44 traveled a few days before being "organized." Gilliam's train was the first to do so. Crockett's journal entry for Sunday, May nineteenth, explained that "Today we were formed ourselves into companies each company consisting of about 20 waggons and elected all necsary [sic] officers both civil and military." But, he added, "a number of wagoons did not organize themselves today."

The organization of the train had been put off at least twice before, according to E. E. Parrish, who wrote on May sixteenth that the "Colony" had "previously elected Honorable C. Gilliam General," though on which date he did not say. Though Parrish did not cite a specific date of the actual organization of the train, he wrote that Gilliam gave a speech on the seventeenth, and on the eighteenth he used the term "companies" in referring to the day's travel progress.

According to William Shaw, "We had not organized when we crossed over the [Missouri] River at all. We started and intended to organize when we got out. We came out fifteen or twenty miles this side [west] of the [Iowa-Sac-Fox Presbyterian] mission and there organized." (Minto estimated "thirty miles" travel from the Missouri River crossing to the site of organization, which occurred, he wrote, on "May twentieth.")

The lengthier narratives by those with the Gilliam train all included some reference to the election of officers of that train. B. F. Nichols explained that "the officers were elected according to military rule. . . The rival candidates stood apart in an open space, [with] those voting, taking place in a line with their candidate at the head. When all had formed into line, the number in the respective lines determined who had been elected. This was repeated for each office . . ." Thereafter, "We were governed, some of the time, by strict military rule." The procedure was observed by a few Indians present at the time.

Willard H. Rees too stated that in early May, when "many of the emigrants were becoming impatient of delay," Gilliam "marshalled the men of the camp, bringing them into single file." He then "addressed the men in a serious yet encouraging manner, reminding them that they had left their old homes and many friends beyond the Missouri River, that they were now in the Indians' country and perhaps would so continue to be for several years to come. He would especially recommend a strict military organization as best for the protection of life and property while on the long dangerous march through the country of savage war-like tribes. The time had come for the election of their officers upon whose judgement and conduct the gravest responsibility must rest."

Then Benjamin Nichols Sr. placed Gilliam's name in nomination as train commander and requested "those who favored the nomination to step one pace forward [upon which] the column advanced unbroken to the front." Thus Gilliam commanded, temporarily as it turned out. And, in like manner the other officers were elected: Michael T. Simmons, Colonel; John Enyart, Lieutenant Colonel; Rees, Sergeant Major "performing the duties of Adjutant." When organized, the train was divided into four companies headed by Robert Wilson Morrison, William Shaw, Allen Saunders, and Richard Woodcock (said by Rees to have been "a border school teacher"). Benjamin Nichols Sr. was elected Judge "invested with power to hear and determine certain causes" in "a court of equity." Joseph Gage was made an "associate justice" as was Theophilus Magruder. "No service I believe was ever performed by this tribunal as the martial law took precedence so long as subordination to the general military organization was maintained." Unfortunately, Rees' commentary about the affairs of the train after leaving the Indian agency in Kansas was lost (see Bibliographical Notes).

Retrospective views of the organizational structure were given by Parrish when he noted the elections that followed a spate of resignations: on July twelfth "Colonel [Michael Troutman] Simmons" resigned whereupon the "General ordered a new election" at which Jacob Hoover became "Lieutenant Colonel" and Alex McQuin "first Lieutenant." Later, in mid July, the General himself resigned in a huff, as did "first Colonel Benjamin Nichols."

After Gilliam's resignation, Parrish wrote that the Saunders company was "called the California Company" and its officers included "Mitchell Gilliam, Lieutenant; James Marshall [who would later find the gold nuggets that would set off the California gold rush of 1848–9], First Sergeant; Gamaliel Parrish [son of E. E. Parrish], Second Sergeant; Solomon Shelton, First Corporal; William Gilliam, Second Corporal; and E. E. Parrish, Judge." The foregoing were perhaps titles copied from the previous all-train organizational structure.

There are several references in the Gilliam train narratives to the size of that train. When they left the Indian agency, John Minto estimated that there were "eighty four white covered wagons." William Shaw told Bancroft that in the company of which he was elected captain, "I had about forty-five wagons. There were about eighty wagons in the train altogether, maybe more. There were about 500 persons in the train."

Several years after the journey, Willard Rees offered another set of statistics for the Gilliam train. In a letter in 1874 to his former trail mate John Minto, he wrote that "our train all told . . . numbered 87 wagons and was divided into four companies." Second, in the pages which Fred Lockley copied from the sparce leavings of Rees' unpublished Trail narrative, Rees recalled that "The brigade was divided into three companies with an average of twenty-seven wagons each." And to these, "there were some half dozen wagons joined the companies later." The three companies which he identified in the second reference were those of Robert Wilson Morrison, William Shaw and Richard Woodcock. In the first citation he had referred also to the company of Allen Saunders. Further, "the muster roll contained 108 men rank and file and was subsequently increased to 115." Rees also included "stock consisting of horses, mules, oxen, cows and young cattle, numbering between eight and nine hundred head . . ."

John Minto, in writing to Bancroft years later, referred to another organizational matter. Once on the west side of the Missouri, Minto wrote, (though whether at the first camp near the river bank or that near the Indian agency he did not say) there occurred "the first act in the interest of safe journey to Oregon": the appointment of a committee of three citizens who were not going to Oregon "to make investigations into the amount and kind of preparation each head of a family or single emigrant coming independent of others had made for the trip." The examination (the stand-ards for which Minto did not give) had little effect, however, for though "it was soon discovered that some were not at all adequately provided for such a journey, none were hindered from starting on that account."

An explanation as to why some, though not adequately provisioned, were permitted to start, can be found perhaps in E. E. Parrish's journal which he recopied in 1867 and to which he may have added some important reflections. Therein Parrish gave the revealing information that though some packed food for the entire trip, an appreciable number intended to subsist on wild game along the way. (Minto stated that R. W. Morrison had much the same intention.) On July twelfth, five days after reaching the Platte River, the camp was "in something of confusion," Parrish wrote, "a part [of which] desire to be off, while the other part wish to remain and improve the oppertunity to save and cure plenty of meat while there is an oppertunity." The "confusion" was caused by two different methods of provisioning. "Some laid in provisions on the start for the journey, while many others, backwoodsmen, as they tolde me, depended on the gun for their meete." The matter was resolved when "the more considerate, and better supplied, gave way to what now appeared to be unbending necesity," and the train remained while the "backwoodsmen" hunted buffalo. It may have been these who intended to get by on hunting to whom Minto referred as those "not at all adequately provided for . . ."

The northsiders of the Stephens-Murphy/Thorp train were organized on the eastern bank of the Missouri near Council Bluffs on May twenty-first after pulling many miles over the hills of northern Missouri and into Iowa Territory. The next day they began crossing the river, a four day affair in which they battled the elements, as well as the differing opinions among themselves about the timing and the method for crossing. Though the other trains may have experienced some of the same difficulties in organizing themselves, Hammer alone complained of contrary attitudes resulting in factions already this early in the journey.

For the Hammers and the other northsiders, there is no clear indication about whether the "Organization Agreement 1844" document attributed to A. C. R. Shaw was used as the contract under which that train operated in the beginning of the journey or whether the "agreement" was just something Shaw had composed and had on hand in late

1843 when answering questions about emigrating. The angry outburst by Shaw on May twenty-ninth was said by Jacob Hammer to have been caused in part because the captain "gave orders contrary to our regulations." Whatever these regulations were, they arose from the same needs and considerations with which all trains had to deal in some way.

Eleven days after leaving Independence, Clyman's train elected Nathaniel Ford their leader on May twenty-fifth at the "Waukarusha" River. Clyman mentioned only this one election. And not until the twenty-sixth was there "a call . . . made this morning for a regular organization," whereupon Clyman and eighteen other men (representing seven wagons) were "formed in to one mess for mutual assistance in traveling and encamping near together." His mess "made some regulations to prepare for keeping of a night and day guard" thought necessary "as we are now not more [than] two days easy travel from the Kaw [Kansas] Indian villages, the first of the wild roveing tribes that we meet with on our way."

The June twelfth issue of the St. Louis Democrat quoted the Independence newspaper the Western Expositor (date not given) in reporting that "the Oregon emigrants started from their place of general rendezvous at the "Lone Elm" on the 14th ult[imo, i.e. May]." But "although they had gone upwards of two weeks, they had in consequence of the high water, only travelled about one hundred miles."

Furthermore, "Major Moses Harris, a native of Union county, South Carolina, is their pilot, and Col. Nathaniel Ford, of Howard county, Mos., is captain of the company. There are several small parties on their route, which have not yet reached Col. Ford's company, embracing in all 27 families, numbering about 125 souls. They also have 10 wagons, 130 cattle, and some few horses."

The report described the "aggregate strength" of the train including "those who have reached him [Col. Ford] by this time" to be fifty-five married men with their wives, their children (83 boys, 85 girls), and eighty single men, for a total of 358. These were traveling in "fifty-four wagons, with 500 head of cattle, sixty horses and twenty-eight mules."

The Ford train then when fully formed "will be about 64 wagons, [483 people by the count above], 640 [i.e. 630] head of cattle, 65 horses and 30 mules—quite a number." (For comparison, see Clyman's count below.)

The *Democrat* article continued to suppose that, "Col. Ford's company it is thought will reach Gen. Gilliam's in about two weeks, the latter having crossed the river near Fort Leavenworth, and being now encamped on the Nimahaw river, waiting for Col. Ford's company."

"In Gen. Gilliam's company, there are 48 families, 108 men, 60 of whom are young men, 167 children, in all 323 persons. There are also in his company 73 wagons, 713 cattle, 54 horses and 11 mules." (See earlier counts above of the Gilliam train.)

It was explained also that, "There were a good many families who came on here for the purpose of going to Oregon, but changed their route and have gone to Texas. This, it is said, was in consequence of the supposed annexation of Texas to the Union."

As for those who opted for the Pacific Northwest, "The Oregon emigrants are well supplied with provisions, and if no unlooked for accident happens to them, will reach their place of destination about the 1st of October." This last assumption, as will be seen, was an estimate ambitious by at least one month.

Once across the "Waukarusha," and twelve days into the journey, Clyman counted "92 men present." But a more dependable estimate was included in a letter which he wrote on May thirtieth, at "Tonga Morga [Nunga] Creek, Four Miles West of Kaw Village" to the *Milwaukee Sentinel* (published therein on August 11; he would post other such periodic reports to this paper, perhaps by an arrangement with the editor, Elisha Starr, an acquaintance from the time Clyman lived in Wisconsin). The train was traveling in four groups (probably "messes") at this time, Clyman indicated, there being at his current vantage "thirty-nine wagons, about one hundred men, and about the same number of women and children . . ." About "twenty or thirty teams [were] yet behind." Exactly "Forty-one teams are north of the Kansas river . . ." A small group of "ten teams" were "three or four days ahead of us." All together, "we muster about one hundred wagons, and from five to seven hundred souls, when we are fairly collected."

By May twenty-sixth, then, all the trains were organized and on the move. The emigration of '44 was under way.

Chapter Five

The Rains of '44

Even as they moved toward their rendezvous sites, the emigrants of '44 were beset by all but intolerable traveling conditions. By all accounts, the spring and summer of 1844 in the Midwest was remarkable for the amount of rain that fell. For several weeks while the emigrants were traveling in eastern Kansas, travel was hindered, even halted altogether for days at a time. The weather and particularly the exhausting, uncomfortable travel conditions which stunned the chroniclers of '44 were characteristic of the monsoon season in some regions of the world where travel by hundreds of people in loaded wagons would never have been contemplated much less attempted.

As early as January, E. E. Parrish had been delayed a week by high water in the One Hundred and Two River when his family was moving to the place where they "put up for the winter." Willard Rees called the spring of '44 "an unusual backward one." He described scenes along the Missouri River where "thick broken ice was still to be seen in places along the timber line that skirted the sand bars, sometimes fifty yards from the water's edge where it had been left at high water when the ice of the upper river was broken up."

The spring rains soon brought a sense of alarm. The *Baptist Missionary Magazine* (Boston, September 1844, vol. 24, page 284) reported that in " 'Kansas' . . . spring opened very early; but after about three weeks' pleasant weather in March, rains commenced, and continued up to the 1st of June so constant as to render it quite impossible to plough or plant . . . ." All across present eastern Kansas streams were flooded and bottom lands inundated.

By mid June the bottom country in some places was twelve feet under water. When the water eventually subsided, crops and fences had been washed away, along with out buildings and livestock. Much topsoil close to the rivers was melted away, silting the waterways to brown surges behind which were deposited overlays of sand in some places several feet deep, making formerly rich farmlots barren. <u>Indians of the region had no oral tradition of the likes of the flood of 1844.</u>

The people themselves were no less threatened than their livestock and other property. The smaller streams particularly rose suddenly, and those living on the banks, or travelers encamped there, were often forced to move quickly to higher ground. Thousands of families reportedly were made homeless. One month after Clyman and the others rode through Westport Landing, that place was nearly completely swept away by the rising floodwaters. Other river landings suffered similarly. The water was moving rapidly toward the larger rivers of course, and the Missouri and the Mississippi soon showed the results. The *St. Louis Democrat* of June 24, 1844, reported the Mississippi "38 feet, 7 inches . . . above low water mark." Four days later, the river crested and began to recede, baring the sodden and devastated country side.

Many people clambered aboard river boats, flatboats and other crafts to ride out the flood, but even that refuge was occasionally threatened. The *Niles Register* of July twentieth reprinted an article from the Liberty (Missouri) *Pioneer* which told of the steamboat *Mary Tompkins* which, laden with flood victims, was swept from the channel of the Missouri thereabouts and out over the neighboring prairie, breaking down cottonwood trees as it went. Other boats carried destitute passengers away from the scene of their heartbreaking losses.

While the southside emigrants were yet in eastern Kansas,

the two hundred persons who boarded the *John Aull* at St. Joseph in mid July included many flood victims who, arriving at St. Louis in mid July, set about their own dejected way, to the east. Those who remained faced bouts of chills and fevers, ravages encouraged by the mosquito infested pools of stagnant water left by the receding rivers. The smudge-pots used incessantly to ward off the mosquitoes created a smoky, reeking pall around cabins and elsewhere. Even by the next fall, travelers in the region were yet complaining that many bridges had not been replaced and fording places at streams long had been reduced to bogs where wagons and draft animals mired. The flood of '44 was not easily forgotten.

In all this, the emigrants continued their travels, sensing perhaps that they were not only leaving familiar scenes, but were escaping a panorama of destruction and despair. Obviously then, their own travel conditions in the nearly continuous rain were exasperating and depressing. From what appears in, and between the lines of, the narratives of '44, one can nearly feel the conditions in which the emigrants toiled, and the many discomforts that came with traveling in such adverse weather. John Minto recalled that in the diary he had kept for the first two months of the journey (an effort he apparently abandoned) he had recorded only eight days without rain.

Jacob Hammer had recorded on April twenty-sixth, the day his family left their former Missouri home, that the streams "between Little Platte and One Hundred and Two rivers in Andrew County, Missouri" were high, causing the family to detour. A few hours later their wagon was mired in mud at a creek bank and they remained there for the night.

Though for the northsiders there was less rain and fewer delays, Jacob Hammer made reference to four days of rain (May fifteenth, sixteenth, seventeenth, and nineteenth) while yet in Missouri and in Iowa Territory. Later, on the west side of the Missouri River and following close to the north bank of the Platte, Jacob reported sloughs—swampy areas no doubt made worse by the excessive rain— along both the Papillion and the Elkhorn rivers.

"The rain came down on us," he wrote on the twenty-seventh, as it did the next day, and the next—days spent in camp in the rain. On the thirtieth the train reached the Elkhorn and ferried across in two "boats" of wagon beds covered with raw hides. After this, however, the train did not lose another day of travel because of rain until June tenth, by which time they were near the Pawnee mission on the Loup River.

B. F. Nichols Jr. remembered the conditions through which his family struggled when they left the Missouri River encampment and headed to the Indian agency rendezvous of the Gilliam train. "The first day's travel was noted, particularly, for the mud and slush encountered while crossing a low tract of land that we were compelled to traverse. There was ample evidence of the difficulties experienced by those who had preceded us. Here and there were sections of logs which had been used as a fulcrum, and long poles for levers to pry the wagons out of the mire."

The Nichols wagon was handled expertly by the family's driver, Charles Smith, who, Nichols said, wielded a ready ox whip and as ready a supply of cuss words for commanding the oxen. Smith's skill and profanity were often for naught. "The incessant rains caused the ground to become so soft that the rear wagons often sank in to the hub, and frequently had to 'double team' to pull out. I do not think there was twenty-four hours at any one time that it did not rain after we left the Missouri and until we reached the Platt River . . ."

Catherine Sager remembered being made to remain inside the wagon with the cover drawn tight against the rain for days at a time, confined in the scant space not otherwise taken by goods packed in barrels and boxes and sacks. For her and the others, to the annoyance of damp clothing was added the nauseating mustiness of the close atmosphere inside the wagon. For several days there was no opportunity to dry out the clothing and bedding. When there was an occasional opportunity to dry out—when the rain ceased for a few hours and clothing and bedding was spread out to "air"—the event was noted thankfully in the journals.

The Ford train, leaving from Independence, had similar rough going. It would appear that this train proceeded in small groups for some miles, filing along, Clyman wrote, on the "Sant a Fee Trace" west from the Missouri River toward the point at which the "Oregon road" branched off from the Trace. The roads were "extremely bad owing to the Leate greate rains," Clyman noted on May fourteenth. He and the others left Westport in midmorning amidst rain that lasted all day and all the next night "in one continued and rapid Shower." The rain continued on May sixteenth and the prairie west of the river was "nearly knee deep in mud and water." Travel conditions the next day, when the train passed the point at which the Santa Fe Trace and the road to Oregon separated, required "doubled teams nearly all the way." Even so, "Both teams Swamped down and [we] had to unload our team, [in the process] breaking an axeltree."

Though the rain apparently slackened somewhat, it continued in mid-morning of the eighteenth "so much so that we could not finish our axeltr[ee]." The rain continued through the night. "Our beds ware overflown in water nearly mid side deep." Sunday dawned a "dismal rainy thick morning" with a "Tremendous Shower" about eleven o'clock. Soon, however, Clyman replaced the axletree, reloaded the wagon, and, seemingly taking it all in stride, (he, after all, was no stranger to journeys with extremely trying circumstances) he took time to pick "a considerable fine mess of ripe Strawberries."

For the emigrant women, there was also the chore of cooking out of doors in the rain. There were days during which no hot meals were prepared because of the nearly impossible task of lighting and keeping a fire in a nearly constant downpour. There were, however, some particularly commendable efforts at doing just that, to be sure. James Clyman wrote on May twenty-eighth that "Our last nights repast" was graced by one young woman who "watched and nursed the fire and held an umblella[sic] over the fire and her skillit with the greatest composure for near 2 hours and baked bread enough to give us a very plentifull super . . ."

Clyman, Parrish, Minto and others traveling from points south on their way across the northeast corner of present Kansas wrote often of the vast wetland which the region had become because of the many succeeding days of rain. Streams were far out of their banks, making the approaches to fords laborious and the actual crossings treacherous. Expanses of water "over shoe mouth deep," Clyman wrote, stood upon prairie meadows.

Even on days when sunlight was seen however briefly, mud sucked at the hooves of the draft animals, and gripped at the wagon wheels, making each step burdensome and adding weight to each revolution of the wheels. What's more, the cool dampness of the thick morning fogs seemed to penetrate even to the bone marrow, and certainly to the spirit, of the travelers. On June thirteenth, Clyman wrote of "a great Dejection in camp" while waiting for the Knife River to become passable. From a neighboring bluff he had a panoramic view of the Kansas River, which "shews 8 or 10 miles wide" with flooding.

The conditions may well have caused some to give up the

dream then and there. Clyman wrote about many "brooding over fine houses, dry beds, & pleasant Society all of which are scarce here. . . The distance and circumstances allmost seems to forbid our ever regaining any of the comforts of civilization and verry little encouragement can be given to the fearfull and timerous." Spirits were low, and with a full five months remaining in the journey.

There probably were defections (though none for that specific reason were mentioned in the narratives) by those who threw up their hands, and the chance to reach the distant goal, because of the disheartening sight of floodwaters surrounding them. The "road," little more than a hint of such at best, was churned to mud for mile upon mile. Double teaming was required in many places for the wagons to move at all; sometimes the wagon had to be unloaded as well.

The entire region was similarly affected. On June twenty-second, three men returned to the Ford train from tracking allegedly stolen cattle and reported that the streams to the south and east of the train had risen and floodwaters had ravaged the countryside for hundreds of square miles.

On their way to the Indian Agency on Wolf River, John Minto, Willard Rees, the Morrisons, and others, "were stopped several hours in making a small stream passable, its banks being low and soft . . ." [the] "stream . . . so near the surface that wagons went down to the hubs in the rich soil."

Minto reported no less than a "small cyclone" during the night of June twenty-second after all were across the Big Blue and "camped under large cottonwood trees on the west bank . . ." The twister "blew the most of the tents loose and cast water down upon us in sheets rather than drops. Its roaring through the trees, and casting down branches from them, was fearful for a few minutes." Fortunately, no one was hurt, though all were thoroughly drenched.

Parrish too complained of the mind-boggling conditions.

"Oh the difficulties of this day in crossing the slough and bottom," he wrote on May ninth, the day his family left the Missouri River encampment. "We mired down twice within less than a mile, so that we had to unload in both cases." Thankful for the help from others among their group, they "passed through both mud and water . . ."

The abnormal amounts of rainfall during the spring of '44 pointed up the number of streams which the trains were forced to cross in Kansas. Between the Missouri River and the Platte, Parrish named eleven stream crossings and additional "sloughs" and flooded "bottoms." Clyman, coming from farther south, listed nineteen by name or other direct reference besides a few more he crossed in search of stolen or strayed cattle.

Even in good weather, the crossing of rivers, streams and creeks was a task not taken lightly. But in the spring of 1844, every channel where water ran or had once run, and every low lying spot where water could possibly collect, was made at least bothersome and at worst life-threatening. High water caused many delays. Parrish used the quaint but succinct compound terms "water-stayed" and "water-bound" for that occurrence.

Two days before they were officially organized, the group with which Parrish was camped tried unsuccessfully to take sixteen wagons across the Wolf River using a raft. When this "proved a failure" they built two canoes, probably of the hollowed out log variety. The next day the Cornelius Gilliam extended family and several other families arrived for their turn at the treacherous crossing.

Sometimes the men "prepared the banks" of streams and creeks for the descent and ascent of the wagons by "digging a kind of road down the bank" as Clyman wrote on May twenty-second at the "Waukarusha" River. Here the water level was expected to fall, but it rose instead. Nevertheless, wagons were "let down by cords over a steep rock bluff through mud knee deep an[d] in the rain pouring in torrents." All this moved Clyman to write that he had never seen "more determined resolution even amongst men than most of the female part of our company exhibited." About twenty wagons were taken across by this method with "the utmost exertion" before the river rose to a level which "would swim a horse," whereupon the train members were forced to stop their work and to endure yet another delay.

The river rose another six or seven feet during the night. But the next morning the crossing continued, with the use of "one verry ordinary canoe," an insufficient conveyance which could accommodate but a paltry load on each trip. Clyman's experience at the Waukarusha pointed up the speed with which the water level rose in the streams in this region. It must have been awe inspiring. Later, on June tenth, he noted that during the day, the "Knife River" rose fifteen feet.

The fashioning of crude and cumbersome but apparently servicable pontoons on which to float the wagons was a common practice. Though an occasional raft was tried, the hastily made pontoons were more commonly (and successfully) used. At the "Black Vermillion Creek," Minto and the others "waded into the timber lining the stream, while the water was still knee deep, and cut down the largest cotton wood trees we could find. These we shaped into large canoes, and lashed two together so that the center of the bottom of each would just receive the wheels of the respective sides of a wagon." This worked until the water level of this particular stream fell to a point at which "the bank on the further side became exposed," whereupon "it was necessary to use oxen and log chains . . . to bring the loaded wagons to firm land . . . up the bank."

On June twentieth, the Saunders company, with whom the Parrishes traveled after leaving William Shaw's company on or before May twenty-sixth, "Spent the day in hunting up the canoes used by Woodcock's company." They found two canoes which they "halled out of the brush and fastened together" and made ready for crossing the next day.

During this episode, "a fine young man, James Oen [Owen?]" had set out for the opposite bank to retrieve the canoes but came near drowning when he "cramped while swimming." The next day the Parrish's "Western" was drawn across on the "canoes" while the companies of Shaw and Morrison "came up". On June twenty-second, Morrison's company crossed; Shaw's company followed suit on the twenty-third as did "about half the cattle." The job of crossing the Big Blue was finished the next day.

Though there were no deaths by drowning reported in the records herein considered, fatal accidents of that sort were not unusual during the emigrations. In addition to young Mr. Owen's close call, two more near drownings were reported.

Much later in the journey, A. C. R. Shaw, Jacob Hammer's traveling companion, came near drowning in his efforts to salvage some of the belongings from Mr. Osborn's wagon which upset in the Portneuf River in the Snake River country near Ft. Hall.

Hammer's description (September first) of A. C. R. Shaw's flirtation with a drowning death on the Portneuf River was characteristically brief. But John Minto was actually twice presumed drowned early in the journey while crossing the Big Blue River on June twenty-second.

Minto described in detail both of his own bouts with the grim reaper. Though the water level was high in the Big Blue River, the river was within its banks where Minto first entered at a "ferry landing" (though no actual ferry craft is mentioned). Immediately the filly he was riding with only a bridle sank out of sight. Minto slid off the horse but the frightened animal followed close by and tried to climb on Minto's shoulders as the only object showing above water. Minto narrowly escaped this mismatch. "It was a close call," but both he and the horse were saved.

Later in the day, while attempting to "swim the cattle" at a ford three miles down river, Minto found the current swift and strong, with "barrel head" size "whirls" eddying off the edge of the point of land from which he entered the river for the second time. Taking a lead oxen with him to induce the others to follow, Minto again nearly lost his life as he was pulled under by one "swirl" spout of water and then by another. He let go of the ox, thinking he might be endangering it by adding his weight to that of the animal. In his struggle with the circular motion of the water spouts, he tried to swim for the main current of the river, but just then he touched upon the ox which by brute strength was freeing itself from the miniature malestroms and was swimming for the calmer current of the river. In this way, both man and beast were saved. But Minto's seeming demise, observed from the bank, prompted others to assume, for the second time that day, that he had drowned. Impressed by the strength of the ox, Minto held on tight to the other oxen when on repeated crossings of the river the current threatened again to take him under.

Not only was there real physical danger involved in river crossings, but the delays caused by difficulties in crossing the streams and rivers used up precious time. And time lost in May and June while waiting for swollen streams to recede were not only bothersome then, but caused foreboding also for the weeks ahead. Because of the time lost to rain delays, the travelers faced the pressing danger of being caught in the mountains beyond the Rockies in the snow season, particularly in the Blue Mountains of eastern Oregon. Rain delays also meant that more provisions were used without westward progress being made. And, as a matter of physical strain, the extra effort of double teaming, unloading often to lighten a wagon stuck in the mud, and ferrying an entire wagon train across each of the numerous streams, were all tiring endeavors.

The admonition heard occasionally that, ideally, the trains should reach Independence Rock in west central Wyoming by July fourth was reduced to an absurdity for the trains of '44. By that date, the Ford train, traveling last in line, was as yet ninety-two miles south east of Grand Island in the Platte; the Gilliam train was yet three and one half days from the Platte; the Hammers and others of the northsiders were within sight of "the chimnies" on the south side of the Platte. And ahead of them all was the long haul across the length of Nebraska (though not in the continuous rain) and the many dry, punishing miles of Wyoming as well before reaching Independence Rock.

Clyman, who reached the Rock on August sixteenth, cited the dangers of delay. Earlier, on July nineteenth, he indicated some easing of his concern over "crossing the mountains before winter." But on August eleventh, while near "red Bute mountain" near Casper, Wyoming, he acknowledged that his train's delay on the "Kaw" River was "bringing us through this dry region in [the] warmest and dryest part of the season. Our stock begins to look bad . . ."

Anxiety over being late on the Trail must surely have weighed heavily on the minds of all at this point. The Hammers reached the Rock on July twenty-ninth; Parrish and Clyman on August sixteenth, Minto on August seventeenth.

Though it appears from both the Edmund Bray and Moses Schallenberger narratives that they spent July Fourth, and perhaps an entire week, at the Rock, the daily travel schedule contained in the Hammer journal conflicts with the schedule for the Stephens-Murphy party suggested by Schallenberger editor George Stewart. However that particular mystery may be resolved, it is certain that the great sea of mud created by the rains of '44 during the early weeks of the journey, depressed and slowed the emigrants that season.

Chapter Six

Health

River crossings were sometimes life threatening, even when emigrations were not beset by nearly continuous rain as in 1844. But health was a daily concern on the overland passage. The all-pervading dampness of the spring and summer of '44 intensified the worry. Clyman observed on July seventh that "the season has been the worst possible for Sick persons generally . . ." Parrish, Clyman and Minto noted several more specific instances of illness among their companions than did Hammer or Schallenberger. (It has been assumed that the northsider route was somewhat healthier than the southern route.) Clyman wrote during the journey, and Catherine Sager and John Minto were of the same opinion as they recalled the journey years later, that the unusual wetness of the weather that season and the many discomforts it caused contributed to the health problems of many and even to deaths.

In a time when health services were primitive and one relied on home remedies and herbal concoctions to stabilize illnesses and even cure diseases, sickness was feared as the moribund forerunner of the ebb of life. Because of the inability then of medical science many times to counteract the effects of sicknesses and injuries, the eventual and often inevitable continuation of an illness weakened the patient to the point of death. And so when the writer of a travel journal mentioned the good health of the group, it was not idle chatter; it was thankful affirmation of the positive side of an ever present concern.

Jacob Hammer's first mention of illness among his companions was made on May fourteenth when "F. M. Thorp's wife [Margaret] was not able to travel." John Murphy had "the fever" on June eighteenth. On June twenty-second came the first mention of young Thomas Vance who "is sick and has been for several days;" similarly, "some others [are] not very well." The death of Thomas Vance on June twenty-eighth moved Jacob to record a lengthy entry though no symptoms, causes, or treatment were noted except for Jacob's suspicion that the medicine Dr. Townsend was said to have given Vance accelerated "this mortification."

Travel on the Trails brought many dangers to good health, particularly poor nutrition, exposure to threatening weather conditions, and the loss of refreshing sleep for those unable to rest satisfactorily in the conditions imposed on them.

Any mention of "the fever" in emigrant narratives has potentially serious implications. The reference might be to cholera, the pestilence which swept the Midwest in the 1830's and which would descend on those of the later emigrations. This malady was particularly feared for the speed with which it could inflict persons recently in excellent health. The victim first noticed an inward burning and craved cold drinks. Cramps followed, with vomiting and diarrhea, intestinal spasms, slow circulation, sunken eyes, cold skin, and eventual prostration.

The cholera victim's appearance made the disease particularly fearsome—a wizening effect from much dehydration, discoloration of the skin (to black and blue) from ruptured capillaries—as if the shadow of death was indeed passing over the afflicted. All this might take place in the space of a few days, or a few hours. This acuate gastroenteritis, "cholera morbus," struck in hot summer time and was caused by a bacillus in polluted water which quickly multiplied in the human alimentary tract. If untreated, the victim had less than a 50% chance of survival.

A reference by an emigrant to "camp," "yellow" or "mountain" fever might have meant typhoid, and that infliction was not uncommonly fatal. Ten days (or longer) of incubation by this particular bacillus brought on the fever and thereafter a combination of symptoms including headache, red rashes, bronchitis and coughing, pain in the abdomen, fever for two or more weeks, diarrhea in the final stage and eventually delirium. Near the end, the afflicted suffered from ulcers caused by the typhoid bacteria along the intestinal lining, leading to perforation and internal hemorrhaging. Some references to fevers may have been paratyphoid, a milder form of the dreaded disease the name indicates and of shorter duration.

Laudanum, a tincture of opium, was most often administered for many illnesses. This narcotic relieved the pain but did not affect the cause of the illness. Even this measure however was appreciated by the sufferer with abdominal pain in the final stage of the affliction.

Not all sickness on the Trail was as potentially lethal. More often some indisposition was suffered in due course. With the first mention on June twenty-second of the illness of Thomas Vance, Jacob Hammer referred also to "some others" who had not been well. On July sixth, "William Clemmens . . . sick for several days . . . is getting better." After the mention on September twenty-eighth of a man thrown to the ground by a spooked horse, Hammer made no more references to illness or injuries.

In the Gilliam train, B. F. Nichols, Jr. was ill at the very beginning of the trip. At the first camp after leaving the Missouri River encampment, Nichols recalled that "The night was bad; one of the worst of storms raged and the wind blew a gale." (This was the night too when "Mr. Bishop" died, as mentioned by several of the narrators.) "All this long night," Nichols wrote, "I lay sick nigh unto death, my

father and Charles Smith [the family's teamster] holding the
tent to prevent it from blowing down upon me as I lay inside.
It was not thought that I could live until morning. . . At
that time I was an invalid caused by a long spell of sickness,
lasting from September 22nd, 1843. I was very much reduced
from a physical stand point. I stood six feet one inch in
height; bones, skin and sinews were normal, and adapose
[adipose] tissue nil; weight 120 pounds."

It was not until he reached Ft. Laramie that young Nichols
recovered. There "I bade an affectionate farwell to that
infamous diabolical Missouri disease, called fever and ague.
'Twas here I had the last shake and it was all shaken out of
me. . . I shook and shook a plenty . . . from that time on my
convalescence was very rapid."

Nichols' mention of "ague" introduces this age-old complaint, actually generic for a variety of ailments often referred
to as "the agues" ("dumb ague"—or cerebral malaria;
"shaking ague," "chill fever," etc.). A chill alternating with
fever were common symptoms. The shaking ague, from
which young Nichols suffered, was common also, a bout of
which might begin with the urge to yawn and stretch, then
the fingernails would turn blue and the victim would complain of cold sensations that grew in intensity leading to
chattering of the teeth, followed by waves of fever during
which the head and back ached miserably. After profuse
sweating, the illness eased. Victims could be and often were
inflicted with recurrent bouts, even to the extent of a more
or less routine schedule being established of shaking and/or
chill-fever bouts, so much so that daily activities were sometimes planned around anticipated recurrences of the victim's
particular variety of "the ager."

Ague was not often fatal but did weaken one for attack by
more virulent strains of malaria, of which ague was a lesser
type (the mosquito, present in suffocating masses, was as yet

little suspected for its part in the malady). In the absence of quinine, not always readily available, other would-be remedies included teas made from select tree bark, or from mullen and sassafras roots, bloodwort or boneset tops, or, at one extreme, a selection of items from a catalog of bizarre concoctions not far removed from witches' brew. Though vaccination, as for small pox, was not unheard of (had in fact been introduced in the U.S. in 1800) there is little opportunity to know how many of the emigrants had availed themselves of this preventative measure.

When his train was ordered to "lay at camp" on June sixth, Samuel B. Crockett wrote that it was because of the "sickness which has been common . . . for some time." This indication of time is vague, but since Crockett joined the Gilliam train on May eighteenth, just nineteen days before his notation above, his "for some time" may have meant that several of the train were ill nearly from the official beginning of the journey.

James Clyman made a few references to illness. On May twenty-fifth, prompted perhaps by the distressing traveling conditions resulting from the nearly continuous downpour of rain, Clyman noted thankfully that "all are in good health." On June fifteenth, however, he noted "Several complaining of the chollic" (stomach cramps, often severe).

Clyman reported "the Musketoes troublesome" on July fifth, five days before reaching the Platte, and also wrote of "Several persons complaining of the Rhumatism & Dyentery[sic]." On the fifteenth, the wagons passed through a section of the Trail where mosquitoes were present in impressive, ravenous numbers. On the twenty-second, mosquitoes invaded the camp for the first time (there was no breeze that evening "to keep down the flies & Moketoes[sic]") although for the previous ten days mosquitoes were plentious enough to cover a horse every evening "if he happen to be out alone." Such a host of the infectious insects could certainly bring about the debilitating bouts of chills and fever and other symptoms which tormented those afflicted by the dreaded malaria.

Some who apparently began the journey in poor health were said to have improved. On May twenty-fifth, Clyman noted "Mr. Everhart who is taking a trip for his health . . . is making rapid improvements . . ." On July seventh, he referred to the tubercular "consumptives" among his group, and implied that something about the rigors of the trip so far had helped to improve the health of these afflicted ones. Later that month, on the twenty-eighth, Clyman turned clinician to observe that "all our sick of old cronic disorder begin to ware a healthy appearance and active elastick movement."

Parrish included more references to health than did any other of the chroniclers of '44, particularly about his family members. Though he noted "all in good health" on May twenty-ninth, the train was halted twice in the gloomy rains of early June: on the second for Mrs. Sager who had given birth to a daughter, Henrietta Naomi (referred to also as 'Rosanna') two days earlier on May thirty-first; and on the sixth for Gilliam's daughter, Margaret Louisa (Mrs. Joseph) Gage for what Parrish called "another family frolic," his way of announcing childbirth (though the child was not born until August third).

On June twenty-second, Parrish again noted that the camp was "all in good health." His own family was similarly blessed according to an entry four days later. On the thirtieth, the train had a welcome opportunity to air out the clothing, certainly contributing thereby to better health.

The journey also was not without the danger of accidents. On July third, one of the three wagons which upset that day contained Mrs. William Bowman who was already ill. The little son of Reverend Mr. Cave was injured in one of the wrecks. The next day, "a number are reported sick in camp."

Catherine Sager wrote of two accidents which her family had before her father's death. On July eighteenth, their wagon upset after they had crossed the South Platte. Mrs. Sager was knocked unconscious. (Parrish did not note this wagon wreck though he too crossed this fork of the Platte on that day and his own vehicle nearly upset when getting off the "track.") Two weeks later, on August first, Catherine's leg was broken just below the knee in a fall from the moving wagon. Without the aid of a doctor, Henry Sager set the child's leg himself, though it was later checked by Dr. Theophilos Degen who was traveling in a company behind William Shaw's company with which the Sagers traveled. Often before, the children had jumped onto the wagon tongue before bounding clear of the wheels when leaving the wagon while it was in motion. But this time Catherine's dress caught on an axe handle causing her to fall in the path of the wheels. As she lay on the ground both wheels on one side of the wagon passed over her left leg. She was confined to the interminable jarring and jolting of the wagon for the remainder of the journey. That evening the family reached Ft. Laramie.

Parrish's own family was in but "midling health" on July fourteenth. On the eighteenth he complained of being sick, apparently from a cold which he blamed on his having waded across the Platte River. Of a more serious nature, Captain Saunders "came into camp bad with cramp cholick" on July twentieth. On the twenty-fourth, the "camp" remained in place, to "rest the teams, wash the clothes . . . [and to] doctor the sick . . ."

On August first, Parrish was too ill to write in his journal. On the seventeenth, sixteen year old Elizabeth Ellen Parrish became ill and her father noted her condition for the next several days. His own health was much better on the twenty-second, but on the twenty-fifth, son Thomas Mapel Andrew

Jackson Parrish (age fourteen) "has taken a bad cold. . . I hope his Mother with good Medicines & her skill to apply it, & the blessing of God will soon bring him out." Parrish himself suffered from "bad Diorea" on August twenty-fifth.

The Parrish family suffered their most serious accident on September twenty-second when ten year old daughter Rebecca fell beneath the wheels of the wagon and suffered a badly injured thigh. Though she would recover, with seemingly no other complications during the journey, she is referred to in later life as walking with a slight limp from the injury she suffered while on the Trail. On October twenty-third, at the Whitman mission, son Edward suffered a similar accident, though seemingly with little effect when "two wheels roled across his head and breast, directly over one ear. We picked him up supposing he was about killed. But thank God he soon recovered again. And by the next day he was seemingly as well as ever. . ."

Little Edward had apparently fallen on uneven ground which allowed some clearance for his head as the wheel bumped from one higher spot to the next. Otherwise the child obviously would have been much more grievously injured.

Parrish was apparently in relatively good health himself by the time he reached the Whitman mission on October twenty-third. There he slept in a tent for two nights since no other accommodations were available. Perhaps his joy at reaching the mission under his own steam and not as an invalid or worse after hundreds of miles of often difficult and always tiring travel was sufficient to forestall any complaining he may have felt disposed to do because of uncomfortable sleeping conditions.

At the mission Parrish worked "threshing out corn" on October twenty-fifth and the twenty-sixth when "we moved into the house." On Sunday the twenty-seventh, the family attended the worship services. Parrish tended the cattle on Monday, butchered a beef on Tuesday, looked after the cattle again on Wednesday and the next day tried his hand at trading "cows with the Indians for oxen." He also began to load the wagons for the departure from the mission, "having declined the idea of wintering with the Dr." whom he called "a Christian gentleman . . . and his wife a Christian lady of the first water."

Thus Parrish occupied himself to some benefit for the mission for a few days before setting out again on the Trail to the Valley, despite his earlier intention, stated on October twentieth, that his family, and that of the Caves and Hawleys, intended to winter at the mission "and try it again [continue to the Valley] in the spring." On November fourth, three days back on the Trail, Parrish reported good health all around.

John Minto referred to a few cases of sickness. Though he gave no other details, he wrote that "In our traveling family of ten, [Willard] Rees and Captain Morrison's oldest daughter [Martha Ann Morrison, twelve years old, the future Mrs. John Minto] had severe attacks of 'camp fever' as it was called." Rees was ill when the "family" reached Ft. Laramie on June thirtieth (Rees did not mention his illness in the few pages of his recollections extant when local historian Fred Lockley copied them). Minto also referred to having excused young J. S. Smith from guard duty at Pacific Springs because of illness.

Minto was present during the worsening illness of Henry Sager and on about August twenty-sixth he spent the night watching over Sager while the sick man's wife, Naomi, slept fitfully between times of administering medicine to her dying husband. Mr. Sager died on August twenty-eighth, one day before reaching Ft. Bridger and was buried on the west bank of the Green River. Catherine Sager Pringle wrote that her

father died in the morning. Minto recalled that "we camped
for the day [after crossing the Green] and buried the body."
Parrish made no mention of this death. Minto wrote of
arriving at Ft. Bridger on August twenty-ninth, Parrish on
the thirtieth, so Minto, with Morrison's company, was
apparently traveling one day's march ahead of the Saunders
company.

In an illness-related incident, Minto confessed to the
reproof which he earned for refusing to give way when
another wagon driver tried to pass him as he drove one of the
Morrison wagons near Bear River west of Fort Bridger. After
exchanging heated words with the other driver, and being
told by Captain Morrison to let the other wagon pass, Minto
was embarrassed to see that it contained a sick person whom
the driver was trying to relieve from breathing the dust raised
by Minto's wagon.

Regarding illnesses, the small train led by Andrew Sublette
was unique in composition and corresponding purpose. This
group was referred to in the narratives by Parrish, Crockett
and Minto. Clyman specified that the group was made up of
"20 men 11 of whom are sick and traveling for health."

It should be pointed out that most of those who mentioned
this small train actually referred to it as being led by "Sublette"
(or some phonetically spelled variation thereof). Minto
specifically wrote "William" Sublette in his reminiscences
compiled years later. Only Washington Smith Gilliam
referred to "Andrew" Sublette.

It was Andrew Sublette however. In Independence he had
found a company of emigrants gathering for the grand trek.
Sublette was looking for paying work and his knowledge of
the outback was certainly a marketable commodity.

With the small group of those looking to improve their
health in the western mountains, Sublette left Independence on the twelfth of May, arriving in Westport the next

day intending to begin the trip on the fifteenth though he
questioned the strength of two or three of the party to make
the trip at all. None of them, he knew, would be able to
travel at a normal pace.

But Sublette and his small party were yet at Wesport on
the twenty-first, delayed by the rain which had persisted for
several days. He found there were eight men in the group
who could not be expected to start in such weather. Sublette
himself was bothered by a bad cough, he informed his brother
William. It has been said that the Sublette brothers—
William, Milton, Solomon and Andrew—had a predisposi-
tion to tuberculosis and this has been given as but one reason
for their many trips to the Rocky Mountains.

Sublette's band was first mentioned by Clyman on June
twenty-seventh when they appeared on the opposite bank of
the Blue River the morning after Clyman and his group had
crossed. One of Sublette's party, "Marshall by name," had
died that morning and had been buried "about 15 miles East
of this [place]. Marshall's "fair companion accompanied him
from St Louis and tenderly watched over him to Indipendence
whare thy seperated." From this point forward, the Sublette
party mingled occasionally with the Gilliam and Ford trains
when they met on the Trail or at a camp site.

Minto, in his commentary on the Parrish journal entry for
July nineteenth, wrote that "Some of the sick, who were
traveling with us under the guidance of William [actually
Andrew] Sublette, rapidly improved. They ate lean buffalo
meat. It may have been that the air of this region was their
principal medicine."

Minto's narrative also contains a reference to at least a
portion of the Sublette party at a date much later than that
given by any of the other narrators. Presumably on hand to
view the incident, Minto gave August twenty-eighth as the
time when "the party who had come from Saint Louis with

William Sublette" left the Trail (shortly after Minto and the others had "crossed Green River") to go "down the river to Brown's Hole." That destination was formerly a famous meeting place for trappers and was located southeast of Ft. Bridger. Here, apparently, the invalids intended on wintering in the high altitude.

Before reaching the forks of the Platte, both Crockett and Parrish noted the presence of the Sublette party on July thirteenth, Crockett writing simply that "sublets company overtook us."

Deaths

The journals of Hammer and Clyman, and the recollections of Minto, Sager-Pringle, William Shaw, Willard Rees, and B. F. Nichols, all contain at least one description each of deaths along the Trails.

William Shaw was called upon early in the journey to take charge of the wagon and "property" of a Mr. Bishop who died while groups forming the Gilliam train were on the St. Joseph approach to the Trail, somewhere "between Wolf Creek and the Missouri." Shaw "examined him before he was moved," then took the body to the Wolf River mission where he requested that the Indian agent also receive the man's belongings. A Presbyterian minister from the mission conducted the burial service.

E. E. Parrish wrote on May thirteenth that during the previous evening "the sick man Mr. Bishop . . . bound for the Rocky Mountains for his health . . . died at the Mosquitoe creek camp." B. F. Nichols well remembered that "one of the worst storms raged and the wind blew a gale" the night Bishop died, for young Nichols himself "lay sick nigh unto death."

John Minto called Bishop "a nice gentleman beginning his second trip to secure the life-preserving quality of the arid country air," who "died of the continued dampness." Bishop "had a costly and complete outfit, the care of which, together with his burial, delayed us somewhat." Minto perhaps relied on Parrish's journal for the date of May twelfth for Bishop's burial but added that the event took place "about thirty miles west of St. Joseph."

Among those who noted the presence of the Sublette party, James Clyman reported on June twenty-seventh, having crossed the Big Blue River the night before, that Sublette's group arrived at the opposite side of the river the next day and he learned that one of the health-seekers had died "and was Buried this morning about 15 miles East of this [perhaps near their crossing of the Black Vermillion]. Poor fellow [James H.] Marshall by name"

Again on July third, when Sublette's group "came up," Clyman learned that they "had buried one more of his invalids, Mr. Kechup by name, three days since at his camp . . . 10 miles West of Blue river. The young man (also called Ketchum) was "attended" by his brother who saw him buried. Three days later Sublette and party passed Clyman on the Trail and the next morning, July seventh, Clyman came up on the party just after the "intering [of] Mr. Browning who left this troublesome world last night at 11 o'Clock."

A fourth death in the Sublette party was indicated by E. E. Parrish. On July thirteenth, after "four and a half days [travel] up the Platte," he made his first reference to the party: "A Mr. Sublette came up this afternoon with a company of sick folks going to the mountains for their health. They have had four deaths in their company since they left St. Louis." (William Findley noted in his journal the next year that on June second, just after crossing the Big Blue, he "Passed the grave of Mr. I. P. W. Chutheson[?] of St. Louis. Died June 29, 1844.")

Jacob Hammer noted on June twenty-second that Thomas

Vance had been sick for several days. The company stayed in camp on the twenty-fourth "for Vance to get better," but the young man died about sunset on the twenty-eighth. Hammer, a member of the Society of Friends (Quaker), described the dying moments of Vance who though a believer in the "hard doctrine" of the Baptists, "his faith appeared to be good."

The mourners wrapped Vance in a quilt and, having no coffin, "dug the grave deep," laid the body to rest on dry grass, then replaced the sod on top of the grave to hide the gravesite. The burial took place "before midnight . . . about ten miles up the north fork of the Platte River [on] the north side . . . in the bottom a few rods from the river."

Two more deaths among the Gilliam train occurred, John Minto stated, when "Mrs. Seabren . . . died on August 4, and Mrs. Frost . . . died on the twelfth." Both deaths, he said, were caused in large part by "that exposure to the almost constant rains . . ." Parrish noted on the thirteenth that two deaths had occurred earlier in the Shaw and Morrison companies, "Mrs. Sebring, & Mrs. Frost." (The transcript of Bancroft's interview with William Shaw does not include references to either death.)

B. F. Nichols too wrote that the Shaw company, with which his family traveled when coming from the South Platte to the North Platte, traveled last in line for awhile because it "had been delayed on account of sickness; Mrs. Sebring and Mrs. Frost were not expected to live but a few days at most." The Nichols family left the Shaw company and moved on ahead. Nichols guessed that the two women died somewhere west of Ft. Laramie. ("The Roll of 1844" included in the 1876 *Transactions* of the Oregon Pioneer Association's "fourth annual reunion" includes the name William Sebring without any reference to the deceased Mrs. Sebring/Seabren.)

References in local history publications indicate that "Mrs. Frost" was Elizabeth Cogdill who married Gilbert Frost in 1829 in Clay County, Missouri. She was another who gave birth in 1844. Her illness has been listed variously as "mountain fever" and cholera, and her burial as being near Ash Hollow. It was not until two days before he reached the Sweetwater River, however, that on August thirteenth, E. E. Parrish wrote that "They have had 2 deaths in Shaw and Morrison companies, Mrs. Sebring & Mrs. Frost." What is more certain is that her husband continued the journey with their five children.

B. F. Nichols wrote of a death in his extended family while on the Trail in western Wyoming when "during the night my brother's little daughter Elizabeth died of a protracted fever. She was about 10 years old and a general favorite with the emigrants. We remained in camp during the next day to prepare for the funeral and bury the remains of the departed little one." Nichols described the pathetic scene of the parents standing on the "brink" of the grave, and later having to "leave her alone on the almost trackless wild." Minto too remembered the death of Elizabeth Nichols. Though in his eight years a coal miner he had seen the more bloody and otherwise ghastly deaths of miners "maimed, crushed, and burned," the death of Elizabeth Nichols who was "just budding into womanhood" affected him, he said, like no other death he had seen.

According to Minto, Mrs. Shaw and Mrs. Morrison asked him to prepare a grave for the young woman after others had refused claiming exhaustion from the day's travel (and many such days previously). He also stated that Elizabeth was buried at night on August fifteenth at the crossing of the North Platte (near Casper, Wyoming) after which he and some women burned wood and brush over the grave to obscure the location. Parrish wrote on the fifteenth that the girl had died "last night," and that "she had lain long in a fever."

These three accounts differ markedly in one important aspect. Nichols, a cousin, recalled that the girl died while the family was on the Sweetwater River. Minto, also writing many years later, placed the death at the North Platte crossing site. Parrish, in in his journal kept while on the Trail, indicated that the girl died and was buried at a point between these two locations. Also, Minto at first implied that he alone had consented to dig the grave, then he added that, "We dug Miss Nichols' grave in loose soil and stones, near where she died . . ." Nichols did not state specifically that he helped dig the grave for his niece; he had stated earlier that he was no longer as ill as he had been earlier in the journey.

James Clyman's journal entries from August twenty-first to the twenty-sixth included references to the final days of "Mr. Barnette" (he spelled the name both with and without the final 'e') as the Ford train approached South Pass. Unlike even the few details Jacob Hammer offered about Thomas Vance, Clyman wrote little about Barnette, perhaps because he knew little about the man (perhaps the "J. M. Barnette" who he listed on May twenty-sixth as one of the nineteen men in his mess). On August twenty-first, Clyman wrote that "Mr. Barnette whom has been confined 5 or 6 days with a fever has the appearance of being quite dangerous and has been delerious during the whole of the night."

On the twenty-third, Barnette's worsening condition required that he be spared the further discomfort of contin-ued travel, and so Clyman and the others remained in camp that day. As Barnette lay dying from "a Typhus Fever," the others were "all Buiseed in mending, washing . . ." On the next morning the "camp . . . roled out," their "circumstances not permitting delay," but Clyman remained with Barnette until the end, which was expected momentarily. When the others left, a "spade was thrown out & left, which looked rather ominous."

For a few daylight hours, Clyman, Barnette and Moses "Black" Harris were alone with the ravens and a wolf which came "to see if the way was clear to contend . . . for the Fragment of the camp." Later that afternoon, the Shaw and Morrison companies "hove in sight" and camped about a half mile away. Some women from these groups came to offer their help. On the twenty-fifth, two men, "Perkins and [Levi?] Scott," dropped out of the procession to remain with the two mountain men in their solemn duty during the night. The next day, "Mr. Scott's company" remained at this camp and women from this group tried to make Barnette comfortable. But "about noon Mr. Barnette commenced with severe Spasms & seemd to be in the gratest agony imaginable continually driving his teame or calling on some friend to do something or other, all those called being absent. Late in the evening howeveer he became at spells more camlm & even Stupid & about 10 oclock he deprted this life verry easy without a struggle or a groan & all his troubles ware in Silent death." Thus did Barnette die in the waning hours of August twenty-sixth. The four who awaited his passing laid him out on a bed of green willows. Then they huddled against the chill and, obligingly, listened to "Black" Harris's tales of "hair breadth escapes." The setting, the occasion, and those present must have made for a most compelling storytelling session. Early the next morning, Clyman and the others buried Barnette, "the first white man that ever rested his bones on [the Sweetwater River]" Clyman wrote for the record.

There is some indication that Clyman may even have

carved a gravemarker for Barnette. For the design he used as a surveyor chiseling milestones on the Vincennes-Springfield (Illinois) turnpike is said (by editor Camp) to have been similar to that of Barnette's grave marker which remained until the 1930s on the Sweetwater nine miles east of South Pass on Burnt Ranch.

Child emigrant Catherine Sager Pringle later wrote about the sad circumstance of the deaths of both her parents on the Trail; her father's death preceded that of her mother by less than a month.

GRAVESITE OF JOE BARNETTE (1844) AND MRS. BRYAN (1845)
Scattered stones at left mark Barnette site, and large stone at right marks Mrs. Bryan's grave; as they appeared in July 1974. The present Burnt Ranch buildings are just beyond the line of trees marking the course of the Sweetwater River.
Courtesy of Lawrence Eno

Henry Sager had been ill for several days after leaving Ft. Laramie. He had contracted typhoid fever, called variously the "yellow," the "mountain," and the "camp" fever by family members who later wrote or told of it. A few days before he died, he had taken up the chase of four buffalo which had run between his wagon and the one following behind. This unwise exertion proved too strenuous for his condition and he died on August twenty-eighth, the morning after crossing over Green River. John Minto later wrote that he had been asked by Mrs. William Shaw to sit up during the night with Sager to help his wife, Naomi, who also had the fever by this time, as she tried periodically to administer medicine. Henry Sager was buried on the western bank of the river, "His coffin," daughter Catherine later wrote, "consisting of two troughs hastily dug out of the trunk of a tree."

And so to Mrs. Sager's frail health following the wagon accident on July eighteenth at a steep embankment just after the crossing of the South Platte River, was added the sorrow of losing her husband. For she too, her daughters said, had contracted typhoid fever. Now her condition worsened.

About the time the train reached Ft. Hall, Mrs. Sager became so distraught and physically weak ("consumed with fever and afflicted with the sore mouth that was the forerunner of the fatal camp fever" her daughter wrote) that she became delirious and on September twenty-fifth, west of Salmon Falls, she was found to be near death by one of the women of the train who came to wash from her face the day's travel grime. Naomi Carney Sager died in her sleep soon thereafter. The next morning the children were taken to see their mother for the last time. Her grave was softened somewhat by a layer of willow brush. The corpse, in a calico dress, was sewn in a sheet and laid to rest. Her body was covered with more willow brush and the covering earth. After a "head board" was placed over the grave, "the teams were then hitched to the wagon and the train drove on . . ." The Sagers, mother and father, left seven children including a sixteen week old infant, Henrietta, born May thirty-first. (Parrish, traveling slightly in advance, and Minto who had left the train a week or so earlier, were not present when Mrs. Sager died and so did not comment.)

These descriptions of the dying moments of the few unfortunates who succumbed along the Trail add pathos to the record of '44. In all, these narratives include reference to a total of twelve deaths: one reported for the northsider train, six for the three most often mentioned companies of the Gilliam train, one by Clyman for the Ford train, four of the Sublette party (a cumulative total from duplicate references by Minto, Clyman and Parrish). The burials for the four women (Mmes. Frost, Sebring, Sager and Miss Nichols) and eight men occurred in the rain of the early weeks, on the plains of central Nebraska, along the parched expanse of Idaho desert, in the chilled mountain air of South Pass, and on the western bank of the Green River.

Four of the five deaths among the three companies of the Gilliam train occurred in August (the fifth came in late September). The reported deaths among Sublette's convalescents and health seekers all occurred before that group reached the Platte River. Some of those who died were said to have lain in feverish torment for several days before dying.

It should not be assumed that this is a complete list of all these sad occurrences that season. There is little opportunity so far, for example, to gain a view of the health of the Woodcock company which seemingly traveled most of the journey in advance of the other three companies of the Gilliam train and ahead also of the various groups of the Ford train. Others traveling in the wake of Woodcock's group might be expected to notice gravesites had there been any, though burial sites such as those of Thomas Vance and Elizabeth Nichols were purposely obscured to save being disturbed. Some graves were marked as indicated.

It may be that the vantages from which the documented deaths were reported may have allowed at times for a fairly reliable cumulative tally. The companies of the Gilliam train and the Ford train intermingled several times on the Trail and there was therefore an opportunity to trade information about those occurrences in the neighboring trains and in Sublette's group as well. There were obvious gaps, however, in the reporting of deaths even in the same train. Parrish, as noted, did not record the deaths of the Sagers. Minto had gone on ahead before Mrs. Sager died and so did not comment on that event, even when composing his recollections years later. Other deaths, then, may have gone unrecorded.

And so the chronicles of '44 refer to eleven deaths, indicating a relatively healthy emigration, especially in contrast to those of later years when cholera took a heavy toll. To be sure, there had been risks to good health. There were the unhealthy early weeks of drenching rain which quarantined the emigrants to dank, foul smelling wagons and to wearing damp clothing for days at a time and to sleeping on damp bedding. There were many weeks of travel along the Platte and particularly the Snake in oppressive heat and dryness that sapped body moisture and energy. There were the many cold miles traveled in the Blue Mountains. And, for the last hundred or so miles on the Columbia River, the pilgrims, especially those toughing out the ordeal in November and December, suffered much during the trip down the expanse of the wide Columbia, swept as it was by stunning chilled winds. After days spent on the river, the emigrants huddled at camp fires on the river bank, tormented by chilblains.

Their downcast despair masked the remnant flicker of hope that had once shown bright at earlier campfires on the west bank of the Missouri.

But such were the sensations of the moment. For most, there were better days ahead.

Chapter Seven

Leadership

It appears that there was no one in the trains of 1844 who, like Marcus Whitman during the much publicized "Great Migration" of '43, inspired followers by personal magnetism. For certain, that emigration had other persons in leadership roles, but Whitman was well known from frequent reports in the newspapers about his past journeys to the Oregon country and also from his public appearances in which he promoted emigration. Many emigrants of '43 and '44 cited Whitman's enthusiasm and example for their decision to make the long trip. Although T. M. Ramsdell stated that "When our emigration of 1844 started the transcontinental trip, we had not heard whether the emigration of 1843 . . . had succeeded in safely getting through," nevertheless he and many others began the journey knowing that the ebullient Whitman preceded them.

The emigration of '44 evolved as a workaday operation successful in transporting persons to Oregon and California. Its success no doubt did much to encourage emigration in the years immediately following.

But it was not all smooth sailing for those of '44, however. The disheartening traveling conditions, especially during May, June, and July, undoubtedly made the emigrants grumpy and overly critical, an attitude further aggravated perhaps by occasional bad judgments by leaders. And a close view of leadership that year reveals difficulties occurring nearly from the moment of organization.

Two train leaders in particular, Cornelius Gilliam and Elisha Stephens, exercised leadership styles which seemingly invited active criticism. Their trains suffered much from divisiveness. The third train, that of Nathaniel Ford, has fewer recorded instances of discord, an observation based admittedly on the single long-running viewpoint composed during the emigration—that by James Clyman.

The fourth train, Sublette's little band, has been said to have disbanded at Ft. Laramie with Sublette heading for Ft. Bent on the Arkansas River, the priest (or priests) following the Joseph Walker-Cornelius Gilliam party, and the convalescents generally unaccounted for except for John Minto's reference on August twenty-eighth to their having made it at least "down the [Green] river to 'Brown's Hole'."

Andrew Sublette had arrived at Independence on May first looking for paying work with the wagon train then assembling, for whom "M. Harris is to be the guide." This he wrote to his brother William on the second, adding that "The company of Catholics will probably start before that time. They have their guide all employed." By the thirteenth, writing from Westport, Andrew reported to William that he had been engaged as a guide, as above, and that they would leave on the fifteenth. He had "undertook to attend to business of men going to the mountains . . . as far as Fort Laramy." He could "get the same or more ["$75 per"] if I wish to go a cross the mountains with them." He was going, he wrote, "with the Priest and a party of young men some of them going for their health!"

Leadership during the various emigrations is a worthy subject of much more extensive study than what is attempted here. But a few points can be considered however cursorily.

For certain, the strict measures used for attaining obedience and discipline in military organizations were not appropriate for wagon trains of emigrant families. Successful leadership of such a unique entourage, therefore, required some alchemic blend of qualities which attracted confidence in these peculiar circumstances and which produced satisfactory results. Thus, an unwise call for delay, an otherwise ineffective travel schedule, or a bad choice in routing directly affected the then-current livelihood of the emigrants—that of the very act of emigrating itself. It is not surprising then that leadership was a matter of criticism continually.

And the fault of leadership was not only that of those who dared call themselves leaders. These strong-willed emigrants were not easy people to lead. The same qualities which were essential for survival on the Trail—independence, determination, and perseverance—were often transmuted to uncooperativeness, stubbornness and pessimism, making leadership particularly difficult even if it had been tried by the most objective and otherwise talented person.

There were two primary categories of leadership: that of the elected train leader, and that of the guide or pilot. (A third category, that of the company captain, is treated sporadically in the chapter entitled "Traffic on the Trail.")

Jacob Hammer indicated plainly that the leadership by Elisha Stephens came in for criticism early. On May twenty-fourth, Hammer refused to follow Stephens' orders to cross the Missouri River with some others who according to Jacob were taking far too great a risk crossing at that particular time. A. C. R. Shaw's threat on Stephens' life, on the twenty-ninth, and Hammer's own less violent opposition, were apparently not isolated events. For no less than four elections had been held (counting the one probably held at the Missouri River crossing) by the time the train left Ft. Platte.

The second election among the Stephens-Murphy/Thorp train occurred on May twenty-ninth following A. C. R. Shaw's outburst, and though Stephens was re-elected, the fact that an election was forced at all is significant.

Then on June twenty-fifth, "We made a division in the company and elected Harmon Higgins captain of our company." The "division" this time, if not before, involved an actual physical separation into two groups.

The fourth and last election (at least that mentioned by Hammer) was on July fourteenth while the train was camped near Ft. Laramie when "Captain Higgins resigns his office" and John Thorp was elected captain. The evening before, "Captain Mudget's company joined us," a group otherwise unmentioned or further identified except on the eighteenth when some of them were said to have withdrawn two days earlier to join Stephens. (This reference to the possibility that Stephens and his party were close-by does not agree with Schallenberger editor George Stewart's assumption that Stephens, the Murphys and others for California, with a few for Oregon, were much farther ahead at about this date.)

It is significant that following the third and fourth elections, there was apparently no mass move to rejoin Stephens and the others. If the chronology Stewart deduced from the Schallenberger and Bray narratives is correct in placing Stephens several days ahead of the others at this point, re-joining his party was not possible without an unlikely rapid trip ahead.

The Hammer narrative however suggests a travel schedule for Stephens which does not agree with that implied by Schallenberger and Bray. The last time Hammer mentioned Stephens (though not by name) was on June twenty-fifth when he wrote that "the old captain denies throwing up his commission" (on the seventeenth he had noted that, "The Captain . . . gets angry and resigns his office"). Thus it seems apparent that on June twenty-fifth, the train was yet fifty-six miles east of the forks of the Platte River. Dr. Townsend, a member of the California-bound and hence original Stephens-Murphy party, was present on or shortly before June twenty-eighth when Vance died, since Hammer referred to medicine the doctor gave Vance. And so for Stephens, Schallenberger, Bray and the others to have reached Independence Rock in nine days is, of course, highly unlikely.

But to return to the subject of leadership — the composition of this train was altered so that Stephens proceeded as leader of the California group and also of some Oregon bound persons, it would appear, since both Schallenberger and Bray referred to the farewells their group bid Oregon emigrants near Ft. Hall. Hammer and others, however, followed Higgins and later John Thorp who in later years was credited with having led the northsider train, an indication that he occupied the leadership role with enough success to be so noted by his peers when they composed their reminiscences or when others wrote Trail history.

Elisha Stephens' continued leadership of the California contingent is dealt with cursorily in the Schallenberger account. Even in hindsight, Schallenberger was neither profuse in commentary about Stephens nor did he impugn his leadership. Similarly, the commentary prepared in later years by and about the many Murphy family members contains neither illuminating details about Stephens nor dispersions cast on his services. Edmund Bray's meager addition to the record included comparatively more praise for Stephens and, when answering historian Bancroft's inquiry in 1872, Bray even knew the man's whereabouts at that time (on the Kern River near Bakersfield, California).

More space in the narratives was given to Cornelius Gilliam's efforts at leadership. Willard Rees described Gilliam as "seemingly not far from forty years of age, he was about five feet, ten inches in height, florid complexion, robust health, weighing some two hundred pounds, a heart overflowing with blunt kindness toward stranger and friend."

Both E. E. Parrish and John Minto however complained of

the leadership style of the "General" in the early weeks of travel. Gilliam, according to Parrish (and John Minto concurred), was given to ill-tempered piques, and when his authority was openly flouted, he staged apoplectic tirades laced with threats. And though Parrish was less critical of Gilliam's abilities, his comments on the General's mannerisms, including his "cantankerousness" and particularly his "abusive" resignation harangue, indicated a lack of total confidence in the man's leadership capabilities.

Rees, an official record keeper for the train, wrote a credible critique of Gilliam's personality which, though more balanced than either that of Parrish or Minto, nevertheless mentioned some significant character flaws. In one of the few surviving pages which Fred Lockley was privileged to view of a book-length manuscript which Rees prepared but never published, Rees wrote that Gilliam "was an unlettered man, possessed of some strong common sense traits, but seemed to give loose reign to his temper . . . was a fair representative pioneer of the Southwest borderland . . ." In a letter to John Minto in 1879, Rees recalled that while Gilliam "was an obstinate, impetuous, uncultivated man, he possessed some kind sympathetic traits of character, a strong will united with a powerful robust frame and sound constitution. He was better fitted to execute than to command."

Gilliam was not a stranger to the leadership role. Again according to Rees, Gilliam "had recruited a small company and participated in the Seminole Indian war" under General Zachary Taylor who, in a report on "the battle of Okee-cho-bee fought on Christmas day 1837 . . . made mention of some disobedience of orders on the part of Capt. Gilliam causing unnecessary exposure and loss of life in consequence of which report . . . [Gilliam and 'John Enyart'] bore an inveterate enmity against the man [Taylor] who became the hero of the Mexican war." As for Enyart, who had "served in several subordinate offices under Capt. Gilliam in Florida," Rees wrote that he "was perhaps an average of poor boys reared in the Southwest[sic] in his day amid the ruinous institution of human slavery the baleful effects of which will descend to generations yet unborn." Gilliam's daughter, Martha Elizabeth (Mrs. Frank Collins) reportedly told Fred Lockley that her father too as a young man "took up tracking runaway slaves."

Gilliam insisted in treating his leadership of the wagon train as a military command according to Rees. And scarcely three weeks into the journey, his leadership had been called into question. His order, for example, for delay on June sixth, based on the ill health of his own daughter, displeased the many who expected to push ahead. Parrish noted "some dissatisfaction in camp," and Minto pointed to this instance as an indication of faulty leadership, stating that it would not be possible "for any man . . . to retain long his control over free men if it is suspected that he cares first for his own." Minto believed, further, that this particular decision by Gilliam revealed another failure—insensitivity to an important travel regimen. "Our men all did everything better when traveling every day," Minto wrote. "Even one day's idleness made them slack in starting the next morning." For this reason, the delay at the banks of the Vermillion, he continued, "was a grave misfortune," since, had the train pushed ahead and forded, it would have been saved the nearly two week delay caused by the quickly rising water of that stream. Parrish too noted, on May seventeenth, that there was "Nothing so disheartening to emigrants as to be detained on the same incampment for a day with out making some progress onward toward the end &c."

Neither Parrish nor Minto complained about remaining in camp on June second because of the illness of Mrs. Sager (she had given birth on May thirty-first). But the much longer, frustrating delay at the Vermillion was bound to be construed as bad judgment by the emigrants. Such a question-able delay that kept the travelers, already rain weary and discouraged, from reaching the solid and relatively dry Great Platte River Road would surely cause murmuring and worse among the ranks.

John Minto complained that it had taken his group sixty-one days to go the two hundred miles from the rendezvous to the Platte River near Grand Island, a poor showing due to rain of course, but also, he wrote, to "bad generalship." This, and Gilliam's seemingly erratic behavior when rushing off after the first buffalo which the train encountered, caused many to openly doubt his suitability as a leader.

Yet another matter which required sensitive leadership was the apparent anxiety of the emigrants over the reactions to be expected from various Indian tribes to the passage of the wagon trains through the territory they inhabited. Whether well founded or not, imminent attack from Indians was a nearly constant concern of the emigrants. Early in the journey, John Minto remarked that he feared for the security of the train when he saw "the undrilled condition we were in." According to Minto, Gilliam never proposed "even a plan of defense in case of a sudden attack." While one might argue that Gilliam rightfully downplayed the supposed threat from the Indians, Minto was not convinced of the train leader's sensitivity to, and perhaps even understanding of this particular matter as well as others involved in shepherding emigrants.

It should be noted that though Parrish and Minto expressed anxiety about the supposed possibility of attacks from Indians, their concern was not only for the want of decisive and otherwise convincing leadership on this subject but also for the lethargic attitude of the others about practice drills and especially when it came time to actually man the guard posts.

Narrators referred to inefficient security at camps and Minto wrote of the occasionally uncooperative attitude he met when trying to place night guards. Such an attitude by the train members could have been forestalled appreciably by capable leadership, yet it was perpetuated by a natural penchant to disregard matters of security until the travelers were scared into reacting to some real or imaginary threat. Here also one must recognize that no such attacks, orchestrated in the noisy and heinous fashion depicted in popular fiction and motion pictures, occurred this year, nor did they generally.

On July fifteenth, before the train had reached Ft. Laramie, Gilliam resigned. As he stalked off trailing the mantle of leadership, he muttered (according to Minto) about the unworthiness of those whom he had tried to lead. But though he stepped down as train leader, he apparently continued as head of a smaller group including several family members and others, former neighbors from Missouri, friends and cohorts, such as John Enyart and other partisans (though not including in-law William Shaw who led a separate company and who, Minto said, "was by nature much more capable of generalship" than was Gilliam).

The manner in which the companies of the Gilliam train would proceed henceforth beyond Ft. Laramie was no doubt affected by the "General's" resignation. John Minto explained that "the three divisions proceeded each on its own account." Parrish's worried mention on July fifteenth that, "we are now in companies," referred to the autonomy handed the three companies upon Gilliam's impulsive dissolution of the former command structure. The companies of Shaw and Morrison chose to remain "within supporting distance of each other."

Some welcomed a less structured traveling arrangement. B. F. Nichols later wrote that "after three or four days travel up the Platte, General Gilliam called the emigrants together and made a speech to them, after which he resigned as commander of the train. My father [Benjamin Nichols], who was second in command, also resigned which left us at liberty to travel in companies under the captains which seemed to be quite an advantage over traveling together as we had heretofore done, [for] we were thus enabled to select camping places at different points and get better pasturage for the animals."

The original company captains remained in office for much of the journey ahead. Apparently their leadership was far less controversial than was that of Gilliam. Soon after Gilliam's dramatic resignation, Captain Saunders issued an order for his company, which included seventeen wagons and a carriage, to "hitch up and roll away." This company at this time included Gilliam and the families of his sons-in-law David Grant and Joseph Gage.

Historian H. H. Bancroft's interview with William Shaw revealed little about the events which led to the resignation of Gilliam, Shaw's brother-in-law. Shaw said only that before the train reached Ft. Laramie, "the emigration had split up . . . as soon as we got into the buffalo country they split up. They fell out, some got mad and left. Morrison and I stayed behind. The General left with the company and went on. Morrison's company and my company kept together until we got to Fort Bridger."

It may have been for the Saunders company, or for another group made up of Gilliam partisans only, that Gilliam acquired the guidance of Joseph Walker just west of Ft. Laramie for the trek to Ft. Bridger. (Parrish and Minto stated that the companies of Shaw and Morrison followed close by so that they could benefit from Walker's guidance.) Walker was returning to Ft. Bridger and to his Indian family there.

As mentioned earlier, Nathaniel Ford, according to James Clyman, was chosen train leader, after that train had been eleven days on the Trail, in "a kind of election" to be "our

capt or leader" and that "by a considerable majority." Alanson
Hinman cited Ford's "considerable reputation" as a politician back in Missouri.

Though the Ford train seemed not to be troubled by
disruption in the same degree as recorded by Jacob Hammer
and others concerning such problems in their trains, James
Clyman noted a few instances in which contrary attitudes
may have led to problems not otherwise recorded. For example, Clyman noted the tendency of train members to belittle
important advice from guide Moses Harris. Here, then, was
some of the same stiff-necked contrariness found in other
trains (granted, not unusual in emigrations, as narratives for
succeeding years bear out). Clyman also noted "dijection"
several times as the apparent mood of his fellow train members. Such a collective attitude could prove to be the breed-
ing ground for more active dissention.

B. F. Nichols later described Ford and his entire family
as being educated well beyond most others of the train.
Nathaniel Ford was born in Virginia in 1795 of French
Huguenot ancestry, according to grandson John T. Ford.
Nathaniel's father was said to have served with George
Washington in the Revolution. The younger Ford moved to
Howard County, Missouri, in 1820. Two years later in July
he and Lucinda Embree were married. Before the emigration
of '44, Ford worked as a surveyor, school teacher, flatboatman,
Clerk and later Sheriff of Howard County. His title "Colonel"
reportedly came from his participation in a fight against
Mormons at New Madrid. The Ford family, when they began
the journey in '44, included one son, Marcus A. (usually
called Mark) and five daughters: Mary Ann, Josephine,
Caroline, Sarah and Miller. Nathaniel and Lucinda were
leaving the graves of three of their children who died in
Missouri. Grandson John T. Ford's sketch of Ford credited
him with putting his flatboating skills to use on the Columbia

on his way into the Valley. The same sketch gave his arrival at Oregon City on December 7 (as does the Donation Land Claim record). But Parrish noted his presence, as but one of the group, on the boat from Ft. Vancouver on November 29 which reached Linnton on the thirtieth.

In light of the troubled and temporary leadership by Ford's counterparts in the other trains, his own leadership can be assumed then to have suffered the same onslaughts of criticism. It should be noted that Ford's train was not hampered by overlong delays, as was Gilliam's. As John Minto had observed, a train that moved with appreciable regularity and which avoided questionable delays remained progress-minded and had less time to carp and complain.

Ford's train had been grouped into "messes" after being organized in the larger, less personal "companies." One might hope that such an arrangement would help offset some internal troubles. These smaller groups—the messes—came together at each camp for necessary functional purposes, a positive motive, while members of the much larger companies were thrown back onto their own individuality in some matters where competitiveness and other negative reactions may have occurred—opportunities for disputes and second guessing, backbiting or other calumnies. It will be noted however that the Shaw and Morrison companies of the Gilliam train seemed to have maintained a workable relationship of leader to followers for the duration organized simply as it had been from the start.

The degree of success of the often disparaged governance by the train leader and the company captains was dependent on the continuing popularity of those persons. But consistant heroic character, popularly acclaimed as such, was difficult to maintain hour by grueling hour on the journey. Questionable decisions (and every decision might be so judged by someone), the occasional indecision, and the outright mistakes, were not likely to be hidden in the close confines of a wagon train.

Official leadership in '44 seemed to have lasted until the travelers reached The Dalles. But by the time the trains reached that point, some apparently had been traveling in small groups of wagons for many miles. The descriptive passages of the record of '44 relating to the arrival of companies and smaller groups at The Dalles indicate that much depended on the individual pace of each family for the order in which they arrived there. The remnant of an organizational structure at least from that point if not before seems to have been dispensed with for a variety of reasons: the pattern of travel dictated by the weariness of draft animals and accompanying loose stock; the reciprocal relationships engaged in for helping one another; the health of individuals; and the procurement of food. "Packers" were sent from some companies, or the remnants thereof, to obtain foodstuffs from the Whitman mission, and these actions may for some have been the final acts of official leadership. Willard Rees explained that he, as "sergeant of the guard," and R. W. Morrison as company captain each performed their duties "until the company arrived at The Dalles Mission."

Though leadership of the trains of '44 was not exemplary, this emigration helped set the pattern for succeeding emigrations in which a duly elected leader was chosen by vote in one or more elections, and company captaincies continued to be relatively effective leadership roles.

Pilots

The Trail pilot represented yet another category of leadership. The pilot chose the route, and in suggesting camping spots helped set the mileage for each day. He also gave counsel about the reactions to be expected to the passage of the emigrants through the respective regions of various Indian tribes. In short, the guide was engaged for his knowledge of the Trail and to anticipate, offset, or circumvent anything (within his power) that might threaten or deter the train.

The presence of the guides (and including former mountain man James Clyman) was probably something of a novelty to the farm families and the young single men from the woodland Midwest and the eastern states. Likely clad in buckskins and carrying the accouterments of the outback (Trail-worn headgear of some highly personal design; all-purpose oversized knife; perhaps even a tomahawk; a rifle carried casually but ever ready) these seasoned travelers in the Rockies and beyond undoubtedly stood apart in appearance and manner. Though assuming a seemingly relaxed and travel-worn posture, they were yet attuned to "signs," their senses keen and their reactions geared to survival means of which the others had little knowledge or need previously.

For the trains of '44, the pilots were Caleb Greenwood, Moses "Black" Harris, Andrew Sublette and Joseph Walker. And briefly there was the elusive "Mr. Hitchcock," a name noted by Schallenberger and Bray and in James Clyman's journal as one who had some knowledge of the Trail and particularly of the direct route to Bear River—what has come to be called the Sublette-Greenwood Cutoff—along which it was said that Hitchcock led the Stephens-Murphy party.

Guides have often been portrayed in pulp fiction (and of late in so-called nonfiction picture books) as larger-than-life figures, unbelievably wily, of incalculative resourcefulness and of course the hands-down favorite for any fisticuffs. But not only did the three hired pilots of '44 appear not to have been revered particularly during the journey, similarly they were not given much space in either the journals of that year or in emigrants' reminiscences composed years later. (B. F.

Nichols, for example, made no mention at all of guides or pilots in his recollections.)

This is not altogether surprising. The pilot's guidance was usually given the train leader who was more visible and vocal, and, of importance, was elected to the position and therefore more accountable to the others. The guide/pilot was hired for a specific duty and it was the job of the train leader to incorporate that specialized counsel into his own generalship.

And, as noted by Hammer, Clyman and Parrish, it was not unknown for the emigrants to be of the set-jaw attitude that they could guide themselves, at least as far as each day's beckoning horizon. Some may have had with them, or had memorized, the few sketchy forerunners of the guidebooks published later for emigrants and were therefore convinced that they could find their own way. No doubt many persisted in this myopic naivete for much of the journey, to the frustration of train leaders and to the amusement of the guides.

Willard Rees characterized the men of his train as "in general but little enlightened, with minds dwarfed by super-stition and prejudice, yet strong in maintaining their native freedom." Not the type, it would seem, to have their imagi-nations swept away by so-called living legends, these wanderers who dressed partly in animal skins, who had failed to send down roots in the land, and who were relatively, suspiciously, comfortable with Indians.

While the guides were useful for some things, the emi-grants themselves were nearly consumed daily with the main tasks: plodding along, remaining healthy, and maintaining their "outfits." And so, for whatever reason, the narrators of '44 did not elaborate on the services or the physical appear-ance of the guides. Jacob Hammer wasn't favorably impressed with Caleb Greenwood or even with the need for his services. After but two references to the man, Hammer mentioned him no more, nor did he mention Greenwood's grown sons, two of whom, John and Britain, were assumed by George Stewart to have accompanied their father on this trip.

Though said to be illiterate, Caleb Greenwood left his mark on the pages of trans-Mississippi literature by being seen in action at wide ranging locales over a number of years by others who did record their observations. First known as a hunter for the trappers working for John Jacob Astor and then Manuel Lisa, Greenwood was later employed by the Missouri Fur Company. He attended the first rendezvous of his counterparts in the Green River country (at Henry's Fork) in 1825 as an employee of W. H. Ashley. He was said to be a fixture at the subsequent gatherings. In his early sixties he married an Indian woman and one or more of the three sons she bore him were present on some of his later travels in the 1840's.

In addition to getting credit in 1844 for being with the first wagons to cross the Sierra, "Old Greenwood" as he was generally known, was said to have helped in a rescue party for the Donners and to have joined the goldseekers of 1849 in California. It has been said also that he played the part of a would-be oracle, offering advice for a price to naive flatlanders looking for get-rich-quick schemes involving land or other treasures. It is generally thought that Caleb Greenwood died in 1850, though substantial corroboration is lacking.

There were but four references to Greenwood in Schallenberger's recollections. There it is implied that Greenwood was able to translate some Indian dialects, but that the usefulness thereof was of no great importance. It seemed also that Greenwood was a stranger to the Humboldt route later in the trip. Specifically, Schallenberger was reported to have said that "Old Mr. Greenwood's contract as pilot had expired" upon reaching the Rocky Mountains.

As a footnote to the emigration of '44, Clyman referred to Greenwood as present in a party in which the two were traveling back East from California in the summer of 1846. From the way he worded his journal entry for July 15, 1846, when the group was at the Blue River in Kansas, it appears that it was the first time he had met Greenwood: "on our Return from California a Mr Greenwood and his two sons made a part of our company. This man the Elder is now from his best recolection 80 years of age and has made the trip 4 times in 2 yares in part."

The piloting of Moses "Black" Harris in '44 is chiefly known through the journal of James Clyman whose second entry, on May fifteenth, noted a loan of $15.25 he made to Harris whose overland kit apparently was not bulging with burdensome cash. About Harris, Clyman, whose own experiences in the wild were encyclopedic, made a particularly telling remark on June twenty-ninth when referring to the fresh-faced impertinance of many in his train who ignorantly disparaged the twenty-plus years of experience which "Black" Harris offered (just staying alive that long in the outback of the American West was like a lifetime elsewhere). Harris' expertise, Clyman wrote, "is perfectly useless in this age of improvement when human intelect not only strides but actually Jumps & flies into conclusions." There were many of these "nominal pilots" as Clyman called them a few days later, members of his train who insisted on forging ahead on their own tack.

As former mountain men, Clyman and Harris were fellow members of an exclusive brotherhood of wanderers and sufferers. They shared the stuff on which true camaraderie depended for initiates of such wonders and horrors as they likely had experienced in common.

Harris was apparently in Independence as early as January 1844, according to an article in the *New Orleans Picayune*

(January seventh) which stated that the "famous old traveler. . . Major . . . 'Black' Harris" was there "preparing for a great expedition to Oregon next spring." Another *Picayune* article of March thirteenth referred to an earlier article published in an Independence paper (the issue date not cited) in which Harris reportedly "contradicted" some statements of T. J. Farnham about conditions along the Trail.

Farnham had "promulgated some just and very valuable information in regard to the extreme West, but [in] his representations [of] the nature of the roads from the States, and in some other particulars, he has most assuredly fallen into error . . ." This Harris sought to correct, particularly trying to assuage the "discouraging influence" which Farnham's statements about hardships on the Trails were "calculated" to have had on "the adventurous throngs . . . now preparing to start for that country in the spring." Farnham reportedly had stated that there were "distances of many days travel where no wood can be obtained and where travlers are sure to suffer." Not so, this article stated. "It is only along the South Fork of the Platte, and even there for not more than two or three encampents, that wood can not be obtained." The article, presumably quoting Harris, advised gathering wood when available and also to "tie all the fuel they want upon their wagons." Furthermore, when wood was unavailable, there was, in buffalo country, the "bois de vache [which] except in rainy weather . . . supplies every use for which wood is needed."

As for guides—"with an experienced mountaineer to direct, no party need fear ever being out of wood. . . Let the emigrants secure a good guide and they are safe enough."

Like Greenwood, Harris was well known for his adventures, which were not diminished in his self-promotion. But it was also claimed by well known trapper and early Oregonian

"TRAPPERS" 1837
Moses "Black" Harris
and a companion

A watercolor by
Alfred Jacob Miller,
courtesy of Walters
Art Gallery, Baltimore

JAMES CLYMAN
Courtesy of the California
Historical Society

Robert Newell that in 1840 Harris shot at him then ran and hid when Newell underbid the exhorbitant price Harris had set on his services to guide missionaries to Ft. Hall. Several others however who wrote about him acknowledged his sense of humor. Along with the notability for his solitary treks in wondrous if dangerous territory, Harris had acquired the nickname "Black" for a combination of physical traits cited in W. H. Gray's *History of Oregon* (1870) in which he was described as "of medium height, black hair, black whiskers, dark brown eyes" and with "very dark complexion."

Harris was sketched by artist Alfred Jacob Miller who toured the mountains in the 1830's and depicted numerous scenes and persons of historical importance. Miller surmised that the "Black" which had become Harris' nickname "must have arisen from an appearance as if gunpowder had been burnt into his face . . ." He further described Harris, from the viewpoint of an artist, as being "of wiry form, made of bone and muscle, with a face apparently composed of tan leather and whipcord," which was "lighted up with a lively & restless eye."

Even as early as 1823, when Harris was with the W. H. Ashley trapping party, he was said to have been an experienced mountain man. He and William L. Sublette came out of the mountains together (and otherwise alone) in the winter of 1825–26 traveling on snow-shoes to St. Louis, beating starvation by eating their pack dog. Harris returned to the mountains the next spring through South Pass. While a trapper himself, Harris served also as a guide for other trappers in the 1830's.

In 1836, in company with Thomas Fitzpatrick, Harris had guided the Whitmans as least as far as the Green River, since at that point Narcissa Whitman noted in her diary that she had invited him to tea on June fourth. In 1838, Harris made another journey across the plains, this time with missionaries sponsored by the American Board of Commissioners for Foreign Missions.

In June 1841, Harris wrote a letter to Thornton Grimsley claiming twenty years experience "in the mountains." He complained about the British having taken possession of Ft. Hall and for their "putting it in military customs." He offered his services to "make a clean sweep" of the "Origon" country to drive out the British and Indians. "Why our Government suffers these things I know not," he mused.

James Clyman indicated that Harris was present from the beginning of the journey. But though working as guide, Harris took the time to stop with Clyman at South Pass to while away the evening after the death of Mr. Barnette and to help bury the deceased the next morning.

Alanson Hinman stated to an interviewer years later that when his party reached the present site of Baker City, Oregon, he "left his companions and under the guidance of Black Harris . . . went to the mission station at Waiilatpu for supplies." No dates were given by Hinman for this important sidetrip, nor did he identify others who may have been present.

After the '44 journey, Harris remained in Oregon for three years, exploring new land routes into the Valley to be used for emigration and trade. According to the St. Louis Reveille of June 9, 1845, he was still "preferring the wild haunts of the Indian and the buffalo to the tameness of civilized life." A week earlier, his old friend James Clyman had noted in yet another of his journals that on May thirty-first Harris had visited him in his camp on the "Lukimute" River which "falls out of the Killimook mountains." Clyman was awaiting others bound for California.

That year Harris was credited with the rescue of emigrants who in October had been led astray by piloting errors before reaching the Columbia River. Similarly, his name was associated with additional feats of succor for those who became endangered by weather or other conditions on the Trails into the Valley.

In May 1847, Harris returned east along the Trail. In late June, Howard Egan, a member of an advance group of Mormons, recorded that "near the headwaters of the Green River" he met Harris leading two pack mules loaded with skins for trading. Orson Pratt, another Mormon, met Harris at Pacific Springs. Both Egan and Pratt stated that Harris was hoping to offer his services to trains heading for Oregon.

Harris continued along the Trail back to Missouri. The December third issue of the St. Joseph Gazette included an article addressed "To Emigrants" announcing Harris's "extensive and accurate acquaintance with Oregon and California" and that "his services as pilot should by all means be engaged by the emigrants" the next spring. The article was reprinted in the Liberty Weekly Gazette (Liberty County, Missouri) on December tenth.

How Harris occupied his time during 1848 is unclear, but the March 5, 1848, issue of the St. Joseph Gazette, in reporting the town "literally crowded" for the past two weeks with those "laying in their supplies" for the journey to Oregon and California, also referred to the arrival of Moses Harris "from the front camp of the Oregon emigrants" (apparently several miles out) who in turn told of what he found there as the emigrants made their final preparations. Little more was said about Harris's plans for this emigration season. Whether or not he met up with his friend James Clyman, who was leading the Lambert McComb family of Indiana and a few others to California that year, is not known.

He was again on the scene in 1849. The Jefferson Inquirer of March fifth reported that "Major Harris better known as Black Harris arrived in St. Joseph on Wednesday last from

Fort John, and that Harris "will leave for California in a few weeks."

But it was not to be. Two months later *The Republican* reported that "Black Harris, the well known mountain pioneer" was "among the latest victims of the Cholera at Independence" when that scourge swept among the emigrant camps as elsewhere. Another source noted his death as occuring on May sixth. From somewhere in his wanderings, James Clyman heard of his friend's death and on a slip of paper kept thereafter with his journals he jotted a memorial which has come to be a well known Western doggerel:

> "Here lies the bones of old Black Harris
> who often traveled beyond the far west
> and for the freedom of Equal rights
> He crossed the snowy mountin Hights
> was free and easy kind of soul
> Especially with a Belly full."

Piloting for the Gilliam train seemed almost to be an afterthought, and here too Harris may have been involved, at least temporarily. Parrish indicated that no pilot was present in the Gilliam train on July sixth when he wrote that "we fear we lose ground for want of a competent pilot" (and this seven weeks after leaving the Wolf River Indian agency). Later, he complained on July twenty-first, while yet on the South Platte, that his company had not reached the North Platte when expected because "our pilot missed the way," indicating the presence of someone, though unnamed, purportedly acting as guide. (Parrish reached the North Platte the next day.)

Samuel Black Crockett may have provided a clue to the identity of the pilot in question. On Friday, July nineteenth, he noted that the Morrison and Shaw companies hired Harris after having "raised subscription money." John Minto, who arrived at the Platte possibly on the twenty-fourth (he did not say exactly) recalled that Morrison's company had been following Moses Harris from a point between the two forks of the Platte.

If the pilot to whom Parrish referred was not Harris, it may have been Andrew Sublette. On the fifteenth Parrish wrote that his company had hoped to overtake the Sublette party but "he had gone further." But by the nineteenth, Sublette and his group had camped within sight of Parrish and the others for the "last two nights."

Washington Smith Gilliam, son of the "General," credited Andrew Sublette with guiding his father from a point at which the Gilliams and others reached the Platte (he did not distinguish between the south and the north forks) to Ft. Laramie. The elder Gilliam's daughter, Martha Elizabeth Gilliam Collins, later wrote that both Sublette and Harris "acted as guides as far as Ft. Laramie."

Andrew Whitley Sublette was the fourth son of five in a family famous for Western travels. If not earlier, he was at least active on the Trails in 1832 in the fur trade caravan led by his more famous elder brother William. Another member of the party, John B. Wyeth, credited Andrew as an expert marksman, able to "crease" the necks of wild horses to aid in their capture.

In 1834, Andrew Sublette was again in the mountains, returning in mid-winter to the states. Two years later he was a partner with Louis Vasquez in the fur trade on the South Platte River. Vasquez wrote to his brother Benito from "Platte River, Oct. 9, 1836" that Sublette was returning with part of their furs. Andrew, he wrote, "is a good youngster."

Young Sublette continued to work with Vasquez; the two were issued trading licenses by the Superintendent of Indian Affairs in July 1837 and again in June 1838. Their trapping group consisted of some twenty-two men, including the well-known James P. Beckwourth, and the venture was secured by brother William. The partners built an adobe trading post on the South Platte about one mile south of present Platteville, Colorado.

Known to Indians of the Platte Valley as "Left Hand," Andrew Sublette gained much knowledge of the Trails of the region in the four or five years he worked with Vasquez. He returned many times from the wilds to the states, bringing furs out and taking supplies back. In early 1839, he reportedly advised the Thomas J. Farnham party to take the route along the Arkansas River rather than the Platte River road. Later that year, he, Vasquez, and thirty-two men left Independence outfitted for trade with the Indians and packed in four wagons each pulled by six mules. The next spring the partners sent a huge mackinaw boat, thirty-six feet long and eight feet wide carrying seven hundred buffalo robes and four hundred buffalo tongues, to St. Louis. In perhaps 1841, the partners sold their fort and business to Lock and Randolph, and Sublette dedicated himself to his farm in Missouri until the emigration of '44 when he was hired to guide the small party west.

By most accounts, Sublette went no farther than Fort Laramie. (Harris may have continued to serve as pilot for the Shaw and Morrison companies of the original Gilliam train as well as the Ford train.) And from Fort Laramie, Joseph Walker, the fourth pilot mentioned in the narratives of '44, led Gilliam and others from that train, and some from Ford's train, to Bridger's post. Parrish wrote on August fifth, three and one half days after leaving Ft. Laramie, that his group halted to await "Walker's party who wish to join us." W. S. Gilliam stated for the Oregon Pioneers Association *Transactions* of 1905 that Walker was "an old friend of my father's."

From May twenty-fifth to July fifth, Walker had guided Fremont on a portion of the expedition of '44. When his services were ended at Bent's Fort on the Arkansas, Walker went north to Fort Laramie. It was from there that he caught up with the Gilliam train and worked as guide at least to Fort Bridger.

Like his contemporaries the Sublettes, Thomas Fitzpatrick, Kit Carson, Black Harris and Jim Bridger, Walker had a well known reputation as a mountain man. But for all his Trail savvy and familiarity with this particular route, he was not immune to criticism if Parrish's comments were typical of the others. Though Parrish wrote on August twentieth that "Colonel" Ford's company was waiting "on the creek below us . . . to avail themselves of the experience of our pilot Mr. Walker," Parrish himself and apparently a few others did not always follow Walker's advice.

For example, shortly after he noted Ford's wish to rely on Walker's guidance, and following his note on the twenty-fifth on the practice of the companies to "all camp near each other while captain Walker stays with us as pilot," his family and that of Mr. Hawley chose on the twenty-seventh to follow their own noses rather than Walker's example. On this occasion, these two families followed "the mule tracks of the Roman Catholics and missed the road" that Walker and the others had taken. When they rejoined Walker and the others, Parrish stated that Walker's way was longer and harder. "The people are getting tired of leaving the road to follow Captain Walker in new routes, and I think they will quit it," he added. (The "Roman Catholics" to whom Parrish referred were possibly those formerly traveling with Sublette.)

On August twelfth, after hurrying "to be off ahead of Ford's company," Parrish's group was ordered to camp to cure the buffalo meat they had just acquired, and "to give Walker a chance to kill more, as he has not enough, it seems." Parrish appeared ambivalent about all this, trying perhaps to balance the time lost with the need to procure more meat for the journey ahead, and with the advantage of

Walker's familiarity with the Trail through present Wyoming.

Arriving at Bridger's post, Parrish acknowledged that Walker "kindly conducted us to the place of encampent" before going himself to his Indian "wigwam" near the post. Parrish added that "Mr. Walker has taken some pains to pilot this company from Fort Larimo to Fort Bridger."

Though the emphasis on Walker's piloting was chiefly on the road between forts Laramie and Bridger, Parrish referred on October ninth, when the company was five weeks beyond Ft. Bridger, to the advice of "Mr. Walker" on choosing a campsite when the company was six days west of Ft. Boise. Since this is likely counsel from a pilot, one might first assume that the guide Joseph Walker had agreed to continue in that capacity for some undisclosed destination beyond Ft. Bridger.

But in searching Parrish's narrative for hints of piloting beyond Ft. Bridger, one sees also that on October eleventh, he and the others in his immediate company met "Captain" James Waters who was "just from Oregon City" coming east along the Trail in search of his family whom he expected to be among the emigration that season. On September twenty-seventh, Waters had already met Clyman on the Grande Ronde and may have learned that his family was not among the Ford train. From Gilliam and the others he would now learn that his family was not with that train either. Martha Elizabeth Gilliam called James Waters "an old friend of father's" whom they met "at Burnt river" and who "took us to his cabin on Tualatin Plains where we stayed while father traveled over the valley looking for a land claim." Washington S. Gilliam said more to the point that Waters, "an old friend of my father's and also . . . of several persons in our party . . . had gone to Oregon the year before, and had kindly come to meet us and help us in . . .," along the way aiding in "locating camps . . ."

It appears then that Waters returned to the Valley with the Gilliams and possibly others, serving thereby as guide. And so it may have been that Joseph Walker's services as guide were dispensed with here, if indeed he had come that far, for those of Waters—a reasonable assumption not otherwise proven. After October ninth, the name Walker was not mentioned again in the Parrish journal. But to further confuse matters, there were at least three emigrant men named Walker on the Trail this season. (Gilbert, in *Westering Man,* p. 209, states that Walker left the 1844 train at Ft. Bridger and spent the winter in the Green and Bear rivers vicinity.)

Another who acted as guide, if only for a short spell, was the "Mr. Hitchcock" of the few fleeting references in three of the narratives of '44, those of Schallenberger, Bray, and Clyman. (In George R. Stewart's second work on the subject, *The California Trail,* 1962, he supplied a first name "Isaac" for the man.) Bray, in his letter to Bancroft in 1874, credited Hitchcock with having been "with the Sublettes in their expeditions." If that was true he may have had some knowledge about the Rockies and the country beyond. Bray first wrote "Greenwood" then scratched it out and substituted "Mr. Hitchcock" as the "old trapper and mountaineer [who] . . . gave us much information about the country to which we were bound." Of some significance also, Bray stated that it was Hitchcock, not Greenwood, who led the party along the Sublette Cutoff. And, Bray continued, Hitchcock provided some guidance near Humboldt Sink.

Sometime around mid July (according to Schallenberger's and Bray's implied chronologies), Hitchcock stepped forward from previous, and succeeding, relative anonymity and led the Stephens-Murphy party along the shortcut which eliminated the trip to Bridger's post. This cutoff was not without its hardships, particularly the two days (and one dry camp) required to cover the fifty or so dry miles on the way to Bear River. This saving in time and mileage also caused desert travel wear and tear on draft animals and vehicles, and on emigrants alike.

Even Hitchcock's short spell as guide was not without complaint. Schallenberger's account called the cutoff the "first real hardship on the march," since "most of the distance [was] across a rough, broken country [with] no water of any kind." According to this rendition, Hitchcock thought the cutoff was about half its actual length, and consequently the travelers did not take a supply of water, hence the dry and otherwise uncomfortable camp on the way to the Bear River. And not only was this routing variation difficult traveling, but some from the party, returning along their tracks to find strayed cattle, reported having to hide from a Sioux war party, and, on the same outing, being set upon by a large party of "whooping and charging" Indians who fortunately proved to be friendly Snake.

The considerable Trail knowledge of James Clyman himself can be added to the overall guidance exercised in '44. Though he seems not to have worked officially as a guide, his advice and counsel was undoubtedly sought, and used if wisdom prevailed. On June twenty-fourth he entered into his journal a brief recollection of piloting he had done in 1827 when with a load of prime beaver pelts he and a few others had returned to St. Louis from a fur trapping expedition.

For all his knowledge of the outback, Clyman appears to have been content following along fairly uncomplainingly with the Ford train for hundreds of miles before leaving the cumbersome caravan east of Ft. Hall for the relatively faster pace on horseback.

Though the keeping of a journal itself can be viewed as somewhat egotistical, it is entirely believable that James Clyman was a self-effacing individual who gave readily of his considerable Trail related knowledge without exhibiting the tedious temperamental conceits of some others whose similar accomplishments were not matched by Clyman's seeming strength of character. A friend, G. C. Pearson, described Clyman as "tall, spare in flesh, [with] keen deep-set blue eyes, face and hands as bronzed as the color of smoked buckskin, hair that fell upon his shoulders . . ." The mountain man also had "a heavy beard which with his hair was the color of dried grass." Clyman often dressed in a linsey woolsey shirt, buckskin pants and moccasins. He carried a "long full stocked flintlock rifle, tomahawk, and knife." And, like anyone who hailed from such exotic places and times, he was known for his store of tales, which he told with apparent pleasure and talent (*Past and Present of Vermillion County, Illinois*. Danville, Illinois, Public Library, n.d.).

Clyman had spent an eventful four years trapping in the Rockies beginning in 1823 as a member of the expedition of William H. Ashley and Andrew Henry. He was then thirty-one years old. His own dues as a mountainman were paid in ways which prompted minor legends: he saved William Sublette's life, was one of the first to traverse South Pass, stitched Jedediah Smith's ear back on after that luminary of the outback lost it briefly to a bear of the grizzly persuasion, and he escaped untold sufferings at the hands of Indian tribes who hunted him like one of the rodents he himself trapped. He was also likely on hand at one or more of the raucous fur trapping rendezvous begun in 1825 in the Green River region by Ashley as an event at which to distribute supplies and collect furs.

But Clyman's most memorable feat was one of Herculean mimickery—his solitary walk in 1824 across Wyoming (east of South Pass) and Nebraska as he returned from the mountains to Ft. Atkinson at Council Bluffs. Fortunately for his own rough and ready career, and for the historical record which he compiled over several decades, he didn't "go under," which he compiled over several decades, he didn't "go under," mountain man's parlance for succumbing to any one of the frightfully long list of bone chilling dangers he and his kind dared to face. Instead, he returned to the mountains to trap, came out again in 1827, and seventeen years later joined the Ford train for Oregon.

Some specific expressions of appreciation for leadership, guidance and other help received on the Trails are included in the record of the emigration this season. Catherine Sager expressed understandable gratitude to Captain William Shaw and his wife Sarah for willingly taking the responsibility for the seven Sager children and conducting them to the Whitman mission. The Sagers would henceforth refer to the Shaws as "Uncle Billy and Aunt Sally."

Not all acknowledgements were specified or as emotion laden as that of the once destitute Sager children. There is, for example, the implied appreciation for Thorp, Ford, and even Gilliam in their being listed years later in emigrant society publications as leaders of wagon trains. Here the implication seems to be that regardless of squabbles and patience-trying, nerve-jangling episodes along the Trail, each leader had followers who remained loyal, and the epithets of leadership were forever attached to their names.

And though the emigrants did not heap unbounded praise on the pilots, they undoubtedly benefited in many ways from the presence of those picturesque figures from the mountains who represented much life-saving experience. For example, there were no doubt some useful things to be learned from them about living in the out-of-doors for an extended period of time, such as how to hunt wild game on the Great Plains. And the writers of the journals probably learned many place names from the guides. In general, the advice and the example of the guides counted for more than the narratives indicated.

No long-term or temporary elected leader of '44 arrived in the Valley completely discredited, or shamed by odious charges of cowardice, egregious misconduct or other serious and reprehensible conduct. Among the few so designated as leaders, one faded, quite willingly it seemed, into the scenery of a California river valley. One continued to pursue the life of the hunter and died from wounds received during a bear hunt. One was killed during the period of war with the Cayuse. One lived out a career of nearly three decades as public official among his fellows of the evolving Oregon landed gentry.

Except for a biographical sketch in the *San Francisco Post* of December 28, 1883, Elisha Stephens was little heard from after the emigration of '44. And that seemed to his liking if a true picture of his temperament has been achieved by the few who have written about him over the years. Stephens was said to have worked as a blacksmith at Monterey during the Mexican War and later to have lived as a hermit beside the Rio Bravo (or "Kern" River) near Bakersfield, California, becoming proficient in beekeeping among other farming endeavors.

While supposedly reporting about him, the *Post* article did not actually quote Stephens. Only an artist's sketch of the man's distinct profile hints at his presence at all, much less any compliance with the person who wrote the article. The journalist, apparently a devotee of phrenology, added that Stephens wore a hat indoors and out, and that he "carries a brain of moderate size, but of compact material," a dispatch that would have us believe Stephens obligingly doffed his hat so that the bumps on his head could be measured.

Unfortunately, some misinformation also appeared in this article which along with a dose of journalistic supposition about details of the emigration of '44 casts doubt on other tidbits which indeed may have been useful information about this one whose contribution to Trail history has not been adequately understood.

One source of information however is particularly noteworthy. When young Thomas A. Baker came to the site in 1863 which would later be called Bakersfield, his family's nearest neighbor, though several miles distant, was Stephens. A few days after the family began their first log cabin, Stephens appeared with a crate containing six hens and a rooster for their new farm. After that, young Baker became better acquainted with the reclusive Stephens. Though Baker took notes on Stephens' tales of adventure about trapping and about the 1844 emigration, the notes and the composition he later prepared were destroyed by a fire in 1893.

A brief description of Stephens by Baker appeared in *History of Kern County, California* (Chicago: J. S. Clarke, 1929, pp. 122–127) in which the former train leader was said to be "of the 'eagle' type; aquiline of feature, aggressive but reserved, not overbearing like many men of this type . . . of medium height; active, quick, wiry and untiring . . . he had learned in a strenuous school [as a trapper] to look out for himself and protect his rights, though he never went out of his way to seek trouble."

Official acknowledgement of Stephens' contribution to pathfinding which led to the settlement of California has been confined largely to a creek (spelled "Stevens" on which he owned a ranch in 1848 according to Baker) in the Santa Cruz Mountains in Santa Clara County near Cupertino, and a highway leading from San Jose to the creek. Stephens was in the southern end of the San Joaquin Valley in about 1861, Baker reportedly said, and established the ranch there which Baker visited many times. Stephens was said to have been born in 1801, possibly in South Carolina. He died in 1884 and was buried in Union Cemetery in Bakersfield.

Andrew Sublette remained active on the Trails following

the journey in '44. In early March of the next year he wrote
to his brother William from somewhere on the South Platte
that he and brother Solomon would start the fourth for Taos
or Santa Fe, hoping to return to the North Fork of the Platte
by late May or early June so he could meet with more
emigrants for Oregon and offer his services as guide. He was
enjoying such good health that he hesitated to leave the
higher country, he said. A few years later, according to
noted fur trade and Yellowstone historian Hiram Martin
Chittenden, Andrew was in California shortly after the
discovery of gold.

A printed notice, dated "Los Angeles, December 19,
1853," announced "funeral services at 10 o'clock tomorrow
at the El Dorado" for "The Friends and Acquaintances of
Andrew W. Sublette." He had been mauled by a bear in May
and a second such encounter later in the winter caused his
death on December eighteenth.

Four years after settling in the Valley, Cornelius Gilliam
led a group of volunteers against Cayuse Indians allegedly
involved in the Whitman massacre. After engaging the
Indians in battle near Walla Walla, Gilliam set out for the
Valley to confer with Territorial officials. But in late March
1848, at a camp on the way, he was killed by the accidental
discharge of a loaded gun left against his orders in a baggage
wagon. Previously, Gilliam had been appointed to establish
a postal system for the Valley. Gilliam was buried near the
Upper Well Spring, an emigrant watering place inland from
the Columbia on the dry stretch of Trail between Butter and
Willow creeks in present Morrow County, Oregon.

Nathaniel Ford became a well known public office holder
in Oregon, though he was said to have declined at first his
election as a judge by the Champoeg convention of 1845.
Later he served as a county treasurer (1847), a state senator

(1866–68) and in other public offices. Ford, "a refined south-ern gentleman," B. F. Nichols wrote, was also said to have "brought with him a family of Negroes" on the emigration. Nichols once attended a church service at the Fords' and was obviously impressed by the setting and the courtly manners of the family. "To visit at Col. Ford's was like going to the Governor's," he wrote. Nathaniel Ford died on January 9, 1870.

Regarding the Fords and the former slaves who accompa-nied them, Ford family descendant Pauline Burch is on record (Oregon State Library, Salem, 1953) as stating that the young single man Scott, and Robin and Polly Holmes and their three children had requested to come to Oregon. But there unfolded in Polk County court records in the early 1850's a scenario of contention regarding that arrangement. For after working with the Fords in Oregon and in the gold fields of California, Robin Holmes swore out a petition claiming that Ford had not lived up to an agreement to treat him and the others as free persons. Since Section Four of the Organic Act of 1845, the basis of a temporary Oregon Provisional government, forbade slavery, a justice of the Oregon Supreme Court ruled for Holmes, later the owner of a nursery business in Salem.

Chapter Eight

Traffic on the Trail

There were eventually five emigrant processions in '44. In chronological order, the northsiders were first, and at least from Ft. Laramie westward they traveled as two trains: the Stephens-Murphy party bound for California (along with some for Oregon), and those often referred to as the Thorp train bound for Oregon. From the south of the Platte came the Gilliam and Ford trains in third and fourth place (and that occasionally interchanging).

Finally, there came the small party led by Andrew Sublette. The Sublette train left Westport about the third week of May and overtook the Ford train at least by June twenty-seventh, when Clyman referred to them for the first time as having appeared "on the opposite side" of the Blue River. Along the way thereafter to Ft. Laramie, Sublette's group occasionally traveled with or in sight of the Gilliam and/or Ford trains.

The trains of the emigration of 1844 got underway at about the same time, but travel conditions and leadership affected the progress each made along the various initial routes. And while the northsiders traveled in relative isolation, the trains coming to the Platte from the south were occasionally intermingled.

The journal of Jacob Hammer provides a major contribution toward the understanding of the travel schedule of the northsider train of '44 which was the first party on record comprised truly of emigrants to use what has been called the Council Bluffs-Bellevue road. These northsiders generally traveled alone, except for meeting Indians and a few traders along the way. The official start for Hammer's train began with the dispirited crossing of the Missouri River which took four days—May twenty-second to twenty-fifth. And though they began last chronologically, the northsiders were soon first in line on the Trail.

It should be remembered that the vantages from which observations were reported in the journals were that of the individual narrator and not necessarily of an entire train or even a company. Later on the Trail, when the trains were less apt to be traveling in company-sized formations, the narrators' vantages, though no less enlightening, were further restricted.

For the Gilliam train particularly it is helpful to remember the four companies into which the train was divided after its "organization": those led by Richard Woodcock, William Shaw, Robert Wilson Morrison and Allen Saunders.

As for the narrators for the Gilliam train, Parrish was first a member of Shaw's company but at least by May twenty-sixth had joined the Saunders company. Minto and Willard Rees were employees of R. W. Morrison. Samuel B. Crockett, a young man reportedly employed by James Gerrish to drive cattle, may have traveled with the Shaw company though his brief journal does not indicate a particular company affiliation. Crockett indicated that some did not organize themselves into a company when the others did. Whether or not these ever organized he did not say.

Both Parrish and Minto confirmed that Woodcock's company had moved out the next morning after the train's formal organization. This vanguard company, perhaps formed by those with the least number of "loose" cattle and consequently fewer demands on time that such encumbrances required, apparently set a quicker pace than the others and traveled well in advance for most of the journey. While the consistency with which they maintained the lead position may imply efficient piloting, no reference appears in the records of '44 to their having that advantage. On May twenty-seventh, Crockett noted that the Woodcock company had "missed the way and turned back," and had camped "on the main nimihau [River]" while "the other three companies had encamped on the same stream." On the thirtieth also he noted that "captain Woodcock's company started today to take a circuitous rout round the creek [Parrish called it a "branch of the Nimehaw"] we are bridgeing." This apparent eagerness of Woodcock and his group indeed may have correctly characterized this company. But the question remains as to how this group was consistently able to maintain its lead. As partial answer, Minto stated that Woodcock's group had been particularly well provisioned and otherwise properly outfitted.

James Clyman and the Ford train left Independence on the fourteenth and on the fifteenth passed through Westport, heading out on the Santa Fe Trail and to an arduous crossing of the Wakarusa River. Led by Nathaniel Ford and guided by Moses "Black" Harris, this train was divided into messes (Clyman referred also to companies, though the latter seemed in a generic sense). Clyman's narrative, so appreciably detailed and descriptive of many aspects of the overland experience, is not always clear about exactly which portion of the Ford train is being described at specific locations, nor about the train's general progress. It can be assumed, however that the units of this train generally traveled close together for much of the journey since Clyman did not mention nearly as much discontent among the Ford train as that which Parrish, Minto, and Hammer stated plagued their trains.

In early May, Gilliam had publicly announced his intention for linking his train with Ford's. The *Daily Missouri Republican* issue of May twenty-eighth had included (along with the occupations of the emigrants in the encampment on the Missouri River) the text of his letter to Ford in which he stated, in a nearly patronizing tone, that "our company when joined with yours, will be very large—much the largest that has ever crossed the Rocky Mountains. . . We shall be exceedingly happy to join you and you may rest assured that we will not leave you."

On June fourth, Parrish noted that Gilliam had returned from scouting ahead some ten miles or more after the train had crossed the Nemaha on May thirty-first (he had gone to find "Burnett's trace" which marked the route of a previous year's emigration) during which excursion the "General" had seen "ten wagons of C. L. [sic] Ford's company encamped on the west side of a creek." Crockett apparently heard the same news, writing that day that, "Gen Gillum and Mag. [Major] Simons returned to us and informed us . . . that the Independence company was close by and that we would meet them in a day or two."

Assuming that Gilliam knew who drove these ten wagons (as simple a matter as halooing across the stream) this was quite possibly the advance party of ten wagons to which Clyman referred on May thirtieth in his letter to the *Milwaukee Sentinel.* The main body of Ford's train however was many miles to the south on June fourth and on its fifth day of ferrying across the Kansas (Kaw) River. Clyman, meanwhile, was searching the muddy countryside for his stolen mule.

On the fifth, Crockett noted that "three men with pack horses overtook us today and told us that the independence company was 50 miles behind us." The next day, Crockett reported that "four men were dispatched today with an express to fords comp."

Here it is important to note that while the junction of the Independence Road with what would emerge as the St.

Joseph Road has been located by Trail historians at a point in section thirteen just southeast of present Hanover, Kansas (Washington County), the trains of 1844 originating at the two jumping off sites above apparently traveled the same route from some point east of the Black/Big Vermillion River. For not only does it appear from the reference above by Parrish about Gilliam's having seen wagons from the Ford train, but more dependably from Clyman's subsequent notation that the Gilliam train had crossed the Black/Big Vermillion River four days before the Ford train arrived there, that the two trains were sharing some routing in common several miles before reaching the generally accepted "junction" of the two roads.

And it should be added here that John Minto's recollection narrative, published at the turn of the century, included a list of towns in Kansas "on or near the route" west of the Indian Agency—"Hamlin, Fairview, Woodlawn, [crossing of the Nemaha], Centralia"—which he said generally marked the route the Gilliam train took to the "crossing of the Black Vermillion River near Bassett." If correct, Minto thereby described a route angling decidedly south of the now established St. Joe Road.

Two more observations relate to the routing puzzle of 1844. This early year of emigration was one of experimentation, and particularly of rain-impeded travel which no doubt caused many twists and turns in seeking higher, dryer ground where that existed.

Also, Parrish noted on June sixth that, "Yesterday we were much cheered by the striking of the Bernets trale," which he also called the "Burnets trace," for they could then hope "to be able to keep the course better, having lost both time & distance by missing our way, etc." previously. Several miles southeast, James Clyman too was thankful for having "Struck the oregon trace on Cannon Ball Creek [Rock Creek]" on June twenty-third. He noted "greate Joy at finding the trail and a good ford."

"General" Gilliam arrived at the Black Vermillion Creek (Marshall County) on June seventh after calling a one-day halt because of the illness of his daughter Margaret Louisa, (Mrs. Joseph Gage; four weeks later on August third she gave birth). Consequently, with the creek rising at an alarming rate, the train was forced to remain on the spot for the next eleven days waiting for the water to recede or for some other means of crossing to be employed. This was the first event, Minto and Parrish said, which would cause Gilliam's generalship to be seriously and actively questioned.

On June eighth, ten men from the Gilliam train tried to cross the Black/Big Vermillion, hoping to go to the Blue River in search of "canoes" (the hollowed-out log pontoons) which, it was assumed, Woodcock had used to cross that river. The next day train members began work on canoes of their own. Crockett wrote that one craft was completed on the ninth, the other on the fifteenth. By the nineteenth, all wagons were across.

B. F. Nichols described a memorable scene in which "mothers went splashing through this mud and slime to reach the ferry [of rough-cut canoe pontoons for transporting the wagons]. One I remember carrying a small child on one arm and leading or pulling another, scarcely larger, through the mud [who called] 'Mamma, my shoe has come off.' The mother turned and fished it out, and then went forward again, the children squalling, until at last she reaches a wagon fastened on the two canoes, into which she climbs with her children and is pulled across the muddy waters, is landed and finally stands on solid ground, safe with her little brood."

Parrish arrived at the Blue River on the nineteenth where

his—the Saunders—company crossed on the twenty-first using Woodcock's canoes. Morrison's company crossed the next day, and Shaw's on the twenty-third. On the twenty-fourth the last of the cattle were taken across.

Farther south, Ford's train was halted on June thirteenth by the "Knife River" (Cross Creek, Shawnee County) which rose no less than fifteen feet during the day of their arrival. A crossing, by means of a raft built for that purpose, was not accomplished until the seventeenth. The Ford train reached the "Black Vermillion" (actually the Red or Little Vermillion) on the twentieth, the day after Parrish reached the Blue River. When he reached "Burr Oak Creek" (Black Vermillion) on the twenty-fourth, Clyman "found the date of Mr Gilhams company having crossed four days previous." Here the Ford train found a passable ford (the water level apparently had subsided considerably) and therefore was not detained as the Gilliam train had been for two weeks. On the twenty-fifth, Clyman and the others "found two canoes left by those ahead" on a branch of the Big Blue River.

While Clyman struggled on June thirtieth with the crossing of "Rock Creek" (the name for which "seems arbitrary, there being but one rock . . . & that . . . lying right in the middle of the ford"), the companies of the Gilliam train had stopped on that day for a time of both drying out and washing their long-sodden clothing. It was one of the few relatively dry days for the southsiders in a month and a half. At the site where they aired out their belongings, Parrish called the stream by which they camped the "Air fork of the Republican River."

On July first, Crockett and Parrish wrote of a false alarm Indian scare, and Parrish again referred to being "water-stayed," this time on an unnamed branch. On the third, two wagons were upset and the Gilliam train spent the Fourth of July fixing the wagons, washing clothes and resting. In his

inimitable spelling, James Clyman described a celebration of
sorts in his train on the Fourth in which Sublette's group
joined when those "owt on the morning watch [began]
shooting guns at sunrise . . ." But the festivities were not
extensive: "The american Jubilee was but little further noticed
than that the star Spangled Banner floated from Esqr Rolands
waggon throughout the day." (A "J Roland" is listed in the
Transactions "Roll of '44" of 1876. Other sources list a Levi L.
Roland.)

One can assume that piloting was at least one of the points
Gilliam touched upon earlier when he dispatched the four
men to Ford on June sixth. Why Gilliam moved on ahead
rather than waiting on Ford as his letter printed in the
newspapers indicated he would do is not clear. Undoubtedly
the delay on the Black/Big Vermillion made all eager to
proceed. Perhaps that convinced Gilliam not to wait for
Ford's train to arrive from the south.

Ford's train reached the Platte on July tenth, now but
three days behind Gilliam's train. Though, as Crockett
mentioned on July eighth, the wet season had caused muddy
going here as well, the southsider narrators were obviously
thankful for having come beyond the worst mud in which, as
Clyman wrote on July first, they "ate, drank, traveled, slept,
and breathed continually ever since we left the settlements."

Only at this point, as Clyman wrote on the eighth, was
there some appreciable order to the camping routine possible
now that there was less rain. "We are beginning to camp in
tolerable order," Clyman wrote then, "running the wagons
on a level piece of ground and forming a Square, round, or
oblong Krale [corral] the tents Pitched on the outside, the
fires still on the outside of the tents and the guard outside of
all, [with] the horses & other valuables in the Koral." Before,
there had been stragglers to each evening camp who were
delayed by mired wagons, and the campsites had often been

moved hastily when threatened during the night by rising water. Now, on dryer, firmer, ground, the wagons could travel in a more orderly fashion and camps could be set up in relative comfort.

John Minto provided a memorable description of the train in his recollection of July eleventh when he told of the official order of march while moving up the south side of the Platte River. The plan called for Captain Morrison's company to be in the lead "setting the pace," with Morrison himself out ahead "four or five miles" scouting camp sites which offered the essential grass, water and campfire fuel.

Clyman too was moved to describe "our camp" as it moved along on July twelfth. From atop a bluff about a mile from the train, he scanned the length of the procession. "They made Quite a picturesque [appearance]. First came a few strag[g]ling foot & horse men ahead & on the left flank, the right being on the river. Next a thick squad of horsemen in front followeed by a long string of white looking wagon covers flanked with gentlemen & Ladies. Occasionally in the rear a long string of Loose cattle, horses and mules, the tout [total?] assemble being rather uneque."

It was on this stretch of Trail, along the wide River Platte with its gritty shallow flow contained in a wide, aberrant riverbed, that the emigrants would first see the fabled buffalo. And they would have numerous opportunities for several hundred miles (from Grand Island nearly all the way to South Pass) to shoot buffalo and to prepare the meat for use on the Trail. These southsider trains particularly had been delayed many days past the ideal travel schedule and no doubt appreciated the fresh meat from these animals.

The Gilliam train stopped on July eleventh for the frenzied buffalo hunt in which the "General" was conspicuously involved. The resulting erosion of respect for Gilliam's leadership culminated in his resignation as train leader (Parrish wrote that it occurred on the fifteenth, Crockett however entered it in his journal on the fourteenth).

Propitiously perhaps for those who were made apprehensive by the apparent lack of leadership, Ford's train came on the scene (Crockett noted their arrival on the fourteenth; Parrish made no mention of it) and some assurances may have been gained with another train close by.

Clyman wrote on the seventeenth that "La[s]t night we passed Mr Gilhams company & they repassed us again this morning." Parrish and Crockett referred to Sublette's group on the thirteenth, and Parrish mentioned them again on the fifteenth (when he expected to see Sublette but didn't, implying here perhaps that he for one hoped Sublette would provide some guidance). He then reported Sublette close by on the eighteenth and nineteenth.

At this point, Parrish remarked about competent piloting being wanted, and Crockett referred to the hiring of Harris by captains Morrison and Shaw. Crockett had noted that Ford's train was falling behind. And for this Clyman offered one possible though vague explanation. After crossing the "south fork" of the Platte River on the eighteenth, his train remained in camp the next day, "one of the Ladies being to[o] sick to travel." A restless Clyman took a ride out between the forks of the Platte looking at the land and searching for drinking water.

William Shaw's company had been delayed also. B. F. Nichols stated that he was traveling with Shaw's company when that group left the South Platte River on their way to the North Platte and that at that point Shaw's company was "behind most of the other wagons of the train . . . on account of sickness, Mrs. Sebring and Mrs. Frost were not expected to live but a few days at most." (Both women did die. According to John Minto, Mrs. Sebring died on August fourth, and Mrs. Frost on August twelfth.)

Parrish, with the Saunders company, was among the first of the southsiders to reach the "north fork" of the Platte River (the North Platte), arriving there on the twenty-first. Crockett reached the North Platte on the twenty-third. While Parrish spent a day in camp on the twenty-fourth, Crockett and some others two days to the rear, "moved a few miles up to the river to get their catle sepparated from [those of] fords [train]."

On the approach from the South Platte River to the North Platte there occurs one of the more intriguing conundrums of the emigration of 1844: How was it that some southsider companies did not descend the tortuous Windlass Hill to the rewarding Ash Hollow? Named after the emigration period, Windless Hill was a 25° slope (a drop of 150 feet in the space of 300) and the customary approach to a real prize three miles farther on—the only stand of trees, and spring water unexcelled, for miles around. Yet though pilots Moses Harris and Andrew Sublette were at work guiding, one or both of them led the wagons around the site which offered fresh water and wood for cooking.

Of the narrators, Parrish was the one who complained most, though in a delayed reaction. Having come to the Platte River on July seventh at or near Grand Island, Parrish noted on the fifteenth that "We are now above the fork of the Platt" but then corrected himself later in the same entry. At least by the seventeenth, if not before, however, he did pass the juncture of the two forks of the Platte. On the eighteenth he with the Saunders company crossed the south fork, without stating clearly at what distance from the juncture of the forks. He with the others then traveled up the north bank of the south fork on the nineteenth and twentieth, starting the crossing to the north fork on the morning of the twenty-first.

But on that day he got around to recording his displeasure: ". . . camped in the prairai, could not reach the north fork. Our pilot missed the way. . . We were greatly disappointed when we had to camp in the open Prairai, & use pond water in stad of that beautiful spring water so much talked of, & Bufalow chip instid of the beautiful Ash promised."

He was still irritated the next day. "We reached the North platt a little before noon, some distance above the Ash grove and fine spring alluded to above, had bad road to day . . ."

John Minto's narrative, written many years after the journey and for which he relied many times on the daily entries of the Parrish journal published by the Oregon Pioneer Association in 1888, specifically indicated a by-passing of the Upper Ford-Ash Hollow route between the two forks of the Platte River.

But regarding this section of the Trail, Minto's account includes a confusing contradiction arising in part from his own comments becoming confused with his paraphrasing of the Parrish journal about these series of events.

In one instance, the Minto narrative states that on July nineteenth, the Morrison Company with whom he traveled forded the South Platte "four or five miles from the junction of the two branches" whereupon they followed along the north bank of the South Platte for two days, then on July twenty-first "we started across to the North Platte." This involved taking "the decline" along which "we passed trunks and big limbs of cedar trees" which they chopped and put into the wagons for fuel. They came to the North Platte "about twelve miles west of Ash Hollow" he was told by "our guide, Black Harris."

Earlier in his narrative, however, when outlining a general route through Nebraska, Minto reported that his company had reached "the main Platte River about six miles west of [the town of] Prosser." Continuing along the south bank of the Platte, they passed the forks of the river and continued along "its South bank to west of Big Spring" where, according to this version, they crossed the South Platte, "striking the North Platte nearly opposite Oshkosh." Such a route would indeed have led them to a point on the North Platte about the distance west of Ash Hollow that Moses Harris was said to have estimated. But the difference here is that the crossing of the South Platte is implied to have occurred much farther west, at or near Big Spring, than the Parrish journal indicated.

But though by either version of Minto's rendition the Morrison and Saunders companies of the Gilliam train missed Ash Hollow, which was confirmed by Parrish, the William Shaw company apparently did arrive there and enjoyed the benefits of that spot.

For B. F. Nichols, in compiling his narrative shortly after the turn of the century, recalled that while crossing from the South to the North Platte, "We traveled over a beautiful plain to a place called Ash Hollow and down the hollow until we came to an ash grove where we camped at a spring." The next day they reached the North Platte. The William Shaw company at this time had been delayed by the illness of Mrs. Sebring and Mrs. Frost, and so was at the rear of the procession of the Gilliam train. And so whoever was piloting this company at this particular time can be credited with steering the group to Ash Hollow.

James Clyman with the Ford train arrived at the forks of the Platte on July seventeenth, crossed the next day and continued up the north bank of the South Platte for several miles. On the twenty-second this group continued "to the point whare we leave the S. Fork & cross over the ridge to the N. Fork." After traveling twenty-two miles by Clyman's reckoning on "nearly a north course," they arrived at the North Platte the next evening after dark at a spot which offered "not a stick of Standing timber in sight in any direction"—not, apparently, Ash Hollow, a site not otherwise mentioned by this former mountainman and pilot in his narrative of '44.

At this general locale on the Trail also there is in two of the journals yet another of the occasional fortunate intertwining of happenstance references which, in this instance, help explain how the emigrants resolved the problems resulting from two large groups traveling close together.

On July twentieth, Clyman noted that "yesterday an arrangement was entered into for the traveling in the neare vicinity of each other & encamping no further apart than necessary for the good of our stock . . ." He was probably referring to the combination of portions of his and Gilliam's train traveling close together when he wrote about "our entire company making 96 teams, wagons & occupies with loose stock & all, more than two miles of tolerable close column," since the total wagons in his own train and those in Gilliam's train numbered more than ninety-six.

Crockett on the twenty-sixth contributed the second, and complementary, reference which matched with Clyman's when he wrote that his company stopped at 1:00 p.m. "to let Ford's company pass for their weeks travel before; that being our way of traveling." Thus one gains some insight into an attempt at traffic management on the Trail.

Most of the narrators of '44 recorded their arrival at one of the Trail's most famous features. Parrish camped near Chimney Rock on July twenty-sixth. Clyman nooned at the Chimney on July twenty-eighth; Crockett passed it sometime during the same day, on a twenty-five mile march.

Scotts Bluff was the next site of interest, viewed from across the North Platte River by Jacob Hammer in the northsider train, but close up by the southsiders. James

Clyman, on July twenty-ninth writing fetchingly as usual in phonetics of his own construction, was the most creatively descriptive of all. "Left the River and struck S. of W. 14 miles and encamped in the midst of Scotts blufs By a cool spring in a romantic & picturisque vally surrounded except to the E. by high & allmost impassably steepclay cliffs of all immagenary shapes & forms . . ." The former mountain man bagged a "fat Black tailed Buck" for supper, then served as sentinel for "a Beautifull covey of young Ladies & misses" who gathered "wild currants & choke chirries." The next morning he described the anomoly of the bluffs with impressive geological supposition. This localized range of bluffs, he wrote, represented "once the common level of the country."

To Minto the bluffs, viewed from some distance, "looks so like large city buildings." Parrish, who was ill at the time, remarked only that on July twenty-eighth they stopped by a good spring "running out of the bluff or sandy mountains" about five miles from the river. The next day's camp was back on the south bank of the North Platte.

The procession to Ft. Laramie from Scotts Bluff involved more changes in the order of march. Minto recalled arriving at the fort with the Morrison and Shaw companies "late" on July thirtieth. On the thirty-first, Crockett camped fifteen miles southeast of the fort. Parrish made no entry in his journal on the thirtieth, but on the thirty-first he "passed Ft. Larimo one mile and camped."

Clyman stated that from Scotts Bluff some of his train went on ahead to the fort, while he and the remainder proceeded in usual fashion, with about one third of the train remaining at the Bluffs "to recruit their lame stock." He reached "Ft. Larrimie" about 4:00 p.m. on August first, the same day Minto, with the Morrison and Shaw companies, left the fort. Clyman must have remained at the fort longer than most of his train, or mess, for Parrish passed "two

companies and Ford's company" on August second and
Clyman didn't leave the fort until the morning of the third.
On the third, Crockett "camped with Ford at a large
spring . . ."

B. F. Nichols explained that on the stretch west of Ft.
Laramie, "The wagons of the entire train were scattered
along the route, some being as much as two or three days
travel behind others of the train" (and this while yet in the
much feared Sioux country).

After three full days back on the Trail, James Clyman
wrote on August fifth that, "at our camp on horse shoe creek
we over took all the different companies of emigrants except
Hitchcock's and encamped in a Jumbled mass of Stock,
tents, people, &c &c." If this all-inclusive communal
encampment did not include Woodcock's company, then
Clyman had not learned yet that that group, in addition to
the Stephens-Murphy party (which he called by the name of
Hitchcock), was out in front.

As noted before, Clyman referred to Hitchcock in reference to the northsiders and not to train leader Elisha Stephens
or pilot Caleb Greenwood. Clyman gave no hint of how he
knew of the progress of the northsider group. Word undoubtedly traveled up and down the Missouri River earlier in the
spring about the trains that were about to form for the trip
west. Later, on the Trail, some eastbound traveler met along
the way, such as the men in the few mackinaw boats on the
Platte whom Hammer, Parrish and Minto mentioned, may
have told of passing the northsiders, or of having heard of
their progress. Clyman did not mention having seen the
boatmen, but he may have heard of their news from someone
in the Gilliam train which he overtook shortly after the
boatmen had passed.

Though the electric telegraph was but a newfangled con-
trivance in '44 (on May twenty-fourth, the day before the

Hammers crossed the Missouri River, Samuel F. B. Morse in Washington, D. C. had received the famous "What hath God wrought?" message from fellow inventor Alfred Vail over a line stretched the forty miles from Baltimore), the wilderness telegraph—whereby scraps of news were relayed over hundreds of miles by the chance meetings of the few persons astir on wilderness trails—often worked to inform people of happenings far away.

At the place on the North Platte where the trains crossed to the north bank (near present Casper, Wyoming) Parrish's "camp" on August twelfth was eager and wanted to be off before Ford's train broke camp. Parrish crossed the river, then in hurry-up-and-wait consternation, his group set to camp again on the north bank "to cure the [buffalo] meat we have, and to give Walker a chance to kill more, as he has not enough it seems." Some members of Ford's train apparently took the lead again at that point, for Crockett, who would soon range thirty miles ahead to hunt, reached Independence Rock on the fifteenth and "stayed with Fords company all night."

Clyman too noted camping "one half mile below Independence Rock" on the fifteenth. At the Rock the next day, he could claim actual acquaintanceship with some of the names inscribed there, "names of its numerous visitors most of which are nearly obliterated by the weather & ravages of time" (even in 1844!). He saw the names of former companions "Thos. Fitzpatrick and W. L. Sublette," and was amused to find the names of Henry Clay and Martin Van Buren forged by some devotee no doubt ready to argue politics at this open air forum far west of the ornate chambers of Congress.

In the vicinity of Independence Rock, the emigrants first viewed the snowcapped mountains to the west. Perhaps it was this view of the mountains that caused Clyman to reflect in his entry for August twentieth on his trip of 1824. In January of that year "under J. Smith and T Fitzpatrick [we] first traversed the now well known South pass and camped on green river on the 19th of march." The peaks of the Rockies, and their timelessness, moved the former mountain man once again to reflect. He had not seen the mountains for seventeen years, but that many "summers last past had not in the least diminished the snow that then crowned their lofty heads which still ware the white appearance of old age."

Parrish came to the Rock on the sixteenth, passed the site, and nooned at Devil's Gate. Along the way that day he "passed Ford's company this afternoon, so we are before again."

The two trains, or some portions thereof, continued to travel close together on August twentieth. Ford's group "camped on the creek below us," Parrish wrote. "They say they do not desire to go before [us], but wish to avail themselves of the experience of our pilot, Mr. Walker." Ford's train was the first to break camp the next morning.

Here, then, there occurred the apparent turnaround from a similar arrangement earlier in which Moses Harris, originally engaged by the Ford train, pointed the way for some of the Gilliam train as well. And the leap-frog passing of one train by another continued. On the twenty-first, "Col. Ford's company passed us this morning with the priests who left us some days ago," Parrish wrote.

For his part, Harris seems to have struck an unhurried pace on this stretch of Trail. He took the time to remain with Clyman just east of South Pass during the death watch for Mr. Barnette and the subsequent wake. At that point, Clyman had got ahead of the others again, for as he sat with Barnette on the twenty-third, "several teams [from his group or mess] went on & Mr Gilhams company passed our encampment." The next day, "Early in the afternoon, Capt. Shaw and Morrisons company hove in sight" and camped "about ½ a mile below us."

If John Minto's memory served him correctly, it was on August twenty-sixth that he passed "the Ford company" along the way to his own camp that evening at Pacific Springs. And here Minto helped to point out that not only did companies and smaller groups move at will up and down the line of march, but individuals too exercised similar mobility. For in this context he referred to "a single hunter, I. W. Alderman, from Ford's company" who overtook him at lunchtime. Writing over fifty years later, Minto showed editorial nonchalance in recalling that he detected something distrustful in Alderman's looks and that the man had seemed "to talk for effect." (Others by that name have been mentioned: an Alderman, no first name or initials given, was listed as deceased in the "Roll of '44" published in 1876 as part of the Oregon Pioneer Association's *Transactions* of that year. "Mr. Alderman" helped find James Clyman's stolen horse. Later, local history sources listed an Isaac Wesley Alderman as a justice of the peace in Tillamook County for several years.)

After Clyman and his camp mates buried Barnette on the morning of August twenty-seventh, they followed the others west and south from South Pass, along the Little Sandy, the Big Sandy, the Green and the Black Fork of the Green River, to Ft. Bridger. Clyman arrived at "Bridgers & Vasqueses trading house" on August thirty-first, the day after Parrish camped near "the Green River Fort," and two days after Minto had arrived. (Crockett's journal, unfortunately, ended on the twenty-seventh, before he reached Ft. Bridger.)

Among the narrators, Clyman gave the best explanation for why one might choose to take the time and effort to go to Bridger's new "fort." For though the "rout" along the Green

River "has been verry crooked . . . the only object of this zigzag road is to pass the trading hous which however is some convenienc as we ware able to trade every extra article we had for mokisens & leather clothing. Exchanged of all our worn out mules & horses."

(Several weeks earlier, Elisha Stephens' party which possibly included some going to Oregon was apparently led over the Sublette-Greenwood Cutoff, bypassing Ft. Bridger, according to Bray and Schallenberger.)

About the drive away from Bridger's post, John Minto added the curious recollection that on August thirty-first he met an "old . . . Irishman . . . trader from Bridger," who "came with the Ford company." From this occurrence, "We judged the Ford and Saunders company, who followed the Walker cut-off, to be very little behind us." There are at least two points to ponder here: why Minto didn't ask the old trader where Ford and Saunders were rather than merely "judging", and what was meant by the "Walker cut-off" if not one of the deviations from the Trail of which Parrish complained earlier?

Along the Trail northwest from Ft. Bridger, the companies of Shaw and Morrison were apparently divided into small groups. They continued to travel close together; but not to everyone's liking. John Minto hindered a fellow Shaw company wagon driver from passing him on the Trail along the Bear River. This was the first of two such incidents, the second of which was resolved when Minto's employer Morrison signalled for him to give way whereupon Minto saw that an occupant of this wagon was ill and that the driver sought a less dusty ride for his passenger than when following Minto's wagon. Shaw's company and his own, Minto wrote, "drove much mixed," and there was competition "to get the lead" on some sections of the Trail.

William Shaw told H. H. Bancroft that, "Morrison's

company and my company kept together until we got to Fort Bridger." But beyond that place, their closeness came to be a matter of contention. At Ft. Bridger, "I agreed to stop and wash. My company wanted to wash and Morrison was going on. We thought best from that [point] on to separate and they started on. My folks washed up their things and we started on [the] next day. The oxen were so keen to go after the track and trail of the others that they caught up with them the second day. Some of them [Morrison's company] were not well pleased about us overtaking them after we agreed to stop. We could not help that; our cattle just pushed on, on the scent of the others. Then I halted again, and let them go on and I traveled about five or six miles a day down Bear River and let them get ahead. I never saw them again."

Yet another example of the dissolution of some company units was the resignation on August twenty-fourth of Mitchell Gilliam, while yet between South Pass and Ft. Bridger, from the leadership of the group with which Parrish traveled. The guide Joseph Walker had said, according to Parrish, that "there was no danger after this," and so Mitchell Gilliam disbanded the group. The "danger" referred to was that supposedly threatened by Indians.

Consequently, it was not unusual to find small units of emigrants traveling relatively independently along the Trail from this point forward. On the second day beyond Ft. Bridger, "Neal [Cornelius, referred to in other narratives as "Neil"] Gilliam with ten wagons goes ahead" Parrish wrote, while "Michael[Mitchell] Gilliam and ten more take a different route . . ."

That sense of security figured also in the decision made at this point by John Minto, and perhaps by James Clyman also, when within three days of each other they left their trains to continue the journey on horseback. Minto, whose wagon driving habits of late had caused the Morrisons to send him fishing for three days, had talked with Daniel Clark on the evening of September third and had learned of the intention of Clark and Crockett to ride on ahead of the train. Minto returned to Morrison and asked to be released from employment. Morrison "could see nothing against this, if there was no danger from the Indians, and these people [Indians] seemed glad, rather than otherwise, to see us." And so, on the tenth, Minto set out, perhaps riding double with Daniel Clark since he stated that at that point he hoped to trade his gun for a horse at Ft. Hall.

On September third, Clyman too made preparations to go on ahead on horseback. He left the next day from a point three days beyond Ft. Bridger in company with three others. Unencumbered by the slow moving vehicles, the three made thirty miles before camping for the night. By September seventh, they had reached Soda Springs where Clyman saw that "a company of hunters from Fort hall had Just arived & Likewise a few persons (to hunt and make dried meat) For California."

One wonders immediately at Clyman's casual mention of a group "For California." By the Schallenberger/Stewart travel chronology, the Californians Clyman saw here were not those of the Stephens-Murphy party since they would have been much farther along toward California by this time. But if the travel schedule for the California emigrants which is implied in the Hammer journal is stretched to the limit of credence, these "Californians" may have been a detachment from the Stephens-Murphy party. It is safer, however, to say that it is not easy to surmise just who they were. They remain but fleeting silhouettes, much like Sublette's group, the Platte River boatmen, the traders met on the slopes of the Rockies, and a few others who appear in the periphery of the view of emigration this year.

Clyman and his saddle chums camped two miles "above" Fort Hall on the tenth and the next morning rode past the "white washed mud walled Battlements" of the fort. They camped near American Falls on the Snake that evening. Minto came to the fort on the eleventh and remained there until the Shaw and Morrison companies came up a few days later. Thus the paths of the young Englishman and the former mountain man came near to crossing at the fort. This is one of a few near-misses whereby the record of '44 could have been enriched even more; the observations of these two, each of the other, would have been worthy footnotes to the chronicles.

Minto stated, in a manuscript version of his trail story which he prepared at the request of historian H. H. Bancroft, that he had been sent on ahead to report the company's need for supplies. He added that "Here [at Ft. Hall] we were met by a letter from Peter H. Burnett to the effect that if the emigrants were likely to need assistance before reaching Oregon, and would let the fact be known, such assitance, he [Burnett] thought, would be rendered by those who had preceded us to the Willamette Valley. As it was manifest that many of the company would be very short of provisions before they could reach western Oregon, it was considered well that S. B. Crocket, Daniel Clark and myself should here leave the train and come forward on horse back in order to let the condition of the people be known."

A similar mission for Clyman is suggested by a note which he wrote on the inside back cover of his notebook: "Tell these Gentlemen that Gnel Gilham is on the road and scarce of Provisions." Those he listed as persons to whom such a message might be delivered were "Madison Gilmire, Joel Walker, Peter H. Burnett, Anarson Smith, James Watters." James W. Waters came into Clyman's camp on the Powder River on September twenty-seventh, and perhaps Clyman

ALONG THE SNAKE RIVER, TEN MILES BEYOND AMERICAN FALLS
In Massacre Rocks State Park, Idaho. Author's photo.

delivered the message then. Waters, according to Clyman and other narrators, was traveling east on the Trail in the hope of finding his family emigrating that season; Parrish met him on October eleventh, two days travel east of the Grande Ronde. John Minto had met Waters, William C. Dement and a Mr. Rice near where Minto and his companions began on the steep Trail down into Grande Ronde where "we were compelled to give him the disappointing information that his family was not on the way."

On the journey west of Ft. Hall, food would be scarce. Clyman could well imagine the conditions though he had not been farther west than the Wind River and Green River country. Others in '44, however, ventured into the region happily unaware. Minto and his young cohorts began the trip from Ft. Hall with fifteen pounds of "buffalo pemmican." George Washington Bush, a black emigrant of '44 and who hosted Minto and Willard Rees at the Missouri

River rendezvous site, was one "always watchful" who now cautioned Minto and friends about what lay ahead. "Boys, you are going through hard country. . . Take my advice; anything you see as big as a blackbird, kill it and eat it." At times, on the desolate Trail from Ft. Hall to at least the Grande Ronde, Minto and the others would have been glad for fricasseed blackbird.

Minto came to "the little adobe trading post" of Ft. Boise hungry as usual on this stretch of the Trail. Here he and his companions "purchased twenty pounds of Oregon flour." Earlier, four days out of Ft. Hall, one of the three had killed a duck. They had traded for a few fish at Salmon Falls, and later Crockett had killed a cottontail rabbit. Such was the eating fare for what eventually was a party of six young men during the trip across Idaho.

From this point in Clyman's journal and Minto's recollections, neither could know as readily as before about the progress of the trains with which they had begun the trip. Parrish meanwhile continued to log the progress of those with whom he traveled: two days beyond Ft. Bridger, Ford and the elder Gilliam camped "below us" on September third; there also he heard that the companies led by Shaw and Morrison were about two days behind. On the next day, "Mr. Ford's company reached camp ground two hours after dark" but Gilliam "and his squad, consisting of his own and two sons-in-law families, did not come . . . to camp." The day before, the occupants of five wagons and a mule carriage left Gilliam and joined Parrish and his companions.

There was talk at this time of further cooperation between the two trains. "It is supposed," Parrish wrote on September third, that "he [Gilliam] and Mr. Ford will join companies." He also heard that Gilliam and Ford had made mistaken assumptions about the availabilty of grass up ahead on the Trail. If what he heard was true, once again there not only was a pilot lacking, but also some self-piloting initiative on the part of these leaders. After hundreds of miles on the Trail, the availability of life-sustaining natural feed for the cattle would have been of great importance and the practice of sending a rider ahead to scout camping sites would seem to have been the accepted practice by now.

Parrish also complained about the Gilliams when, three miles into the day's trek on September eleventh, "Neal" Gilliam branched to the right and Mitchell Gilliam to the left, "carrying out what . . . [they] . . . had arranged the afternoon previous, the object being to get rid of us." To this Parrish simply remarked, "So let it be."

That evening, the Parrish and Hawley families came into the camp of the Jacob Hoover, James Cave and George Nelson families who had passed them earlier when the first two had "nooned." In camp that evening, while Parrish sat writing in his journal, "Captain Ford with fifteen wagons passed us again." The next morning, Parrish and Hawley left camp first, Ford's group (having camped nearby) followed, and "Mr. Hoover's company" brought up the rear.

Two days after reaching Soda Springs, Parrish was passed by Ford "and fifteen wagons in the afternoon." The next day, the twelfth, he "rolled out before Ford's company" and maintained the lead. He arrived at Ft. Hall about 3:00 p.m. on the thirteenth, passed the fort and camped six or seven miles farther on. On that day, Hoover's company had passed and had arrived ahead of him at the fort, but "The two Gilliams and Captain Ford are behind us." On September fourteenth, one day beyond Ft. Hall, Parrish logged fifteen miles and camped at a point beyond which, he was told, was twenty-five miles without grass. Along the way that day he had overtaken "six wagons that left us some weeks past."

If the "six wagons" were part of Richard Woodcock's company, which pulled ahead of the others at the beginning of the trip and continued to travel ahead, the "some weeks" Parrish estimated amounted to more like four months. If not Woodcock's, then perhaps these wagons belonged to yet another unidentified splinter group from one of the original Gilliam train companies.

Though Parrish camped with Jacob Hoover and some others on the fifteenth, he and the Hawley family "camped alone for the first time" on the sixteenth and the next morning started early and "stayed ahead." Parrish implied that others also were traveling in small groups at this time: "Mr. Welch found a camping place on the bank of the river. . . The bachelors stayed at the camp of bad water today to rest the cattle . . . [We] camped . . . on a branch . . . Mr. Hoover a little below."

When he had set up camp on the nineteenth, Parrish assumed that "we are now a hundred miles below Fort Hall, a good drive for five days." Hoover was camped "a little below" and "Mr. Saunders came up . . . and let us hear from the camps behind us" (news which Parrish did not impart in his entry on the twentieth).

Minto too was close by. On the seventeenth, after crossing the Portneuf west of Ft. Hall (the Trail led across this river on the way in to the fort as well) he "passed Col. Ford's train" and thereupon Minto, Clark and Crockett were joined by "three young men" (Ramsey, Murray, Ferguson) making up the party of six referred to above. Perhaps on the next day, or the day after that, Minto and his companions "overtook Major Thorp's company" near Salmon Falls on the Snake River and were involved briefly in an argument about the ownership of a horse recently acquired by Ramsey from Indians but which one of Thorp's party said had been as recently stolen from him. Minto implied that William Case (whom Jacob Hammer had mentioned early in his journal) was present at this time and place since years later he and

Case reminisced about the event. This is one of but a few instances reported in the narratives of '44 of possible meetings of northsiders and southsiders.

Clyman was now well ahead of the others. On September fifteenth he passed Thousand Springs, an awe inspiring profusion of waterfalls on the north wall of the Snake River Canyon not far from Upper Salmon Falls where he camped that evening. (Jacob Hammer passed these springs five days earlier on September tenth.) About 10 a.m. on the seventeenth, he was fording the "upper crossing" of the Snake where he saw "a few teams that had left Ft. Hall six days before us."

These may have been northsiders, though Clyman did not say so. The Hammers had left the vicinity of Ft. Hall on August thirty-first, ten days before Clyman left there. They crossed the Snake at Three Island Crossing on September twelfth, five days ahead of Clyman.

After crossing the river, Clyman camped on September seventeenth with the occupants of several wagons and noted the presence of "Some Ney Percee . . . & a few Snakes." On that day he made a reference in his journal to "Some difficulty [which] was likely to grow out of a Stolen horse" and one jumps to conclude that he was referring to the same event about which John Minto and William Case reminisced years later— when Minto's companion Ramsey was said by someone in northsider John Thorp's train to be riding a horse recently stolen by Indians. Perhaps when Clyman came on the scene, the horse had just turned up missing, and Minto, coming along later with Ramsey (who had just bought "a small bay horse" from an Indian) and Daniel Clark were yet to arrive for their part in the unfolding drama.

By the nineteenth Clyman had reached the Boise River. He camped with "two teams" on the twentieth, passing nine wagons "in camp" and "fourteen or fifteen more" the next day, the twenty-first. That day he crossed the Boise to the north side, set a course "north of west" and, camping two miles east of Ft. Boise "on a beautifull clear evening," he watched the sun go "tranquilly down behind the Blue Mountains without a cloud to be seen."

The wagons and "teams" Clyman passed along this stretch could have been Woodcock's, or even northsiders. For Clyman reached the fort on the twenty-second; Jacob Hammer "crossed the Snake River at Boisers fort" on the twenty-third.

But while the "clerk" at the fort "made out a sketch of the route to Walla Walla" for Clyman, the same person was probably too busy to leisurely chart the course ahead for Hammer. For when Jacob Hammer passed there "those that kept the fort . . . made ready for battle" in anticipation of a fight threatened by the none too agreeable swapping of horses between Snake Indians and some of "Captain J. Thorp's band," Hammer wrote. Three horses had allegedly been stolen from the emigrants "a few nights since" and "they ['Thorp's band'] then went and took nine horses from the natives . . ." Thorp and the others crossed the Snake River before the Indians arrived and the fight did not come off.

Clyman, passing through the scene the day before, was unaware of this. At his camp twenty-six miles west of the fort on the twenty-second, he was peacefully using the last of the "saleratas" he had picked up a few miles east of Independence Rock. Had he been but a few hours later in leaving the fort, however, his comments would have added much to the record of the event.

After striking "what we Supposed to be Burnt River" along "the worst road yet," Clyman nooned on the twenty-sixth "at what is called the lone Tree in the middle of a vally & a fine one it has been of the pine Spicies now cut down &

all the branches used for fuel." (This "particularly prominent landmark" according to historian Aubrey Haines was
"probably at the first crossing of the Baldock Slough" in
Baker County, Oregon. Peter Burnett, at the site in September 1843, bemoaned the loss of the tree "about 10 miles from
any other timber." Fremont complained on October 15,
1843, of "the 'wretch and vandal' who destroyed it.") Continuing past the site, Clyman camped on the night of the
twenty-sixth at the Powder River where there "came to our
camp . . . Mr. [William C.] Dement and four Indians going
to meet the wagons, their object I did not assertain, but some
speculation no doubt." Clyman entered the Grande Ronde
the next day and found James Waters to be "waiting for his
family which he expects to come in this seasons imigration."

Many miles behind Clyman and the Hammers, Parrish
had logged thirty miles on the twenty-first, traveling from 6
a.m. to 7 p.m., "the longest day's drive we have had." He did
not get to Salmon Falls until the twenty-third where he too
traded for salmon. He then proceeded to Three Island Crossing. On the twenty-fourth he crossed the Snake River. Two
days later he nooned about midway between the Snake and
Boise River at the "Hot Boiling Spring" where, eleven days
earlier, Jacob Hammer had "cooked a piece of meat done in
fifteen minutes."

On the twenty-eighth, the day that Clyman, then on the
Grande Ronde, "concluded to ly[sic] still and rest ourselves
and horses before taking the Blue Mountains," the Parrish's
"Western" rolled on for about twelve hours but didn't come
to the Boise River as expected. (He reached the environs of
the Boise River on the twenty-ninth.) Clyman crossed the
Blue mountains on the twenty-ninth and the thirtieth, and
on October first he passed the trail branching off to the
Whitman mission.

On October third, when Parrish pulled in to Fort Boise about one o'clock, Clyman had come "on the banks of the great river [the Columbia] about 11 o'clock." On the seventh, Clyman first viewed Mt. Hood just before he reached The Dalles mission in the forenoon where he was amused at getting no thanks from the man in charge, the Reverend Alvan F. Waller, for letters he delivered into the Reverend's hands from "the [post] office at Westport." Clyman good-naturedly supposed that it was his unkempt appearance that put Waller off.

Back along the Burnt River, Parrish guessed on October seventh (his second day along that river) that he was about ten or twelve days from "Walley Walley." The next day, when Parrish, five days after leaving Ft. Boise, was complaining of "the steepest hill I ever saw teams cross" on October eighth, both Clyman and his horse had worked up a sweat on the land route around Mt. Hood where on a dangerously steep path his pack horse pitched its load over its head because of the sharp angle of descent.

On the ninth, Parrish and the others traveled from 7 a.m. to 10 p.m. only because "Mr. Walker thinks it would not be safe to go further for fear of failing to find water and grass." Unfortunately he did not explain whether he meant the guide Joseph Walker, or perhaps James, James Jr., or Robert Walker, persons listed on the "Roll of '44" (or even former trapper Joel Pickens Walker noted by Clyman as one of the men whom he should tell that "Gnel Gilham is on the road and scarce of Provision") and therefore conceivably present on the scene at that time and place.

October ninth was also John Minto's twenty-second birthday and about noon he "emerged from the timber on the west slope of the Blue Mountains" and saw the "immense white cones called . . . Mount Hood and Mount Adams [the latter in Washington State]" dominating a vista to which "there are no bounds in sight."

Earlier, Minto had come upon a portion of Woodcock's company after entering Burnt River canyon and observed that these emigrants "had done better than we, both in expedition of movement and in keeping up their food supply." Later, "in a deep valley in the Blue Mountains," he found "the most advanced section of Woodcock's company."

If one could have viewed Parrish, Clyman and Minto simultaneously on October eleventh, the travel conditions under which each toiled would have characterized eastern and central Oregon impressively.

On that day, the Parrishes toiled along the Trail approach to Grande Ronde, double-teaming to cross "an allmost impassable muddy hollow." The day was cold and cloudy; at the campsite that evening the grass was scarce, "branch . . . water in holes only." Here "Captain Waters" came into camp.

Minto that day had come to the mouth of the Umatilla River where it met the Columbia (the Hammers would arrive here on the twelfth). He rode along the shoreline no doubt marveling at the size of The River, thinking perhaps that not even the fable-like descriptions he had heard before had truly prepared him for what he now beheld. Here all his considerable ambition was dwarfed by the Columbia Gorge, the majesty of it all so much the opposite to his own penury. But in the midst of this reflection and wonder, he met M. M. McCarver, Speaker of the House of the Oregon Provisional Government, who had come out to look for his family among the emigrants that season. During this chance meeting, Minto obtained a promise of temporary employment by McCarver on his claim on the Tualatin Plains. Now the former coal miner had at least a grubstake of sorts in the Valley.

On this day also, fifty-two year old James Clyman was farther ahead, riding deep among the fir shrouded ridges surrounding Mt. Hood where he noted "male Fern . . . nine or 10 feet in hight . . ., tall Firr, . . . emmence large Hemlock . . ." But he was anxious each time his mount had to leap the otherwise unavoidable fallen timbers on which the sharp snags of broken limbs threatened the horses with the "greate danger of letting out their entrails." As an outdoorsman who for many years had chosen to range territories where dangers of many kinds threatened, Clyman's senses were yet alert to any hint of stalking figures, animal or otherwise, caught in one's side vision and to sounds such as the gunshot crack of a limb broken nearby. He admitted to being "allmost wearied out with the continual watching it requires to tarvel[sic] through an unsettled country . . ." On the next day, amidst still-smoldering logs downed in a recent forest fire, he "made preparations for shaveing & preparing . . . to see our countrymen tomorrow . . ." His "preparations" required the admirable effort of bathing and shaving "in the cold clear running little brook that passed our present encampment."

And so each of the travelers was experiencing some sensory superabundance so characteristic of the country, impressions which no doubt would remain with them for all their remaining days; "as long as one has life," Minto later said of the view from the crest of the Blue Mountains.

But for all, the toil continued as no respecter of fortunes or the lack of them. Little Rebecca Parrish's broken thigh was yet painfully jolted as she rode in the family's wagon, the "Western," beyond Powder River on the twelfth. On the thirteenth, which began with a covering of frost, the family entered the Grande Ronde.

On the thirteenth, James Clyman, freshly shaved and fresher smelling than for weeks before, topped a ridge and saw cattle feeding in the Clackamas River valley. About four miles from the Falls of the Willamette, where was the "seat and Government and main commercial place for all settlements," he passed the first cabin he had seen in weeks and in "town" the first man he saw was an acquaintance, J. M. Wair, out from Indiana in the emigration of '43.

John Minto crossed the mouth of the John Day River on the bank of the Columbia and though the water was so low and the river bed so rocky that he could nearly cross "dry shod," he found a dangerous ford the next day at the mouth of the "Des Chutes" River. And there also he was nearly robbed, he believed, by several Indians whom he threatened off at the point of his gun.

Minto reached The Dalles on October fifteenth and from there he, S. B. Crockett and Samuel Ferguson, like Clyman a few days before them, rode "across the Cascades [mountains] via the trail the missionaries had used to bring cattle from the Willamete—the only one used until S[amuel] K[imbrough] Barlow and others forced their way through the south side of Mount Hood in 1845–46." They reached Oregon City during the evening of the eighteenth, five days behind Clyman. The next day they were working on the McCarver farm on the Tualatin Plains, as was Daniel Clark who had come down the Columbia in a Chinook canoe.

Minto saw a few fellow emigrants of '44 in the Valley later in November and December. At Linnton on December third, he saw Jacob Hoover, once an officer in the Gilliam train. He also saw John Thorp, "leader of the train that came up the north side of the Platte." Both Thorp and Hoover had recently arrived at Linnton "in the boat we were to get" which Minto and a few others used to return to The Dalles to bring the Morrisons and others to the Valley.

While Clyman and Minto viewed The Valley in October

and November, the Parrishes had much traveling yet to do before they arrived there—a month and a half of wearying travel, some of it mountainous, some along the Columbia, some on the River, and all of it cold. On October fourteenth they entered the Blue Mountains at the western edge of Grande Ronde, struggled down the steep hill to the Grande Ronde River, nooned, and pulled up the hill on the other side. On the evening of the eighteenth they camped at the base of the mountains, having come like the others to the Umatilla River and to the scene which seemed to surprise all who saw it—the well tended farm fields of the Cayuse Indians and their large herds of horses.

How the Parrishes and the five other families with whom they now traveled missed the trail to the Whitman mission was not explained, but their mistake cost them an additional forty mile trek (twenty each way) before starting for the mission on the twentieth. On the way to the mission, the Parrishes were joined by the Hawleys and the Caves. The "packers" who passed them on the nineteenth told of snow three feet deep in the Blue Mountains. Parrish, thankful for his "escape" from the mountains, reached the mission at night on the twenty-third; that day also the packers had passed again on their way back to the trains.

It may be that the "packers" were from the group with which the Benjamin Nichols family traveled. "I think it was at Powder River," B. F. Nichols wrote, "that Bennett Osborn and Thomas Shaw left for Dr. Whitman's to procure flour and corn meal to supply our company of ten wagons with bread as we were running short of this commodity." The Nichols and the others continued into the Grande Ronde, and when they were camped on the Grande Ronde River Shaw and Osborn returned "about dark . . . with an ample supply of flour and corn meal for the entire company."

This group of families which included, in addition to the Nichols, "the families of David Goff, James Howard [both 'of Ford's train'], John Perkins, William Morgan, Solomon Shelton, Theofolus McGruder, William Sebring, Morris Humphry, and [.?.] McCallister," took the side trip to the Whitman mission as had the Parrishes. But unlike the Parrishes and those few with whom they traveled at that time, this group remained at the mission until mid February.

While at the mission, Parrish wrote of others present also. The Hawleys were there on November first, preparing, as were the Parrishes, to travel the Walla Walla River route to the Columbia and thence west to The Dalles. The Parrishes left the mission on November first. When they reached the mouth of the Umatilla River, they found a Mr. Jenkins waiting to join their group. To their camp on the sixth came "Captain Morrison, Mrs. McDaniels, and E. McGruder." The travel for all was rough going here. On the first full day along the Columbia, twelve yoke of oxen were required to pull each wagon up one particularly demanding hill.

On November tenth, "Captain Morrison came up with flour." On the eleventh, the theft of "Wilson's cow," may have referred to R. Wilson Morrison. Morrison's presence was clearly noted on the twelfth when, "the Indians stole Captain Morrison's mare." At The Dalles on the sixteenth, Parrish found "several emigrants, among them Col. Ford and Mr. Grish, [James Gerrish?]" awaiting the return of the boats. On Sunday the seventeenth, Rev. Waller preached first to those in Parrish's group and then in midafternoon to "Mr. Ford's company on the beach of the river."

Parrish spent Wednesday, November twentieth, his fifty-third birthday, waiting for a boat to transport his family on the first leg of the river route. He noted that "Captain Shaw's company came up today and camped on the branch above the Mission. I hope the emigrants will soon all be in."

On Friday evening, "the 'Lady of the Lake,' Captain Smith, commander" arrived. The next morning the Parrishes boarded, along with C. B. Hawley, Widow McDaniel, and others and "got off by seven p.m." The next day, Sunday, they landed at "the cascade Falls" at ten o'clock. Here they portaged to "another boat below," this effort taking all day Monday with the help of "the Indians we hired." On Tuesday, they boarded the second boat "and sailed off . . . for the lower country."

At sunrise on Friday, November twenty-ninth, the Parrishes arrived at Fort Vancouver where they "laid in provisions, flour, salmon, etc." and, after breakfast, started for Linnton. On board this boat were five families, those of "Col. Ford, C. B. Hawley, Mr. Embry, Mr. Packwood, and the Parrishes," along with "some passengers, Mr. Cox, Mr. Saston [Saxton?], etc."

That same day, the party became lost on the Columbia River when, in rowing in a slough around an island, they missed the route and "like the captain who marched his men up hill and back down and then told them 'as you were' " they camped one more night on the river bank when otherwise they would have been in Linnton. The next day they "made the landing [at Linnton] in [the] p.m. . . So now we are to have a little rest."

By the tenth they were at Oregon City where Parrish obtained a basement room also "occupied by Mr. Mudget [perhaps he of the northsider train] and two other young men." Parrish wrote his final entry of '44 on December eleventh. He gave no further information about any emigrants of '44 and their entrance into the Valley.

Minto returned to The Dalles in early December to help Mrs. Morrison and her children complete the journey. He found them instead at the Cascades rapids. Willard Rees was also there. Mr. Morrison was in the mountains trying to reassemble his herd of cattle which had scattered during a snow storm. The family was nearly destitute. The evening before Minto arrived, Mrs. Morrison had traded her last dress for a peck of potatoes, the only food now in their camp. All went back to The Dalles for several days and then, on December twenty-sixth, Minto, the Morrisons and several others boarded the boat for the trip down the Columbia and on into the Valley. Seventeen people were on the boat, along with the running gear of three wagons. They reached the mouth of the Willamette on December twenty-ninth and that night the emigrants were invited aboard the brig Chenamus by the second in command, a nephew of U.S. diplomat Caleb Cushing, who was eager for a detailed description of the overland trail. The next morning the travelers arrived at Linnton.

On December thirty-first, Minto was again in Linnton after returning the boat to Ft. Vancouver. He had already completed his work for M. M. McCarver and so he accompanied the Morrisons to the mouth of the Columbia as they looked for a place to settle.

In reconstructing the travel chronology of the narrators of '44, a few postscripts remain to be added for those who delayed their arrival in the Valley.

While the packers from the small group of families which included the Benjamin Nichols family were at the Whitman mission, Dr. Whitman asked if they knew of a mill-wright among those coming on the Trail. When Whitman learned that Nichols was of that occupation he sent a letter inviting him to the mission to build a saw mill. Nichols complied and his family remained at the Whitman mission for several weeks during which time his son B. F. Nichols "was enabled to attend the school for about sixty days, which constituted the larger portion of my school education." Young Nichols was forever thankful to the Whitmans for convincing his father to allow him to go to school rather than work at building the saw mill. Young Nichols' three sisters, Martha, Elizabeth and Jane, also attended the school.

Unlike others who hurried to the Valley, the Nichols and another nine families, remained at the mission until February 18, 1845, according to B. F. Nichols, at which time they returned to the Umatilla River and proceeded to The Dalles where "we found some of the emigrants with whom we had traveled across the plains the year before and they were also making preparations to go below." The Nichols family stayed here two weeks.

At the Cascades, the big canoe in which the Nichols family rode was "let down over the falls by aid of a rope." From here they were transported in the canoe to "Washbuckle" but waited there while young B. F. Nichols and "Uncle Joe Caples" (a familiar title, not indicating a relative) "went back with the canoe for the remainder of the plunder." That errand took another twenty days. When the two returned, the family "boarded the Callapoola, a small schooner owned and operated by Captain Cook, a jolly old tar. . . We sailed on this vessel for Oregon City where we landed about the first of June 1845." What occupied all the time otherwise not accounted for, Nichols did not say.

Company captain William Shaw reviewed for H. H. Bancroft the last days of his journey when he went to "where Whitman lived at the Walla Walla." He explained that, "We did not take all the emigrants there, but I went there myself to lay in provisions. . . I took the Sager children to Whitman's. . . I left the trail and went on with those children. Dr. Whitman took them . . ." Later, "At the Dalles, my oldest son and another son were sick. And I stayed there

from November until March. I stayed there at the Mission at
Mr. Waller's, the missionary's. . . There were one or two
farmers among us who got out of flour and I came here to
Oregon City and what money I had I spent there for flour and
coffee and one thing and another; and I went back to the
Hudson Bay Company and bought 1,000 pounds of flour
from Douglas [James Douglas, assistant to John McLoughlin].
I was to pay him for it after I came into the Valley. He trusted
me for it although he had never seen me before. I took it up
to the Dalles and distributed it among them. [Later] I stopped
about seventeen miles above the Hudson Bay company's
station at Vancouver on the Columbia River and worked
that summer of 1845 making shingles. I did this to live on
and clothe myself and my family and pay them [Douglas, et.
al.] what I owed them. In September, I left there and moved
up here about eight miles below this town [Oregon City]."

Alanson Hinman, another who remained for awhile at
the Whitman mission, remembered that "Both [McLoughlin
and the Whitmans] suffered from the ingratitude of some of
the immigrants, for many of the promises to pay for the
supplies were never redeemed, and in many cases even the
feeling of gratitude was lacking."
Hinman had a unique vantage for such an observation, for
he stayed at the Whitman mission during the winter of
1844-45 to serve as school teacher at the mission school and
as "commissary" handing out provisions for emigrants' diminished larders. Later he worked as "secular agent" at The
Dalles mission when the Whitmans were killed in late fall,
1847. Hinman was remembered by B. F. Nichols (though as
"Alonzo" Hinman) as the teacher of the mission school.

Yet another routing variation is contained in a letter
written in 1916, wherein a brief account unfolds of a small

group of emigrants who traveled perhaps the most round-about approach of all in '44. This was a detour to the Spalding mission at Lapwai on a branch of the Clearwater River (in present Idaho) many miles north of the customary route which crossed the Snake near Ft. Boise and headed northwest toward the Columbia. The letter, dated November 18, 1916, written by William D. Stillwell and addressed to Oregon historian George H. Hines tells of a few who "left our wagons at the upper crossing of Snake River . . . at Three islands" and then crossed "a beautiful level country" north of Boise River on their way to the Spalding mission. This group included "as far as I remember . . . John Perkins and family . . . and two teamsters, Poe Williams and John Gilmore; Jerry Rowland and family, Ben Nichols and family, Peter Smith and family, James Mulky and family, Thomas Stillwell and family, Glysby and Morgan." (The mention of "Ben Nichols" is noteworthy. For as seen above, that family wintered at the Whitman mission and not at the Spalding mission.)

Along the way, Stillwell wrote, this group built rafts of "drift logs tied together with rope" to cross the streams along the way. Stillwell stopped for two weeks at a "Nespercia" [Nez Perce] village at "the south end of Camus Prairie" to plow five acres of land for Richard Ellis, an Indian "educated in St. Louis" who was also their guide.

Stillwell and the others wintered at the Lapwai mission established by Henry Harmon Spalding and Eliza Spalding in 1836 where the Lapwai Creek empties into the Clearwater River, eleven miles above Lewiston, Idaho. Stillwell and the others left the mission in February, he wrote, to travel "down the Clear Watter to where Lewisten now stands. There we crossed Snake River following the trail to Whitman Station where Walla Walla now is—We followed the foot hills to

near Weston, then crossed the ridge and wild horse creek
—going west to the Umatilla R. at this place, going down on
the west side to Butter Creek."

They were guided in this area by an Indian whom Whitman
sent along to pilot them "to Wells Springs, then to Willow
creek, where we again struck the Emegrant road—from
Willow creek to Rock Creek where we crossed the John Day
river—we followed the Emegrant road to the Dalls . . ."

Even west of The Dalles, the routing of this group continued to be different from that of the others. For difficult as it
was, they took the land route (they were on horseback)
along the Columbia and into the Valley.

"As soon as we crossed Mill Creek, 5 or 6 miles back from
the Columbia, we crossed the hills to Hood River. We
crossed Hood River at [the] mouth coming down the
Columbia, sometimes over high points. Five or six miles
above the Cascades we crossed over to the north side of the
Columbia. The Indians ferryed us over and we swam our
horses. We followed the Columbia 5 or 6 miles, crossed over
Mt. Cape Horn, [and] came down to Washougal. We again
crossed the Columbia below the mouth of the Sandy, followed
an Indian trail, forded the Clackamas near the mouth, [and]
from there [traveled] to Oreg. City." To this Stillwell added,
"I know nothing of the trail north[sic] of Mt. Hood."

One of the last arrivals in the Valley by emigrants of '44
was that of a small party that included J. S. Smith who
started in the Ford train "on the 22nd day of . . . May" but
who joined the company of the Gilliam train that included
W. H. Rees somewhere on the North Platte River. Smith,
who wrote a letter to the Oregonian newspaper in about 1884
to correct the statements of others in previous articles, "left
the emigrants at Ft. Bridger on the first day of September and
spent the fall at Fort Winter [of their own construction?] and

in the neighboring mountains. Early in the winter, our party went into Brown's Hole and I remained there until the 5th day of February when in company with two companions I resumed my journey to Oregon." (John Minto recalled that on the day Henry Sager was buried, "The young man Smith, who had been with us but three days, left us here and went down the river to 'Brown's Hole' with the party who had come from Saint Louis with William[sic] Sublette.")

One of Smith's two companions, returning to Smith's account, was Franklin Sears and the other was named Payne. This little party reached Whitman's mission on March twenty-eighth and Smith remained for "about six weeks and then came down the Wallula [Walla Walla] in a Hudson Bay Company's bateau in company with the noted Father DeSmet . . . I reached Oregon City the 22nd day of May 1845, just a year to the day from the time I left Missouri."

And thus did the former Missourians, and those from points farther east, reach the Valley. At times portions of the two southsider trains had been close together—in the otherwise trackless wilderness of the Great Plains, in the barrenness of South Pass, and among the mountains west of the Rockies. In this way the predominantly individualistic task of emigrating had often been done in distinctly communal circumstances, giving these individualists a sense of belonging to a collective endeavor.

Chapter Nine

Common Experiences

The emigrants of '44 had many experiences in common in addition to the rainy conditions of the first several weeks of travel. A few were particularly memorable.

THE PRAIRIE

Woodland Midwesterners were awed by the first view of the prairie. After they left the wooded hills surrounding the Missouri River and moved into the region of deep-cut streams and long grass, they were struck by the scarcity of trees, as both a point of curiosity and as a concern for the lack of firewood. Several of the southside narrators wrote about evening camps on the final approach to the Platte being strangely and sparsely appointed affairs completely devoid of trees. It made them both marvel and feel uneasy.

John Minto, while "following up the Little Blue . . . [to] the Platte . . . [reached] about twelve miles east of where Fort Kearny was subsequently built," found "only a light fringe of timber on the largest creeks; outside of that all was an ocean of lush green grass, most of which was then in heavy seed stem. Walking in this luxuriance became as laborious as wading in water." On this "divide between that [the Little Blue] and the Platte. . . Not a tree or bush was in sight, but a boundless view of grass-covered country . . . [with] a considerable variety of wild flowers . . ."

A few miles before reaching "Burnets trace," Samuel B. Crockett wrote that "The country through which we are traveling is poor, not verry broken, and nearly destitute of timber." Near this point, before reaching the Vermillion, he and others saw the "blue mound" six miles southeast of Lawrence, Kansas, an oval summit visible for several miles.

Crockett "crossed rich prairies" and camped for the first time "in the open prairie without timber" on July second. Three days later it was "thought . . . expedient to lay in wood" when "leaving the creek which we have traveled up for several days" for the next camp was to be "in the open plane . . ."

The camp on the sixth was "on the brink of a marsh and not a tree in sight;" and the next was pitched "on the bank of the big platte" which he found to be "a broad shallow stream . . ." at which "we had to carry wood off an island." Just before fording the South Platte on the seventeenth, "we had no wood but made a substitute of bufalow dung." Upon reaching the "north fork," Crockett found it to be "quite as destitute of timber" as the south fork.

By June twenty-eighth, E. E. Parrish could report that "the road is now better, the land more roaling. The most of the way from the Big Blue river runs threw a beautiful level country rather flat . . . then it becomes more roaling . . ." Camp on the evening of July second was the "second time we have camped on an open prairie where there was no wood except what we had in the wagons." On the third they camped on "the divide between the Republican and the Platte." The camp on the fifth was "the third time in the open prairie without timber."

Clyman wrote of "uneven Prairie" on June twenty-eighth, the same day he commented on the "fine prairie soile" in the valley of the Blue River. The first day of July he noted "small groves of Timber seen either to the right or left" and was particularly glad to see that "some sand Shews itself in the trail," a pleasing observation since for miles previously their wagons had become stuck several times in the soft prairie soil. (When the Trail later led over deep sand, wagon travel was again difficult.)

"This greate wilderness of Prairie which streches in all most all directions beyond the field of vision" impressed Clyman on July third. Two days later he reported "large intervales as much as 3 miles wide [with] no timber except cottonwood and willows. On the eighth he found "nothing but willows for firewood." He was advised that "we need not expect any beter verry soon." After reaching the Platte on the tenth, Clyman traveled eighteen miles the next day along side the river "over a level Prarie, no timber except a few cotton wood Trees & them all confined to the Islands in the river which are numerous but generally small." He had to make do with "a few dry willows and Quite small" for firewood.

By the fifteenth, Clyman observed that on this "extensive level plain . . . timber [is] still more scarce and for miles nothing seen but now and then a Junt of shrubby Cotonwood or a dwarf willow." The view he gained from atop a bluff on the fifteenth was one of "an undiscribeable country of hills, Bluffs and deep cut ravines through a pale yellow clay soil some of which are 100 feet perpendicular."

Following along the north bank of the Platte, Jacob Hammer reported the view near the mouth of the Loup River. "The land is very rich and nearly all prairie but [with] little timber, which is along the water courses, and is low and scrubby . . . [and] is generally cotton wood." Jacob was favorably impressed by the "up land" along the "Loupfork" which "is rolling, dry, rich, and beautiful country indeed."

Coming to the Platte River "a few miles above Grand Island" on the twenty-first, the Hammers had traversed "very rich land for a few days." But, "this evening the sand is high, hilly, rough and poor." And at the Platte, they found "No timber except a few cottonwood trees . . . with the exception of a few trees in the hills." About forty miles west of the forks of the Platte, Jacob observed that "There is almost no timber in this region . . . for firewood . . . and we have to make our fire of dry buffalo dung or chips" which "is [a] good substitute."

Decades later this region would attract others seeking the hard-earned benefits the land would allow, just as those of '44 sought the distant Oregon valley. But for now these early travelers drew their westering dream closer so as not to have it escape them in this strange open country with few familiar boundaries.

THE PLATTE

Whether counting in miles or time, the emigrants, particularly the northsiders, spent more of both along the wide, shallow, ocher-tinted Platte River (and its north fork) than any other stream or river along the Trail. And the lasting impression from their many miles of walking along the Platte can be summed up by a commonly heard laconic observation such as Parrish's on July ninth that the river "is very wide for the quantity of water" it carried. B. F. Nichols described the Platte as in places being "a mile wide, including the islands which are very numerous, and exceedingly shallow, the water being scarcely two feet deep at any point." The water itself was described by Clyman on the day he reached the Platte (July tenth) as "the most mudy & in fact a grate deal more muddy than the Missourie itself the father of mud."

Southsiders came upon the Platte at Grand Island where they entered thankfully onto the Great Platte River Road. James Clyman made the point effectively: "It was good," he said, after struggling over many miles of flooded prairie, "to get upon more solid ground."

The sight of the Platte, and particularly the travel condi-

tions one could expect in the wide Platte valley, was enough
to bring a cheer from Parrish's group on July seventh. "We
were so glad when we saw the Platte valley and timber," he
wrote, "that some shouted aloud" as they approached a small
"grove of timber on an Island."

By coincidence it was the same day that train members saw
flatboatmen on the Platte who, in this season of abnormal
rain, had more of a flow on which to navigate than in some
years. E. E. Parrish remarked on July eighth, the day after he
saw the "3 flat boats loaded with skins & furs from the upper
country," that "the Platte is up, & has thrown the water
round the timber, between the timber and the camp . . . so
that to git wood we have to wade in water near wast deep, or
over . . ." Two years before, when Fremont returned on the
Platte to Bellevue, he complained of spending more time out
of the boat, pulling it over sand bars, than in it.

With the days behind them of slogging through the mud of
the southern routes, and, for the northsiders, the detours
along the Loup, the travelers were now in a world of rolling
sand hills surpassed only by the Idaho desert for aridness
(though this season the rain storms continued for awhile).
Even in normal seasons however, there were occasionally the
fearsome Platte Valley lightning storms. Most narratives
contained at least one reference to the electrifying assault
of the elements—the cannon bursts of thunder, the blind-
ing eerie blue flash of lightning, and dense oblique waves of
rain, all this combined in an onslaught of surprising force.
Not uncommonly did the storms include hailstones, thrown
like grape-shot against canvas, wood, animals, and anyone
caught outside what inadequate shelter was possible in a
wagon train.

The Parrishes "got a severe weting" when "a tremendous
thundergust came," on July eleventh, during which "from

the clouds torrents of rain poored upon us." Parrish was impressed. "It may have been this was the heaviest fall of rain I ever experienced, or ever will."

After crossing the South Platte, John Minto witnessed a hail storm which struck about noon on July twentieth. Minto professed no comparison in personal experience, labeling this storm "the heaviest . . . I ever saw or felt." Though some of the hailstones were "as large as pigeon eggs," the punishing "shower" lasted no more than five minutes and the cattle, which "could not be kept with their faces toward it," were turned and thus kept from stampeding. Crockett, in his succinct method, referred on the twentieth to "a hard storm of rain and hail."

Clyman wrote that "It thundered & Lightned all night & Several Showers of rain fell during the night" of July eighth, his second day along the river. Again during the night of the eighteenth, "it Thundered and Lightned in several Directions." And on the twenty-ninth, about half way between Chimney Rock and Scotts Bluff, he employed perhaps the most picturesque imagery of any of the narrators in describing a particularly grand storm which included "Keen claps of thunder with a profusion of Electrick fluid playin in all directions in a dry clear sky." This wondrous display of atmospheric might "set the dry grass on fire in several places in sight of our traveling caravan which was soon extinguished by the rain . . ."

The wide and shallow Platte (though "horseback deep" in spots), the cannonading of storms shot through with lightning—these too impressed the travelers with the wonder of it all.

THE BUFFALO

But what caused the most prolonged excitement along the Platte—what truly impressed the emigrants the most—was the sight of the buffalo herds. For a few days before the first buffalo was sighted, antelope were seen and several were shot. But the pronghorns' bounding gait was no match for the fascinating form, and spellbinding numbers, of the slower but much more imposing buffalo. The primitive wood-block engravings that illustrated the few published works on life on the Plains (or the "Great American Desert" of the times) had not adequately prepared the travelers for the sight.

Jacob Hammer, E. E. Parrish, and S. B. Crockett all reported the sight of buffalo bones before seeing any live specimens. Clyman first saw "recent Tracks of Buffaloe . . . in Quanties[sic]" the day before he set out on his own personal quest of them. The first buffalo Moses Schallenberger's group saw were "a few old bulls" which had been run out of the herd by younger ones. But "as they were the first that the boys had seen they must necessarily have a hunt." And so one "old patriarch" was brought to the ground "within fifty feet of the wagons, in the direction of which he had charged when first wounded." The "boys" shot younger buffalo before reaching Ft. Laramie. Like these of the Stephens-Murphy train, others soon saw buffalo in the vast numbers that amazed all who beheld them.

The very size of the buffalo herds darkening the plains for miles it was said was often thought to be a hazard to the travelers. B. F. Nichols remembered being both amazed and frightened at the sight of bison covering the ground "over an area extending four of five miles from the [Platte] river and up the river as far as we could see." When near such an overwhelming number of the "shaggy beasts . . . it was thought advisable and necessary to form a corral of the wagons for our protection." This was accomplished by "drawing one close against another with the tongue of one under the hind axle of the next and placing all in a circle and thus enclosing the camping ground of the families. All camped inside that night and an extra guard was placed to look after the horses and cattle as well as the camp generally in case of a stampede among the buffalo, something greatly dreaded by emigrants crossing . . ."

Sometimes, if the herd had come close enough and wind currents swept the scent of the train out of their reach, the animals would stand stupidly, even after a ragged broadside of gunfire had erupted, as the eager hunters walked toward them.

But more often, upon sighting the first buffalo herds, a light brigade of hunters rode forth, former hunters of rabbits and squirrels inexperienced in the pursuit of buffalo but now emboldened by the thought of downing one or more of the mighty animals, and seemingly unaware of the ever-present dangers associated with riding among the herds. There was also the danger of losing one's bearings after riding hard in pursuit, and suddenly reining up to find oneself lost, with no recognizable reference points for returning to camp.

Clyman wrote of four men who became lost and who did not return to camp for two days. (According to Clyman, Alanson Hinman became lost on July fourteenth while out hunting antelope, an occurrence Hinman did not include in his own brief recollections.)

Parrish described in detail how those around him went about hunting buffalo. "A horse of common speed will run upon [the buffalo] immediately. The hunter then dismounts and fires, then loads and mounts again, and soon comes within gunshot. This process is continued until he has taken in this way what he wants."

Another time, a few men stampeded buffalo "in the forks between the south and north branches" of the Platte which action "brought them over near where we were" where three or four were brought down. All this "was so interesting that some of our women actually joined in the chase."

For some, the shooting of buffalo retained its attraction for the duration of time spent in the buffalo range. But for others, after the initial excitement and challenge had sub-sided somewhat, they deferred to those hunters who had proven to be more skillfull as suppliers of meat. Five days beyond Independence Rock, Parrish referred on August twenty-first to a "hunting 'union' " which appeared to be breaking up because, it was supposed, they were then at the western edge of the buffalo range. "Heretofore," Parrish explained, "the meat killed was brought in and divided among the families . . . but after this the hunters kill for their own benefit."

James Clyman gave specific information as to the chang-ing range of the buffalo when on September fifth, at the "North Bend" of the Bear River, in "this vally" which had been an "early Rendevous of the mountain Trappers & hunters," he had learned from someone who apparently knew that "in the last 7 or 8 years the Buffaloe have entirely left this country & are now seldom seen west of Sweet water."

Clyman shot buffalo on this journey, but, it would appear, not often. It was an activity on which he could advise yet enjoy vicariously. As a man in his early fifties, he perhaps left to younger men the more vigorous and risky activity of dashing about on horseback over rough ground after the buffalo. It may also have been that he chose not to enter the fray in which amateurs handling firearms amidst the rush and tumble of a buffalo herd could be expected to wound more than the animals they pursued.

Perhaps then it was by design that on his sixth day along the Platte River on July sixteenth, he seemingly set a solo course "S. W. over the cut Bluffs" from about twelve miles east of the forks of the river, and finding buffalo "in great Quantities," he "Killed one very fine one, loaded my mule and started for camp." The urge to hunt in this instance had at least two motives, one implied the other stated: the memory from earlier days of campfire-simmered buffalo steaks; and the envious knowledge that "Throughout the night all the companis of Oregon Emigrants mountaineers & californians &c &c ahead of us had had buffaloe for several days . . ."

For the Gilliam train, the first sighting of buffalo brought about a mad dash by some, including the "General" himself who hurried off in pursuit, leaving the train, it was charged, to proceed on its own tack in his absence. The resulting indiscriminate fusillade brought down many buffalo, an over-kill which caused some 40,000 pounds of meat (by Parrish's reckoning, and called conservative by Minto) to go unused. While the event was pointed to as a deciding factor for eventually divesting Gilliam of his authority (a move no less warranted for his having anticipated it perhaps and consequently resigned) it serves as but one particularly obvious example of how the buffalo was to be brought nearly to extinction. No doubt the Indians of the region observed the slaughter of the animals upon which they depended for much of their sustenance. Such a sight must surely have made a lasting impression, a more than merely unsettling portent of what was to come.

Amidst the histrionics of the Gilliam train's first buffalo hunt, John Minto recorded a small scene which was probably repeated many times during the emigrations. It began in disappointment and ended in backslapping camaraderie. For when Gilliam, flush with "the ardor of the hunter," rode off after the first buffalo sighted, Minto was left behind, afoot and saddled with the responsibility of a plodding ox team. But soon Captain Morrison returned from riding the point and announced he had killed a buffalo and needed help in bringing in the meat. On the way there, a companion was pitched from his horse just as he made a killing shot at an antelope "fully one hundred yards" away. Reaching Morrison's buffalo, each member of the group guessed its weight, "two thousand pounds being the average estimate." In the butchering process, "We split the skin up and down the back, and taking out the hump, ribs and loin meat, had more than we could conveniently carry . . ." Though they got wet in a thunderstorm, "we made a jolly party going back." Joseph Watt, "walking beside his mule . . . started us singing, song about. We arrived at camp about 11 P.M., and had the first taste of buffalo meat . . ."

Jacob Hammer's first reference to buffalo was both retrospective and, in contrast to the other narrators, subdued. "Some buffalo occasionally brought in" is all he wrote on June twenty-seventh when the train was near the forks of the Platte. He seemingly did not engage in this hunt or subsequent ones. Thomas Vance died the following day after several days of illness and it appears that the Hammers had taken a special interest in him and his plight, hence, perhaps, the delayed mention of buffalo.

Buffalo continued to fascinate subsequent emigrations, and to be the focal point of complaint by the Indians who foresaw their own diminishment in the useless slaughter of the animals that ensued.

GEOLOGICAL WONDERS

In addition to the assaults on the emigrants' sense of proportion made by the first sight of the expansive and treeless plains, the aberations of the undisciplined Platte River, and the inestimable number of buffalo, they were also especially impressed by two of the many geological features, each greatly different from the other but each representing some special aspect of the journey.

The first of the two, Chimney Rock, was the first truly

"western" localized curiosity for both its unique appearance and for its mile-post function marking their progress. As if fulfilling a requirement of journal keeping as well as reminiscences, all narrators unfailingly referred to the Chimney on first seeing it though it may have been but a pencil-thin exclamation mark on the shimmering horizon and a day's travel away.

Parrish's first mention of "Chimney Mound" was on July twenty-sixth when he camped near the site. Early the next morning, Clyman "came in sight of the noted chimney rock" which, he supposed, was about thirty miles ahead. The former mountain man nearly outdid himself in describing the Rock: "it rises perpendicular and alone and looked like an old dry stub not larger . . . than your finger." A few miles farther on, after viewing Jail Rock and Courthouse Rock, Clyman described the Chimney from about ten miles away as "it changed its appearance & Shewed like a large conicle fort with a Tremendeous large & high flag staff & top taken off with out towers and various fixtures of defence." He "nooned" the next day at the Chimney, "Scotts Bluffs in full vieu ahead" on the "emmence level plains." To the east was "the river a mile wide meandring along . . ."

On July twenty-seventh, Samuel B. Crockett "passed the Great natural chimney today which is one of the greatest natural curiosities known . . . [rising] out of the centre of a cone which is 100 feet above the level of the plane . . . [with] the stem of the chimney 150 feet above the top of the cone."

The second physical feature about which the narrators expressed a special interest was South Pass astride the first mountain segment of the Trail and more a curiosity to those of '44 than the threat it had long been assumed to be. Most of the narrators wrote that traversing the Pass was remarkably

TRAIL RUTS IN SOFT SANDSTONE NEAR GUERNSEY, WYOMING
Author's photo

unlike mountain travel. For although they were at this point living Fremont's vision of settlers breeching the Rockies, they had absorbed enough of the former propaganda about western mountains being impossible to cross with wagons that they all expressed thankful surprise at the ease with which they found themselves crossing the Continental Divide. Of course if they had insurmountable doubts they would not have set out in the first place. And those of '44 may have read articles such as that in the *Niles Register* (October 28, 1843) which sought to correct the misapprehension that the Rockies were "a frozen horror, defying the efforts of man to overleap, and standing frowning at the onrushing tide of civilization [in 1843!] in the midst of a solitude too appalling to be sublime, and which was never broken." Instead, "All these foolish ideas . . . are dissipated" by "Fremont's . . . graphic description of South Pass . . . the bugbear is to disappear." (Fremont's famous simile compared the incline to South Pass to that leading to Capitol Hill in Washington, D. C.)

South Pass, such confident ones said, was desolate and immense, but manageable. B. F. Nichols pictured the view from some otherwise unidentified spot in the Pass: "Here the curtain was raised and one of nature's grand panoramic scenes burst upon the vision in all its sublime grandeur. Far to the north and south was a vast undulating plain, devoid of timber but covered with grass and [a] scattering of sage brush. To the northwest, like a dark cloud resting upon the earth, could be seen the Rocky Mountains extending far to the north. Rising at intervals, and projecting themselves up into the snow above the timber line, were a number of peaks, covered with a white mantle of perpetual snow."

Arrival at the Pass nevertheless was hard earned. Nichols clearly remembered the "stern realities" of "hills, sand, and

ONE OF THE MANY BENDS OF THE SWEETWATER RIVER
Author's Photo

dust, the latter almost unbearable" even "through the dim vistas of so many years . . . like the gosimer outlines of an interminable dream." Sixty years later he yet could call up the discomfort caused by the dust, "diffused through the air . . . entering the eyes, ears, nose and mouth of the one driving the team, covering his garments with a coat . . . and filling every rent (of which there were many) and seam to repletion. . . Often the cloud of dust was so thick and dense that the oxen in front could not be seen by the teamster who was walking by the side of the wheel ox of the team to which they were all attached."

At South Pass, all the narrators also noted the place from which water began flowing west when they reached Pacific Springs in a large marsh 300 feet beyond and below the highest level of the Pass. This was hailed as the first recognizable sign of the Oregon Country. Jacob Hammer "took dinner" where he saw "the first water of the west . . ." on August eighth. Parrish announced on August twenty-fourth that "I am writing in Oregon this morning." The day before, he had "passed the highest ground on the route, summit of the rocky Mountains . . ." On that day also, after Clyman and the three others buried Barnette, they "soon rose the deviding ridge Between the waters of the Atlantic & Pacific . . .," at the same time traversing "nothing more than a plasant assent for about 23 miles & decent of the same distance . . ." Thus were penned more South Pass soliloquies.

Though it was surprisingly easy going, South Pass nevertheless offered some introduction to mountain travel to come. Here was the absence of wood, and the chilly temperatures caused not only by the altitude but also from the season slipping imperceptibly into late fall. There was also an absence of water occasionally. All this allowed some anticipation for the travel conditions in the Blue Mountains. And it was in the Blue Mountains where those following last along the Trail would wade through knee-deep snow.

South Pass then was one of the most important segments of the Trail not only for ease of passage in making an Oregon-California Trail possible but for what its attainment meant to those of '44.

Chapter Ten

The Mobile Community

John Minto called the train with which he traveled "a fully equipped American community." The Trail narratives do indeed show small communities in transit — village-sized populations living not in cabins or clapboard houses but aboard covered wagons for the time being and all engaged in the occupation of inching slowly westward. Along the way, people laughed, loved, quarreled, worked together, suffered, and in general carried on their own private lives of courage and resourcefulness, tinged sometimes with disappointment and despair.

The communities on the move mirrored their stationary counterparts in many happy events. Parrish recorded "frolics" (his quaint way of noting childbirths) on May thirty-first to Mrs. Sager; on August third to Mrs. Gage; on August thirteenth to Mrs. Hoover; on September twenty-eighth to Mrs. Hawley; and while at the Whitman Mission, to Mrs. Cave on October twenty-fourth. According to Moses Schallenberger, little Ellen Independence Miller was born to the James and Mary Miller family at Independence Rock. There were, no doubt, other births, such as that to Calvin and Alcey Neal of the Gilliam train to whom a daughter was born at Grande Ronde.

In addition to the miracle of birth, all these were impressive events for the mother having come the respective number of miles at the time of delivery. One assumes hopefully, lacking evidence to the contrary, that all mothers and infants survived the experience.

Parrish mentioned three weddings in the Gilliam train. The first, occurring while the parties were yet in the Missouri River camp, was an unfortunate episode in which the young wife, Nellie Bunton, refused to follow her husband, Elisha McDaniel, on the journey and returned across the Missouri River. The second occurred on May twenty-first in which ceremony minister Parrish married Martin Gilliam and Elizabeth Asabill, both of whom he called "quite young to start out upon lifes Journey." Parrish wrote of a third wedding in which Reverend Cave married John Kindred to Mary King. But John Minto stated that the groom was "prevented from fulfilling his contract" by his father, David Kindred, who sat up all night with a brace of old cavalry pistols to thwart the consummation. Parrish may have supplied the reason why: Ms. King, he wrote, was said to be "a woman of ill fame."

At least two (but possibly three) ministers of the Gospel were among the Gilliam train. Edward Evans Parrish was a Methodist; James Cave was "of the E.M. church" (Evangelical Methodist?). And Henry Owen, of undesignated denomination, was remembered by B. F. Nichols for the rough-hewn homiletics which woke him one night east of the Blue River crossing when, startled from sleep, he recognized Owen ("of swamp land notoriety") who as camp guard that particular night "was rehearsing a Negro sermon which he had learned back in old Missouri" in full voice which "could have been heard a mile away."

Parrish noted only two "Divine services" while on the Trail—those on June second and sixteenth. He complained on the ninth that the work ordered by train leader Gilliam to be done in preparing pontoons to cross a stream could have been done as easily on Saturday, thereby giving time for a church service, but so "it must be." He deplored the fact that the life-style on the move inhibited observing the sabbath. "We have souls to save," he affirmed.

Thereafter, the wagons rolled out fairly early on subsequent Sundays as other days, and though they often stopped at mid afternoon for the day, no worship services were mentioned. By October twenty-seventh, the Parrishes were at the Whitman mission and enjoying the Sunday services there, including the singing of the Indians at their morning service. On Sunday, November seventeenth, missionary Waller at the Dalles mission preached to two services. Sunday, December first, Parrish and his family were engaged in unloading their "bit of goods yet remaining" from the boat at "Linton" and in pitching a tent "in a dense forest of large fir timbers." They had arrived in the Valley, and to membership of this or other stationary communities beginning to accommodate religious observances.

Jacob Hammer, one who made several references in his journal to adhering to a religious faith, did not refer to nor complain about the absense of organized worship services while on the Trail. The Hammers were members of the Society of Friends, many of whom conducted unprogrammed, non pastoral "meetings for worship" which could have been practiced by the Hammers as matter of course on "First Day" (Sunday) as a family unit. Jacob occasionally recorded his thoughts about how his religious views contrasted with the behavior of some around him. But most of his journal entries related to his observations of new and memorable conditions about which he wanted to tell those in Indiana, to whom he apparently felt the need to justify the trip they had tried to discourage him from taking.

Along with their carefully packed tangible heirlooms, the travelers also bore their social and political inheritances as well. Jacob Hammer's mention on May twenty-first of the disagreements prompted by the company's organization into a self governing entity was the first indication that that group was more than a coterie of families who happened to be driving their wagons near each other on an extended outing. With his mention of majority and minority factions, one begins to see politicking in this village on the move. There-after, Hammer included several references to the lack of solidarity among these whose ultimate goal was to reach the Oregon country, but for whom the accomplishment of that goal meant close, confining, sometimes grating group living.

Politicking was not confined to the immediate business at hand. James Clyman was kept aware of the upcoming presidential election when on June twenty-second he learned from the men who had just returned from hunting stolen cattle that "it appears there has been a great Troubling & Striving of the eliments, the mountain having at last brot forth J. K. Polk, Capt Tyler & the invincible Henry clay as candidates for the Presidency. go it Clay [Presidential Candidate in '44]. Just whigs enough in camp to take the curse off."

Two events in particular offer contrasting views of how individual trains reacted to disputes which at home would have been handled by a criminal court.

When A. C. R. Shaw took offense at something William Prather said on May nineteenth and threatened "to draw his pistol," Jacob Hammer and William Clemmens were called upon to help the potential combatants talk the matter out. And again when on the evening of the twenty-eighth Shaw fired a gun in camp, reloaded, and threatened the life of Elisha Stephens, Hammer did not indicate that a court-like tribunal for dealing with such a potentially explosive affair was convened, even though the "Organization Agreement 1844" which Shaw himself may have helped draft called for the "President [of the Linn Association] to call a court of inquiry at any time that complaint is made to him of any misdemeanour subject to the order of the majority of the association."(See American Trails Series volume XVI for text of the "Agreement.")

Instead, in the case of Shaw's threat on Stephens' life, rather than a court of inquiry, "a new election was held."

A similar embroglio in the Gilliam train however was handled much differently. In that train (when Gilliam was yet the official leader) a court was convened on the evening of June fourth, wherein the defendant, young Clark Eades, was accused of shooting at another man. Eades was "bound over," and though his father Moses Eades paid his bail, the convicted was "tied and staked out in the hot sun from 11 O'clock a.m. until the going down thereoff," according to Willard Rees who had been ordered to arrest Eades and bring him "forthwith to head quarters . . . for violation of a general order."

It was B. F. Nichols' recollection however that rather than being baked by a hot sun, Eades' ire was dampened by "rain [which] came down in torrents." Minto commented on this event also, saying that Eades had but threatened the other man. Minto had been handed the job of guarding the culprit whom he characterized as a particularly unrepentent and otherwise recalcitrant type (one lacks the viewpoint of the accused, of course).

Communal living also involved group security and Minto had more to say about that aspect, perhaps because as a young man otherwise unattached to family responsibilities (except for his day work for the Morrisons) he was selected for regular guard duty and even to supervise that of others. The duty, as pieced together from references by Minto, Clyman and others, appears to have consisted of walking rounds to check on the cattle and to see that the security of the train was not breached or otherwise threatened.

Minto referred to the difficulty in getting many of those given the duty to take it seriously. There appears to have been a general lack of concern for security except for a few times of alarm (always proven false) when the emigrants were probably in more danger from their own excitement and the brandishing of firearms than from the Indians whom they suspected of trying to get into camp by stealth and under cover of darkness.

There was one particular aspect of the Trail experience that seems harsh, even heartless when contrasted with reactions thought normal in a stationary community. When one reads of a seemingly unwarranted social vicissitude such as the refusal by all but one person to dig a grave for a young woman whose deathbed scene should have melted the hardest heart, it may seem that the social tapestry of the mobile community had been rent asunder by abject selfishness and mean-mindedness.

To explain but not to excuse, readers can only attempt to place themselves in the circumstances of the emigrants, in which there occurred a willful but nonetheless complete severing of connections with former homes, and onto which temporary circumstances was added the all-consuming urgency for daily progress westward (especially later in the journey) and that done by an extremely laborious method of traveling. Thus can one recognize how a dominant condition— the essential but exhausting pull across an often inhospitable land—affected this mobile society in ways that seem at first regressive, even repulsive.

Specifically, after walking twenty miles in the oppressive heat and punishing footing of what was then called "The Great American Desert," one is certainly likely to have a different reaction to a death in the group than when all the conveniences of home (even in 1844) could be employed to empathize with the bereaved.

In this environment also, and under these conditions, it may be that the occurrence of death reminded the living of responsibilities to their own family members and of the depressing potential for similar perils to befall them. Movement forward, then, may have satisfied some urge to run from unnerving reflections of their own demise. Meanwhile, however, there were many on the Trail whose last view of the grave of a loved one was seen through the back of a swaying covered wagon.

It should be noted that the most compassionate reactions to deaths reported in the narratives were gender-specific: it was the women who after long hard days themselves implored John Minto to dig the grave of young Elizabeth Nichols, and who, after a day's travel and all the work of preparing the evening meal, sought to ease the passing of Barnette at South Pass. Furthermore, it may have been Hannah Hammer who wrapped young Thomas Vance's fever tortured body in a quilt after his passing. And it was her sister emigrants in the Gilliam train who came to Mrs. Sager's wagon for several evenings to wash the day's travel dust from her face and to care for her children, and, when her passing left seven bewildered and shocked orphans, sewed her in a sheet for her interment.

There were other less dark and gloomy incidents reported in the Trail narratives. Nestled among the more straightforward and less emotional passages are heart-warming tableaux: Views of girls gathering wild flowers; camp sites where weary travelers stretched aching limbs at the close of a long day; conversations around cook fires; Jacob Hammer's efforts at compiling a few amateurish classifications of flora and fauna.

John Minto particularly recorded several personal episodes: singing melancholy songs of Old England upon leaving the Missouri River; viewing flocks of passenger pigeons
that filled the sky; being introduced to the "sensitive plant"
(Mimosa pudica) which wilts when touched, a natural enough
reaction but which was said by Mrs. Morrison to have shown
his lack of honorable character (she then explained the joke
she had played on him); his show-off behavior with the ox
whip; and of listening to a fiddle's high timbre as the glow of
campsite cookfire played among the faces of those who at the
stopover at Ft. Laramie "danced well into the night."

There are views also of mountain man Clyman gathering
strawberries, and of his listening to Moses Harris recite
eyewitness anecdotes, the stuff of which folklore is composed, lost to history on the chilly draughts blowing at South
Pass. Finally, there were the instances of Clyman, Minto
and others standing upon some prominence, or flat on the
level earth, and scanning vistas which they strained to etch
on their memory.

It was a time for absorbing the way it all looked and felt,
but only during some brief respite in the plain hard work of
slowly moving west. Though the majority of the emigrants of
'44, upon their arrival in the Valley, lived for several years on
isolated claims miles from their nearest neighbors, one can
be assured that the memory of living half a year in a wagon
train community remained with them.

Chapter Eleven

Emigrants and Indians

As the emigrants of '44 passed through Indian territories, the very land on which they journeyed with wonder and some trepidation symbolized a telling contrast between them and the native populations residing there. To wit: the Indians assumed the land had some significance in the religious scheme of things, while the whites longed to own the land and made occasional claim to Divine Will as both incentive and proof to that end.

Many of the travelers that year were familiar with the often forceful "removals" of Indian populations from the woodland Midwest and from the Southern states, part of the context in which would be coined in 1845 the term "manifest destiny," a conspicuous, self-accusatory banner flown unabashedly in the crusade for land possession as a base for economic progress. And Oregon was a prominent prize to be won among locales near and far being considered at the time.

Another term had gained a place already in the glossary of these matters. "Savagism," as defined in Noah Webster's *An American Dictionary* (1828) was "the state of rude uncivilized men; the state of men in their native wildness and rudeness."

It would appear that the emigrants of '44 had little difficulty envisioning just such a "state" for the native Americans they met on their westward trek. John Minto recalled that when Wilson Morrison was asked, "Why are you going?" he replied that the United States had the "best right" to the region, and that "there are a great many Indians there that will have to be civilized." Morrison, though said to be "slow of speech," tersely summed up the attitude of those who by their efforts to emigrate were determining the destiny which the promoters said was "manifest."

The statements of the emigrants of '44 about the Indians they met are much like those of others who, historically, have viewed native populations unfamiliar to them: the viewpoint was that of a tourist, mixed with anxiety over personal safety. Hence the attempt to offset these fears by weight of firearms, lead, powder, and serious knives— wagon trains were typically overstocked with weaponry. John Minto, a fairly good-natured young man who had his life, but little else, to defend started the journey with "a nice new rifle . . . a fine double-barreled fowling piece, five pounds of powder, twenty-five pounds of lead, one dozen boxes of percussion caps, five pounds of shot . . . two pocket knives, two sheath knives, a hatchet to answer for a tomahawk, and an axe."

Several emigrant-authors of 1841 identified George Shotwell who died at or near Ash Hollow as one of the first (of numerous) emigrants killed accidentally by gunshot. The aleatoric combination of Shotwell's name along with his manner of demise has often been referred to in comments on Trail literature.

There was also much distrust and anger over attempted and actual thefts by Indians (though many of the "actual" were likely circumstantial in a court of law). In fact, the majority of journal entries in '44 regarding Indians were of this nature.

Of the trail narratives published before the 1844 emigration, Joseph Williams' fear of the Indians when he started out in 1841 was largely not born out. He reported one robbery by the Sioux of a lone hunter from the small Bidwell-Bartleson company of twenty wagons with which he traveled, but pilot "Broken hand" Thomas Fitzpatrick arranged the return of the stolen gear. There were "Indian alarms" in the camp, for though Indians often traveled with this small train, the news came that Sioux had killed a hunter (not of the emigrant party) and his companions. In Oregon, Williams wrote that except for the missionaries, all the white men had Indian wives. Samuel Parker, who made the trip in 1835 with the exuberant Whitman, noted little of which to fear, and had less respect for some of the white men he met than the Indians.

P. L. Edwards, who reportedly gave talks in the vicinity of St. Joseph and elsewhere about Oregon based on his trip there in 1834, largely dismissed Indians met along the way and those residing in the Willamette Valley when writing in his brief *Sketch of the Oregon Territory, or, Emigrants' Guide* published in Liberty, Missouri, 1842.

It is not the intent here to study prejudice against Indians expressed or implied in the narratives of '44. Nor can one believably pretend to know the very thoughts of the emigrants from as personal, yet as staged, a record as the narratives. But a few observations based on statements in the narratives about the numerous times emigrants met Indians on the Trails can be assumed as dependable indications of period attitudes regarding native Americans.

In regard to Indians, one can appreciate again the fortunate selection of narratives for the '44 season. Jacob Hammer, avowed Abolitionist, was somewhat put off by what he saw as the unChristian behavior of the Indians he observed at Bellevue. James Clyman, with many years of experience traveling among Indians, was not dissuaded of the notion that there was an underlying savagery just below the surface of any Indian's often stoic countenance. Not unexpectedly then, the word "savage" occurs several times in Clyman's journal as a trait, taken for granted it seems, of the occupants of a vast portion of the American outback. Edward Evans

Parrish too used the word, even in recopying a version of his journal in 1867. He, in fact, included more hints of anxiety about Indians than did the others. John Minto, on the other hand, took his experiences with Indians in the free and easy stride of a young English bachelor who, until a few days before the Cornelius Gilliam wagon train left the St. Joseph vicinity, hadn't planned to go to Oregon at all. Minto's attitude about Indians is seen to develop as the journey progresses, an engaging process even though the narrative was compiled years later.

Each train encountered Indians early in the journey. Jacob Hammer wrote that "the chiefs and great men of several tribes, the Sac, Foxes, Otoes and . . . Pawnees" were gathered at Bellevue. He may have met Indians before in Indiana, perhaps Potawatomi, and undoubtedly was aware of the militia-conducted removal of most members of that tribe from his former home state of Indiana in the mid and late 1830's. The Society of Friends (Quakers) there occasionally raised money in the mid 1840's to aid the few Indians still living in the central part of the state.

Passages of some length in the Hammer journal relating to Indians are those in which Jacob described the ceremonial dancers at Bellevue, the abandoned Pawnee lodge on the Loup, and the Sioux at Ft. Laramie. All these entries appear to have been composed with a genuine, objective curiosity. Particularly when the Potawatomi chief Pa-reesh aided the Hammers and others in crossing the Missouri river, Jacob's attitude was respectful and thankful.

Jacob's entry in his journal on June seventh unfortunately is obscured in which he reported meeting Pawnees near the mouth of the "Loupfork." It is reasonably plain, however, that these Pawnee requested written passes "so that they might travel amongst the whites." Actually, instances of

Pawnees requiring emigrants to acquire passage permits in this region was more often the pattern. Whatever the order of things, the Pawnee "were very friendly to us" and "wished us all the good wishes that any one could wish." Farther along on the Loup, Jacob witnessed the result of fighting among the Indians themselves as he learned of the Sioux attacks on the Pawnee.

Later in the journey Hammer was more apt to show the prevailing reaction to thefts of personal property by the Indians. He even succumbed twice to the often heard generalization that the Indians thereabouts "will steal everything they can lay their hands on . . . ."

From many statements in the narratives it would appear that the emigrants believed that some quirk of the Indian psyche would at some point trigger an attack in force. Parrish left little doubt that he was aware of being in "the Indian territory" (as indeed it was called at the time) when his family crossed the Missouri and camped for a few days before going to the rendezvous site. The families should stay together, he advised, so they could "go strong and . . . leave no straglers for the Savages to plunder & murder."

James Clyman assumed that many in the train upon setting out fully expected to encounter "the war whoop and the scalping knife." According to B. F. Nichols, writing many years later, the women of the wagon trains were anxious from the start about Indians laying waste their families. And when writing about the fear of what many assumed was imminent attack during the first several weeks of the journey, he even surmised that 4 o'clock in the morning was "an hour best suited to the Indian for an attack upon a wagon train."

Later, deadly encounters did take place, but only after it had been driven home indisputably to the Indians that the emigrations were harming their traditional way of life, as for example the destruction of wild game on which they depended. Later also, when emigrants took an almost sporting attitude about the use of violence, often unprovoked, as a matter of course, did the Indians resort to the kind of tactics the graphic depictions of which gave bad dreams to many who ventured forth in the wild domain.

Yet for all the apprehension found in these Trail narratives about Indians, and the presence of an overabundance of firearms, the wagon trains of '44 were not particularly well secured. As Minto observed, the guards ordered to watch over that train often did not take the job seriously. Others stated that guarding the trains in organized fashion was discontinued once the wagons left Sioux country.

Catherine Sager Pringle recalled that "Each company was organized into a military body, and guards set, and every precaution taken to guard against attack by the Indians. For a few weeks the company drilled of an evening after camping, and at sundown, the drum was beaten to call out the guards, but as the novelty wore away, and we advanced beyond the country of the Sioux and Pawnees, the custom was entirely dropped."

Parrish illustrated the point by reporting on August twenty-fourth, on the way down from South Pass to Ft. Bridger, that "captain Walker says there is no danger of Indians, so we need no guards."

In spite of the common occurrence of theft, the trains often now divided into small groups traveling independently, perhaps in view of others, perhaps not. Just two days beyond Fort Bridger, Clyman reported that "all Subordination and controle haveing been broken up for several days thinking ourselves out of danger at least danger of life" from Indians. After reaching Salmon Falls on the Snake, Clyman and Minto both reported overtaking small groups of wagons on the Trail nearly all the way to Grande Ronde. And this pattern of travel was common also from there to The Dalles.

When the trains reached the environs of Ft. Bridger, and for the duration of the journey thereafter, attention was placed on keeping curious, and the occasional larcenous, Indians from taking anything that interested them and on keeping emigrant cattle from being led off in the night or even during the day. But this too was apparently something each family did for themselves, or as small groups, rather than delegating the job to a few appointed to provide security.

Members of the "General" Gilliam train had a confrontation with Indians early in their journey. E. E. Parrish, Samuel Black Crockett, Willard Rees, and John Minto all told of members of their train who by vigilante action settled in their own fashion the matter of alleged theft while near the "Iowa" agency in present eastern Kansas.

According to Rees, on the night of May eighteenth (Crockett entered the event in his journal on May twenty-first) emigrant cattle stampeded and after train members had gathered the cattle together they found tracks indicating some cattle had been driven away from the herd. "After a gallop of eight or ten miles they overtook the Indians who were engaged in butchering the cattle" but the Indians fled when they saw the riders approaching. The emigrants returned to camp, Rees was ordered to gather forty armed men, and this larger group rode to the Indian agency headquarters. There Gilliam demanded that cattle from the Indians' allotment be given up to replace those killed. Furthermore, he demanded that the individuals responsible for stampeding the cattle and stealing some should be handed over to train members as hostages until all the other cattle were returned. To this the Indian agent actually agreed.

Gilliam and his "troopers" then rode to the Indian village to take the hostages, whereupon the chief, who had already located those he said had been involved in the theft, turned thirteen persons over to the emigrants. Gilliam and the others, with the hostages in tow and the chief following, returned to camp and awaited the return of the missing livestock. The Great Nemaha Sub-agent William P. Richardson, came also to help assure the safekeeping of the hostages. During the night, in a heavy rainstorm, the Indians were allowed to leave.

Parrish wrote on May twenty-first that Indians had been accused of driving off some cattle, and that the next day "mounted soldiers" had gone after the cattle. This service performed by the soldiers from Ft. Leavenworth was probably as much to facilitate a quick passage through the region by the emigrants, thereby shortening the time in which more trouble might occur, as it was to punish Indians who had taken a special liking to emigrant cattle.

James Clyman's first reference to Indians met on the trek west was a few days into the journey when on May twenty-third he reported passing through land belonging to the Shawnee, most of whom "have Quit hunting and gone into a half civilized manner of living" on small truck patches "Productive in both grains and stock." Three days later the mood had changed; he reported the placing of "a night and day guard" since they were but two days from the Kaw Indian villages.

A few days later, on June second, he and another man with the aid of two "friendly" Kaws went in pursuit of Clyman's horse and the other man's mule both of which had been stolen. Searching again on the seventh in one of the drenching downpours common during the early weeks of the journey, they came to an Indian village and, with a pounding hail storm outside, and a fight brewing among Indians gathered inside, boldly entered a lodge where "about 20" Indians were gathered. But when knives were brandished (one was "Flurrished over my head") and as some wallowed in the nearly knee-deep water on the dirt (now mud) floor, Clyman felt lucky to leave unhurt, though apparently without regaining his horse or the mule. His horse was returned to him on the twenty-first by messmates "Robinson, Mr. Morin & Mr. Alderman" who returned to camp that day after searching again for these and other stolen animals.

Unlike novices like Parrish and Minto, and others such as Hammer, Clyman had firsthand knowledge about Plains Indians. As a mountain man, he no doubt had formed the attitude peculiar to men of that persuasion in which he accepted Indian foes and friends as part of the lifestyle. Since Clyman did not weaken his credibility in his narrative by self glorification, one tends to believe him when he assumed he was in danger. He explained on June twenty-sixth that one of the reasons for organizing the wagon train into companies and messes had been for security when they were soon to enter the region of "the wild roveing tribes," the first of whom were the "Kaws" or Kansas Indians.

While passing through the Indian agency, Clyman indicated his displeasure at seeing little evidence so far of the presence of the regional Indian agent who, he hoped, would convince the Kaws that the emigrant trains should be allowed to pass unmolested. Clyman himself on June tenth inveighed the threat of military retaliation in an attempt to convince the Kaws to restrain themselves from continued thievery, telling them that "we had sent to Fort Levenworth for an escort of dragoons."

Five days later on the fifteenth, at "Knife River" (present

Cross Creek, Shawnee County, Kansas) at "10 oclk Maijor Richard Cummings arived on the oposite side of the creek on his way home from running some lines between The Kaws & Pawnees. The maijor is governments agent for the Kaw & Several other tribes of Neighbouring Indians & we ware well pleased to see him so near us."

Unlike Clyman's experienced view of Indians, young John Minto's narrative shows his unfolding enlightenment on the subject.

Minto admitted that his expectations regarding Indians had been based initially on the Leatherstocking tales by James Fenimore Cooper. He began the journey, then, expecting to find the "noble savage." But he was summarily dissuaded from this view when in nearly slapstick fashion he was kissed indelicately by an aged beggarly "chief" at Weston, Missouri, "in requital for a dime." Though perhaps in the telling of it Minto employed hyperbole, the encounter nevertheless dispelled any romantic notion he had retained of the "ideal Indian . . . imbibed" from Cooper's romantic novels.

Minto, as seen earlier, had heard the conversations of the stay-at-homes who came to bid the Morrison family farewell as they spoke, not from experience, of the dangers of traveling in Indian country. Perhaps these conversations came to mind at certain places along the Trail. Back in Missouri, Minto had objected as much, he said, to the tone and the insinuations of the conversations as to the substance. And though his narrative was composed fifty-plus years after the fact, he maintained the most even-tempered and otherwise objective attitude of all the narrators of '44 regarding the Indians he encountered on the overland journey.

For though he characterized some Indians he met as inveterate thieves, he recognized traits, and acts, of nobility in others. He therefore appeared to discern characteristics of individuals and not to blame an entire group for the actions of a few, important insight to have if one is to overcome large scale and all-encompassing prejudice.

It should be noted however that Minto was among those who willingly answered the call to punish the Cayuse for the murders of the Whitmans and others at the mission in late 1847.

The emigrants did not see any Indians on one long stretch of the Trail: from the point at which the trains reached the Platte at Grand Island to the vicinity of Ft. Laramie, in a largely pass-through region for the Indians where various tribes could be found but temporarily. Here the farthest reaches of several Indian groups overlapped. (Clyman did report when a few miles east of Ft. Laramie that "We have been following A recent lodge Trail of moveing Indians for some days But have not been able to overtake them.")

But though Indians were not seen, the possibility of their presence played on the nerves of these strangers in a strange land. There was a "false Indian alarm" in Minto's camp on June thirtieth, about a week after crossing the Big Blue. Parrish wrote of an "Indian alarm" on July twentieth when nearly to the North Platte River. There had been several such scares, he reported, "but no Indians seen."

This cautionary trait wanting of factual reason was evident also in the burials of those who died on the Trail this season. Jacob Hammer reported that Thomas Vance's grave site was purposefully obscured "so that it might not be noticed by the savages, though," he added perhaps self-consciously, "no danger of being robbed that we know of by them." Another grave site was similarly hidden so "that the grave might not be violated," Minto said of young Miss Nichols final resting place, not referring to Indians specifically. Catherine Sager however accused Indians of having "disinterred" her father's grave on the bank of the Green River (about which she heard from emigrants of 1845). Sager also remembered a "head board" being placed on her mother's grave, and editor Charles Camp credited James Clyman with carving a grave marker for the man Barnette who was buried at South Pass.

As a few bold children may have hoped, the emigrants came face to face with the Sioux at Ft. Laramie. The brief stay there meant a day or so for rest, repair and provisioning, and a chance for a close-up view of one of the most impressive Indian assemblages to be imagined. By all accounts, the Sioux arrayed in finery and cutting the classic figure of inveterate machismo, so unlike the image of the Kaws in the narratives, made a lasting impression on the emigrants.

Northsider William Case was alone in stating that there were no Sioux in the immediate vicinity of Ft. Platte. Case's odd statement was included in a Trail narrative pieced together from interviews with him many years later and published in the first volume of the *Oregon Historical Society Quarterly*. In that version, Case reportedly stated that some hint of trouble had been noted by a young Frenchman, "Joe Batonne," who preceded the wagon train to the fort and with a fortuitous understanding of the Sioux language overheard a warrior threaten the approaching emigrants. When told of the threat, "commandant Bisnette" (Joseph Bissonette?) of the fort fabricated a story designed to alarm the Sioux into leaving the scene. He told the chiefs that a death from the pox had occurred in the approaching train. The Indians left forthwith, according to William Case.

All the other narrators, however, reported many Sioux families present at Laramie. Jacob Hammer traded with Sioux on July tenth and on each of the next three days when his train was camped near Ft. Platte. Similarly, Minto, arriving at Fort Laramie on July thirtieth, and Parrish and Clyman, who both arrived there on August first, all traded with the Sioux. Young Minto, ever the affable Britisher, went to observe the Indian village first hand while the others implied that they remained in camp and the Indians approached them.

Crockett and Minto reported that leaders of their trains smoked a "peace" pipe with the Sioux at Ft. Laramie. Parrish described the scene at which presents were given to the Sioux, "then the men sit down & took a smoke all out of the same hatchet pipe, in true Indian stile . . ."

The emigrants had now seen the Sioux close up and had acquired the distinct memory of formidable, uncowering, potential adversaries. On this score, anxiety is apparent in the narratives. One day beyond the fort, Minto quoted Captain Shaw as saying that some of the men were "afeared" that Indians would follow and attack.

Sixteen days beyond the fort, James Clyman on August seventeenth noted "Some recent Signs of a war party of Indians ware discovred yestarddy which caused some uneasiness," though the discovery caused "but verry little more caution." How it was discerned that the Indians who had passed that way comprised a war party was not explained. At South Pass, Clyman again indicated uneasiness. There, while awaiting the doleful duty of burying Mr. Barnette, and listening as Black Harris told "escape" tales about himself and other "Mountaineers," he was uncomfortably aware that they sat "in one of the most prominent Indian passes of the country."

Beyond the Pass, at Ft. Bridger, the pilgrims saw Indians again. The post had been constructed for trade with the "Shoshonees and Eutaws" according to Clyman. Jacob Hammer saw members of the "U-taws, Pawnasc, and Snake tribes" at the fort on August sixteenth. Parrish arrived on August thirtieth in the company of guide Joseph Walker, who was returning there from Ft. Laramie, and Parrish noted that after Walker found the train "a good incampment," he "returned to his Wigwam, or as it is called here a lodge, and his many Indian women . . . of the Snake tribe . . ." The night before, Parrish and the others had camped near a group of Indians and "our stock run together." He was relieved to learn the next morning that there was no trouble brewing; "we had no cause of complaint."

West of Ft. Bridger, the emigrants had numerous meetings with Indians, actually many more than before. Three days beyond "Bridger's Trading House," Clyman saw a group of "Shoshones" riding past as he wrote in his journal. Minto told of being overtaken while afoot on the approach to Ft. Hall by "a single Indian, well mounted, with a loose horse following him." The Indian used sign language to offer the use of the "loose" horse, even taking his own saddle off to let Minto use it. That same day, a young Indian girl brought Minto "the new lid of a gallon tin pail heaped with luscius, ripe blackberries. It was a great treat to me."

Along the Snake River, emigrants often traded for salmon with Nez Perce and Bannocks. Native fishermen reaped an impressive harvest of fish at Salmon Falls, or "Fishing" Falls, where they had erected racks on which to dry the fish for trade and for their own use. Minto and his hungry companions were also given fish soup here during their long and hungry trek along the Snake River.

While the Indians often provided food along the Trail west of the Rockies, the reports of cattle thefts increased in number. Parrish referred to a mare stolen by Indians, then recovered, and the purchase by one in Parrish's party of a horse from an Indian, apparently sight unseen, to whom the horse was never delivered. In early September, Jacob Hammer's group of northsiders hired an Indian to locate stolen horses and bring them back, which, Jacob wrote, was the whole purpose of the theft. Jacob also recovered a stolen ax in the same manner. But his "best cow" was stolen and not returned.

Some narrators referred to the indigence of the Indians farther along the Snake, and particularly those huddled at Ft. Boise near where the Boise River joined the Snake. These Indians were said to live in a feast and famine existence dependent on the seasonal abundance of fish.

Parrish reached "Ft. Boisey" on October third after traveling about four days along the banks of the river of the same name. The day before, he too had acquired fish from the Indians, paying "a load of ammunition for a fish." The family "laid in a supply of fish" as did the others with whom the Parrishes traveled at this point. James Clyman arrived at Ft. Boise on Sunday, September twenty-second, and found that the "Christian Indians" present were unwilling to trade on the sabbath.

There were no outright attacks by Indians on the travelers in '44. But Jacob Hammer, while near Ft. Boise on September twenty-fourth, reported the nearest thing to an armed face-off which happened "a few nights since."

In this episode, John Thorp, train captain of this faction of the northsider Stephens-Murphy train, and some others took horses from some Snake Indians after horses had been stolen from the train. The reaction by the Indians was enough to convince those at the fort ("some of the Hudson Bay Company") to brace for action of a distinctly unfriendly nature. In his none too elaborate writing style, Jacob tells only that those in the fort fired "a small field piece" three times, though only "to try it," which action nevertheless reportedly caused the Snakes to hesitate. Meanwhile, Thorp and the others crossed the Snake River at the fort before the Indians could retaliate. "So ended this career without mischief being done," Jacob Hammer said of this second instance of direct action by emigrants of '44 against Indians.

The punishing trek through Idaho was not the only stretch on which the emigrants welcomed the foodstuffs offered for trade by the Indians. The practice continued as the Hammers pulled onto the Grande Ronde, where they bought "peas, potatoes, and a kind of bread . . . made of leamis root" as well as blueberries. Clyman and Minto too spoke for the many who were thankful to find foodstuffs for sale by Indians at Grande Ronde. When bachelor Minto explained his unfamiliarity with camas roots, an Indian woman gave him a cake made from that ingredient left over from her own lunch.

A few "packers" were sent from the trains while in the Blue Mountains to the Whitman mission for grain and other provisions for the emigrants on the last leg of the journey. But along the Umatilla River and in the vicinity of the mighty Columbia they traded for more fish, camas roots, potatoes and other vegetables. The Parrishes, coming along in early November after a brief stay at the Whitman mission, also bought wood for cook and camp fires.

Such trading at times (and the Indians were said to be always eager to trade) also resulted in disagreements and revoked transactions. On the Umatilla, an Indian to whom John Minto had traded a shirt for a sack of potatoes returned and demanded that the swap be rescinded owing to the worn condition of the garment (a flaw his women companions pointed out in derision of his bargaining abilities). Minto generalized then that such behavior seemed to be a "common trait of Indian trading."

As with the Potawatomi chief Pa-reesh at Bellevue who had impressed Jacob Hammer with his bearing and willingness to help the emigrants cross the Missouri River, so too did the aged Cayuse chief Sticcus impress John Minto who wrote that the chief had aided the Whitman party the year before in finding a manageable route through the Blue Mountains. Washington Smith Gilliam also praised Sticcus, stating in his recollections that not only was Sticcus present again in '44 but that he "came to camp" when a horse had been reported stolen and assured the train members that he would find and return the horse. "The next day Sticcus rode up with the stolen horse, and without hinting about a gift or present [he] mounted his horse and rode off like a king." Young Gilliam thought him "noble."

Several of the narrators, when arriving at the bottom of the western slope of the Blue Mountains, were surprised to see the hundreds of horses belonging to the Cayuse Indians. James Clyman saw that "this vally was nearly covered with horses when we came down the mountain . . ." The Cayuse were "verry anxious to obtain cows & other catle for which they exchang horses of which they have great Quantities." Earlier, while on the Grande Ronde, he had remarked that the Cayuse "appear to be rapidly advancing in civilization." He also provided a view of a "Kyuse farm" as being "Krailed [corralled] in with willows and planted with corn, beans, potatoes, &c &c." When Parrish arrived in the area in mid October, he saw "horses without number."

Some, through envy or other cause, suspected the Cayuse of other than honorable practices in acquiring the impressive herds of horses. Clyman, writing earlier near the side trail to the Whitmans' mission, changed his mind about the Cayuse when he found one whom he took to be of that tribe in the act of stealing his horse. He shouted the thief off ("not haveing brought my gun with me"). "So much for the Kyuse," he quipped, "who are said to be the most honest Savage people on the continent."

Another attempt at theft was reported by young Minto when, crossing a dangerous ford of the Deschutes River near its mouth on the Columbia, he became separated from his companions and an Indian tried to wrest his gun, "an old flintlock," from him while another grabbed for "my horse rope." Minto threatened to fire the gun and shouted the other off. Riding away he counted seventeen others who had hidden from view.

Not only were Indian foodstuffs welcomed during the journey along the Snake, Umatilla and Columbia, but Indians were occasionally employed to help the emigrants in the final stages of the journey to the Valley.

While traveling along the Umatilla, Jacob Hammer hired an Indian named Joseph to drive a cow to the "falls of the Columbia." When Jacob arrived at The Dalles, he hired a Chinook Indian and his large canoe (and later another Indian to assist) to conduct his family and A. C. R. Shaw down the Columbia to Ft. Vancouver. The reference in the Hammer journal to this Chinook Indian reminds one of the Chinook jargon which for many emigrants became an essential means of communication with Indians.

On October seventh, James Clyman and his companions, "after passing the River De Chuttes, took a guide" (presumably Indian) to help them find a campsite in "a small rich vally."

In view of the certain influx of emigrants to the territory, some attempts were made to accommodate the inevitable clash of cultures. In his "Circular to the Oregon Emigrants" dated "Oregon City, April 22, 1847," George Abernethy announced in his dual capacity as Governor of Oregon Territory and Superintendent of Indian Affairs that by an act of the legislature it was his duty "To give such instructions and directions to Emigrants to this Territory, in regard to their conduct toward the natives, by the observance of which, they will be most likely to maintain and promote peace and friendship between themselves and the Indian tribes through which they may pass."

Therefore he advised that "the Indians on the old road [he also advised against taking any of the so-called shortcuts at this time] to this country are friendly to the whites. They should be treated with kindness on all occasions." However, they were "inclined to steal," perhaps, he stated, because a previous party of whites had promised to pay for something purchased from them and failed to do so. Emigrants should "keep in good sized companies" and should watch closely the Indians admitted to their camps, he stated in this notice apparently sent east along the Trail during the spring of 1847.

But the history of emigrants and Indians in Oregon, particularly from the 1840's forward to the time at which the Indians of the region were confined to reservations, is yet another chapter, riddled with confrontation and bloodshed, in the unfolding tragedy of red-white relations.

Many of those of the '44 emigration marched off with militia units to avenge the murders at the Whitman mission in 1847. Cornelius Gilliam was killed (by accidental gunshot, not in battle) during this retaliatory action. There were other skirmishes south in the Valley, and in the Rogue River country.

John McLoughlin of Ft. Vancouver, who had coexisted with the Indians of the region for many years (admittedly with a trade mechanism which greatly enhanced his chances to do so) charged the emigrants of 1844 with a movement to drive out all white men who had Indian wives.

Such residual belligerence was inherent in the manner in which Americans, beginning on the Atlantic coast, had moved ever farther west to occupy "new" land. There were those who adopted a live-and-let-live attitude about their Indian neighbors. But the Valley's subsequent "development," as the whites were wont to call it mandated as it was by popular demand, would include an Indian policy comprised appreciably of attitudes formed in part during the emigration of 1844.

Epilogue

On Attaining the Valley

They had been nearly half a year on a two thousand mile journey, drawn by the rich soil of the Willamette Valley. Though their lot for the first few years in Oregon would be hard, most were satisfied with what they found.

Thus to young B. F. Nichols, "the Valley seemed . . . an earthly paradise indeed" with "grass 12 to 15 inches high and green all winter and waving in the breeze. . . The oak hills which extend from the low prairie lands to the fir timber on the eastern slope of the Coast mountains . . . presented . . . the appearance of a well cultivated orchard. There was no underbrush except in the hollows where there were groves of fir timber. On the eastern slope of the Coast mountains and along the foot hills was the home of the panther, wolf and black tailed deer. Other small bands of deer would feed within gun shot of our cabin. Wild geese and ducks were there by the thousands. Grouse, native pheasants and quail were plentiful as chickens around a barn lot. . . We used in great part the wild game for meat . . ."

To many of the '44 emigration, the bounties of nature were the exact opposite of their material worth. T. M. Ramsdell worked for many days to earn a pair of leather shoes. "I was fortunate, as most of the emigration wore moccasins . . . Buckskin clothing was in large use among us . . . legal tender was more in the form of furs and produce than in cash. I packed butter in boxes on a pack horse 60 miles to pay for my wife's wedding dress. We brought no money from the states and had none till the gold strikes broke out in 1849. We were all broken down . . . financially. I remember taking in but

25 cents from . . . 1844 till 1848. . . From 1844 till the mines [in California] broke out, we lived hard."

Years later, W. S. Gilliam reminisced about growing up on the land where "the town of Dallas now stands." The family arrived on March 16, 1845, at the claim which his father, the "General," had selected earlier. "The whole country was a natural park, and combined with the ideal spring day" of their arrival made it seem to young Gilliam, "like dreamland."

The dreams were nurtured by work and perseverance. "We went to work . . . building a log cabin, but . . . we were over-taken by the equinoctial storm, which gave us some very serious discomfort." Even with a "bountiful yield in both field and garden . . . we suffered some privations in food" for which at times they substituted "boiled wheat for bread," poor fare helped somewhat by their "having plenty of wild meat, milk and butter." In the fall of 1847, the family "moved up the country about twelve miles and bought a place on Pedee."

Another emigrant of '44, Nancy Dickerson Welch, remembered that food was plentiful in the settled part of the country, but the greatest "want" was clothing; the goods in the stores thereabouts quickly sold out. Clothing was pieced together from patches and whatever, with little worry wasted on color or texture. Boots and shoes were to be had at a premium; moccasins were "the universal foot covering."

Others of '44 worked to build a life at the end of the Trail. Though each of course was unique, nearly any one of them could be seen to represent many others in the pattern of settlement they adopted. Jacob and Hannah Hammer, for example, lived for three years on the Tualatin Plains west of present Portland. In 1847 they moved to the newly organized Benton County and took a claim south of Alpine. In addi-tion to tending their claim through which ran Hammer Creek, the Hammers helped populate their corner of "the

Lord's Vineyard" as Jacob, a Quaker, had called the Valley.

Oregon became a Territory in August 1848. But a Provisional Government preceded that status, a home-grown government of which the new Oregonians were indeed proud. As historian Aubrey L. Haines recalls on behalf of his own emigrant forebears, "The Provisional Government of Oregon was, for a time, a sovereign power: it taxed, coined money, raised troops, fought a war, sent out an ambassador, and carried on all the functions of a government—all on a shoestring!"

As in the Conrad Richter trilogy, *The Trees, The Fields, The Town,* set in the Midwest which the new Oregonians had left far to the east (and which region some of them had helped develop in the sequence of the book titles), the Willamette Valley in the early 1850's was undergoing similar development. H. H. Bancroft, in his history of Oregon, noted a "rage for laying out towns" in the early 1850's.

And there was soon much need for towns to process the products of the farms and to supply the needs of the large farm majority. The first U. S. census in Oregon (1850, the Seventh U. S. Census) listed 13,043 residents in the Territory. Historian Bancroft called these the true pioneers. Of that number, 2,206 listed birth places in Missouri, 1,023 in Illinois, over 700 each for Indiana and Ohio, fewer from states farther east and south.

Agriculture, of course, was the mainstay of existence, and wheat was the principal crop. In the 1860's and 70's, the average farm included about forty acres of wheat, representing the extent of the average farm family's capacity for sowing, cultivating, cutting (with hand cradles), threshing (by driving horses over the stalks) and ridding it of chaff by dropping the grain from a tower contraption.

Wheat had another use beyond the obvious in the earliest days. B. F. Nichols wrote that, "As there was no circulating medium or money . . . the Legislature . . . enacted a law declaring wheat at a dollar a bushel as legal tender. . . If one was indebted to another the debt could be paid by delivering one bushel of wheat for every dollar due."

Hay was chiefly timothy or oats, the latter providing a double benefit. Crop yields were hampered considerably by the practice of sowing the same crop repeatedly in the same tilled ground. Much of the claim acreage was left to meadows, where the farmers fought rose briar from taking over pastures. Varieties of sheep were raised and wool was an important product on the farm. Many farmwives knitted heavy wool "Long Tom socks" named for the river in the valley and traded them to local merchants. The socks became popular with the miners traveling south to the California goldfields.

The lot of the emigrant wife and mother was a hard one. Among those who composed their recollections for Bancroft, Martha Ann Morrison (Mrs. John Minto) provided a case in point. Martha Ann was twelve years old in 1844, the eldest child of Nancy Irwin Morrison and Robert Wilson Morrison, the employers of twenty-two year old John Minto. She and Minto were married in 1847 when she was "just a little over fifteen."

At the time of her interview by Mr. and Mrs. Bancroft on June 16, 1878, Mrs. Minto was described as having an "excellent physique." Her face was "full of flesh, with [a] rosy complexion." She had a "matronly bearing still in vigor and prime of life, a clear full voice with deliberate speech enlisting attention and carrying weight."

Martha Ann Minto recalled that "there was only one bolt of calico in Oregon when we came here . . . and that was at Astoria. The women and girls that came here were very destitute." One summer her older sister and she "gathered a

JOHN AND MARTHA MINTO WITH SON JOHN W., ABOUT 1852
Courtesy of the Minto family, by Beverly E. Lowe

barrel of cranberries and sent them to Oregon City and got a little piece of blue drilling that made us a covering . . . it could hardly be considered dresses. There were no shoes nor stockings to buy, and if there [had been] we did not have the money to pay for them. My sister . . . and I managed to send to Vancouver . . . and we got each of us a pair of fine slippers. We used to carry them in our hands nearly up to Mr. [Josiah L.] Parrish's house and just before we got there we put them on and went in to hear Mr. Parrish preach." Believably, "All these things were dreadfully annoying to girls."

When the Mintos "went to housekeeping" near Salem, Martha Ann had "just one stew kettle that belonged to a stove, but there was no thought of a stove. We had that kettle to make coffee, or bread, or fry meat, for we had not even a frying pan. We had three butcher knives . . . nothing else in the shape of knives, forks, or spoons. I got two large flowered plates. That was all we had for three or four years. We had a few tin dishes. The first year we were married we had just seventy-five cents worth of sugar (about 2½ or 3 pounds). We got that [the money] from [a] man who boarded there. We never had a bit of tea or coffee."

The home furnishings were as bleak as the kitchenware. "We had just two sheets, and one little bit of a bed with a few feathers in it. When Mr. Minto started to the Cayuse war, I cut up the sheets to make shirts for him and then I had none. We slept as we could. We had a pile of straw."

When her husband went to the "war," Martha Ann "was left entirely alone, about sixteen years old, three miles from any house." While she remained alone, "wolves destroyed my animals." As for her own mother, "I suppose [she] had more trouble there [on the family's claim on the Clatsop plains] than she had on the road . . ." The Mintos were no doubt representative of many newly married couples in the region.

Though occurring in the unyielding lifestyle of pioneers, family life was preferred by the majority it seems. Not only were nuptials being celebrated by many for the first time, but many of those who had lost husbands or wives to death on the Trail remarried in Oregon. As but one example of those arriving in '44, William Sebring, whose wife had died in early August on the Platte River, was married in July 1845, to Martha Nichols, the oldest sister of B. F. Nichols.

Each of the emigrants of '44 contributed in his and her own way to the development of the Oregon territory. They exercised individuality (especially those of the early emigrations) in the selection of their claim site, choosing a particular tract of land from some deep-well personal reservoir in which was combined a sense of the practical and the esthetic, as if selecting a particularly appealing *objet d'art*. William Shaw, company captain in the Gilliam train, explained to H. H. Bancroft years later that, "It [his claim near Salem] was just the sort of land I started from Missouri to find, all good, rich, deep soil, and first rate timber right around it, and handy close by."

Some occupied two or more farmsites during their farming careers. If they did so it was for reasons again peculiar to their particular circumstances. There were also those who seemingly did not find contentment after seeing the Valley, those who paced the wall created by the Pacific Ocean shoreline in search of some inner peace to be had at finding just the right setting in which to act out the particular life's-drama they felt impelled to perform. The observant James Clyman wrote in late October 1844 of the restlessness of some (with whom he readily admitted some affinity): "Notwithstanding the ease with which the necessaries of life are acquired, I never saw a more discontented community, owing principally to natural disposition. Nearly all, like myself, having been of a roving discontented character before leaving their eastern homes. The long tiresome trip from the States has taught them what they are capable of performing and enduring. They talk of removing to the [Sandwich] Islands, California, Chili, and other parts of South America with as much composure as you in Wisconsin talk of removing to Indiana or Michigan." Excursionist Clyman would lead a party of fellow discontents from Oregon to California during the summer of 1845.

A year after Samuel Black Crockett arrived, he moved to the Puget Sound country and helped found one of the first American settlements there, near present Olympia. Gold fever required a brief stay in California in 1848–49, from which he returned to the soon-to-be Washington Territory where his entire family moved to Whidbey Island.

Emigrants-turned-Oregonians retained some remnant of the dream which had prompted their emigration even as they faced the realities and exigencies of the moment. Such a candle-stub remnant of the high expectations which had burned within when crossing the Missouri River all those years ago was apparent, for example, in the many interviews arranged by H. H. Bancroft at the pioneers' reunions in the 1870's. Even then, thirty years after their great protracted adventure, the interviewees would indulge themselves in reflections on the euphoria they experienced when they sat squarely if not too comfortably in the first structure to be called a home in the Willamette Valley and congratulated themselves for having survived the six month trek west.

Not surprisingly, the emigrants of '44 were people of their times. But they managed to distinguish their times with the symbols of their grand adventure. Consequently they have been remembered when others have been forgotten.

The Neal Family in Oregon
A descendant writes about her forebears,
individuals all, yet typical of many others.
by Norma Eid

Among the able-bodied men in the Nathaniel Ford wagon train
were five brothers by the name of Neal. Like many others who
traveled the Oregon and California Trails, they weren't beginners
at managing an ox team and living in a wagon. They had spent the
better part of a decade moving across Tennessee.

The restless search by the Neal brothers for something better
apparently had precluded an education. Even the spelling of the
family name had been left up to the census-taker or county clerk to
record; thus the O'Neals of Virginia became the Neils of Missouri,
and, some 2,000 miles later, the Neals of Oregon.

The end of the emigration of 1844 found the Neals all together
at Ale, now West Stayton, in Marion (formerly Champoeg)
County by December 24, 1844. They had left Calvin's wife Alcey
at Fort Vancouver to recover from the birth of her first child who
had entered this world along the banks of the Grande Ronde River
which flows along the edge of the Wallowa Mountains. Appropri-
ately, the child was named Martha Grand Ronde Neal.

Calvin was the only brother who stayed on the original piece of
land that he selected to farm. His Donation Land Claim states
that he settled his claim in Marion County on December 25,
1845, and his death notice in 1891 reported that he died there
having raised nineteen children of his own and three step-children
belonging to his third wife. He also gave a home to his young
nephew Daniel, who was the sole survivor of the family of Valentine
Neal, another brother, who emigrated in 1852. Seven members of
that Neal family died of cholera on the Trail.

George William Neal stayed on his claim in Marion County for
several years but eventually sold out and moved to Salem where he
followed his trade of blacksmithing until his death in 1897. He was
a gunsmith of merit too even indulging in the art of silver inlay on

the guns that he produced and on which he always attached a small plate engraved "Made by George Neal."

The other three brothers continued to suffer from wanderlust. Alexander sold his claim and headed for the Washington Territory where there was more breathing room. Tiring of that location, he eventually returned to Oregon where he died in 1889 near Grants Pass. Aldy, the oldest brother, owned land in Montana where he lived part of the time.

Perhaps Peter Neal scorned the farmer's life more than the others for he tried his hand at a variety of other pursuits. A skilled blacksmith, gunsmith, and millwright, he found immediate employment with the Hudson's Bay Company. During the gold rush he saw a good thing in running a supply wagon between the Willamette Valley and the gold fields. Making almost six thousand dollars from this venture, he always claimed it was more profitable than mining had been for many of his friends.

By 1852, Peter had returned to Marion County where he held D.L.C. No.11. This certainly did not mean that he had become reconciled to life behind the plow; instead he was cutting timber and sawing lumber. The records of the Old School Presbyterian Church at West Stayton list his contribution to this historic building not as cash, nails, service or Bibles, but as lumber.

Not all of the Neals remained in the Willamette Valley. Before reaching there in 1844, the bateaux carrying the Neals put in at the mouth of Dog River for a rest period. And while lunch was being prepared, Peter Neal took his young son Jesse and wandered upstream to the middle valley. With its rushing streams and majestic forest of yellow pine and Douglas fir dominated by the crystal beauty of Mt. Hood, the scene became one that he carried in his memory for the next seventeen years.

In 1861 he returned as he had come—by boat—to the valley which by that time had been renamed the Hood River Valley. As they disembarked to portage around the Cascades, he noticed the Parker waterwheel from the Bradford Mill lying in the water where it had fallen when the Indians attacked the settlement and burned the mill in 1856. After settling his family on a piece of land in the

A SCENE IN THE HOOD RIVER VALLEY
Copyright by Cy Eid

valley along the edge of a creek that now bears his name, he returned for the waterwheel. For the next twenty-five years it powered the mill that he built.

He also built a road on the east side of the valley which except for a modern surface remains little changed today. He transported his lumber from the Middle Valley to the Columbia River over this road. On many a favorable west wind, he also rafted the lumber upstream to The Dalles where it found a ready market.

During the first year in the Hood River Valley, the last child of Peter and Mahala Neal was born, bringing the total to nine children. But the family had suffered grievously with child mortality; seven of the children died from consumption, the killer disease of the nineteenth century.

Though Peter Neal continued to work the mill, the old restlessness returned. He began to feel that the valley was getting too heavily populated for his liking, and he started thinking and talking about a place in Douglas County where he had laid over and rested his teams when he was freighting cargo to the gold fields. He sent his youngest child, Jerome, who was now a young man of twenty-four, to check out the area. Jerome sent along a favorable report and in the fall of 1886, Peter sold the mill and left the Hood River Valley.

The spring of 1887 brought a chinook wind that swept over Mt. Hood causing a run-off that far exceeded the flow that Neal Creek could handle. The logs in the mill pond pounded against the dam and in a thundering roar breached the dam, wiping out all traces of the mill. The new owner of the mill opined that "many pieces of the mill had joined the waste of the ocean." Later, one lone iron bucket from the original Parker waterwheel was recovered and presented to the Oregon Historical Society.

With their pioneering days behind them, Peter and Mahala Neal's lives in Douglas County were serene and uneventful. Mahala died in 1892 at age seventy-two and Peter died in 1902, age eighty-eight. They are buried side by side in the Old Pioneer Cemetery in Roseburg.

Bibliographical Notes

The historical record has been enriched by several narratives of the emigration of 1844.

The Nathaniel Ford wagon train is represented by the most impressive day-to-day journal of 1844 to come to light so far, that by former mountain man James Clyman. It is an essential record not only for '44 but as required reading for any who wish to read the classics of the genre. Clyman was one of an exclusive few who in imparting hard-earned knowledge of the western wilderness can be counted on to inspire readers' imagination to the fullest.

The Ford party [handwritten marginal note]

Clyman's journal is compelling documentation, straight-talk of the times enlivened by occasional dry wit and decidedly unimpeded by self-promotion. Clyman downplayed his own role as resident authority, indicating a kind of hemming and hawing, 'aw-shucks-ma'am' mien which didn't allow for opulent self-praise, not even in the privacy of his own journal when referring to earlier trips on the Trail and the deprivations successfully overcome.

This former mountain man was traveling, it would seem, fairly free of responsibilities to others. It is to his credit, then, that he wrote as much as he did about the affairs of the train with which he traveled. Near South Pass he took time out to remain with Barnette, a dying man similarly alone it appears, later interring that unfortunate one along the Sweetwater River.

At fifty-two years of age, Clyman traveled uncomplainingly though he recorded the miserable conditions of the first rainy weeks, and the natural enough discomfort of other stretches of the Trail. He traveled apparently by horse or mule the entire distance, some of it through difficult going close in to Mt. Hood.

The Clyman journal of 1844 (along with the others he compiled on earlier and later journeys) was first edited by Charles L. Camp, *James Clyman, American Frontiersman, 1792–1881* (San Francisco: Calif. Hist. Soc., 1928) and more recently by Linda M. Hasselstrom as *Journal of a Mountain Man* (Missoula, MT: Mountain Press Pub. Co., 1984). The

Camp edition contains many helpful notes and maps of importance. The notes added by Hasselstrom are also helpful and she is to be thanked for bringing the Clyman journals back into circulation.

The published recollections of Alanson Hinman, another of the Ford train, were prepared from "a series of conversations" with him by James R. Robertson and appeared in the *Quarterly of the Oreg. Hist. Soc.*, vol. two, 1901, pp. 266–86.

The Cornelius Gilliam train is represented by several narratives of varying length and importance. The version of the journal of Edward Evans Parrish used for this study is the manuscript at the Idaho State Hist. Soc., Boise: "E. E. Parrish's Traveling Diary Across the Plains" handwritten by Parrish in 1867. Another version of Parrish's journal was published in the *Transactions, 16th Annual Reunion of Oreg. Pioneer Assn., 1888* (Portland, 1889), pages 82–121. One may assume that the version which Parrish hand copied in 1867 contained some reflective commentary and therefore is of importance.

Samuel Black Crockett provided a brief but valuable account from April twenty-fifth to August twenty-seventh. An initial page or pages of his journal have been lost, and this journal ends two days (possibly) before he reached Ft. Bridger. Crockett was another young single man who, with John Minto and Daniel Clark, left the Gilliam train before reaching Ft. Hall and rode on ahead to arrange for re-provisioning for that train from the beneficence of Dr. Whitman. But their ride thenceforward was relatively free of other responsibilities except for their own daily sustenance and safety as innocents abroad, foot-loose bachelors meeting each occurrence with the strength of youth and much of its ignorance. Yet they made their way successfully, happily observant of all that was around them, and all this in such a time and place to make envious today's time-bound Trail enthusiasts. Crockett's journal was adequately edited by Vernon Carstensen in *Building A State: Washington, 1889–1939* (Tacoma: Wash. State Hist. Soc. Pubns., vol. three, 1940, pp. 594–607). Though an incomplete narrative, it has corroborative and descriptive significance.

The narrative of John Minto, another member of the Gilliam train and one of the group of bachelors, is an important addition to the literature of '44 and is notable for, among other things, believable youthful enthusiasm with which his recollections were imbued though compiled fifty-plus years later.

Minto acquired a special place among the emigrants as one who did much to keep the memory of that emigration alive by emphasizing the importance of it all. He published several articles about various aspects of Trail history and took an active part in the Oregon Pioneer Association. His most complete narrative was published in *The Quarterly of Oreg. Hist. Soc.*, 1901, vol. II, no. 3, pp. 119–167. In 1980, that version was enlarged upon with the addition of biographical commentary by Minto descendant Beverly Elizabeth Lowe and published as *John Minto, Man of Courage, 1822–1915. A Biography of an Oregon Pioneer* (Salem, OR: Kingston Price and Co., 1980).

The recollections of B. F. Nichols are contained in a series of weekly newspaper articles in the *Laidlaw Chronicle* (Crook County, OR), the first of which appeared in the November 16, 1906 issue. Thereafter the articles continued at least through April 5, 1907. The series read for this study is contained in the Oregon Historical Society Library.

Information about Andrew Sublette and the small train he guided in 1844 came from *The Colorado Magazine*, vol. 10, Sept. 1933, pp. 179–84; one of the "Mountain Men" series of articles by LeRoy R. Hafen; and from the Sublette Papers, Missouri Hist. Soc.

Two brief accounts tell of variant routing and scheduling for the journey of 1844. The November 18, 1916 letter of William D. Stillwell to Oregon historian George H. Hines briefly recounts the last few days of the Thomas Stillwell family's trip from the Snake River into the Willamette Valley along with a small group of persons from both the Gilliam and the Ford trains. The undated transcript of a letter J. S. Smith wrote to the *Oregonian* in response to what he cited as mistaken references to him in previous articles, particularly about his journey "forty years ago," is in the Oreg. Hist. Soc. Library, as is the Stillwell letter.

Fewer narratives by northsiders have surfaced. Formerly, the reminiscences of Moses Schallenberger served as the chief source of information about the Stephens-Murphy party (sometimes referred to also as the Thorp party). The most complete treatment of that narrative is in George R. Stewart's *The Opening of the California Trail* (Berkeley: Univ. of Calif. Press, 1953). Stewart traces the provenance of the Schallenberger narrative beginning with references by H. H. Bancroft in his *History of California* (vol. IV, p. 446, n. 9), who stated that Schallenberger's "Overland in 1844" arrived too late for publication. Bancroft however did interject a 500 word summary of the narrative, explaining in his volume V that the narrative was written by Schallenberger's daughter in 1884 or '85. It has been assumed that the complete narrative was destroyed in a fire in 1894 or '98. But another version of the narrative appeared in an 1888 county history and biographical compendium, *Pen Pictures [of] Santa Clara County, California*, edited by H. S. Foote, in which appeared "The Story of the Murphy Party," (pp. 38–58) which is credited to Moses Schallenberger. Author-editor Stewart has reasoned that the the narrative to which Bancroft referred and that in *Pen Pictures* are the same, with, possibly, some additions by Murphy family members. The Schallenberger narrative is also cited in Stewart's *The California Trail: An Epic With Many Heroes* (N. Y: McGraw-Hill, 1962; and Lincoln: Univ. of Nebr. Press, 1983).

The recent publication of the Jacob Hammer journal (*This Emigrating Company . . .*, vol. XVI of The American Trails Series, Glendale, CA: Arthur H. Clark Co., 1990) provides for the first time a specific chronology for the Stephens-Murphy-Thorp wagon train which crossed the Missouri at Council Bluffs-Bellevue. This journal sheds new and important light on the composition and travel schedule of both the California-bound party and those bound for Oregon.

Two other northsiders are represented by brief recollections: William M. Case in *The Quarterly of Oreg. Hist. Soc.*, vol. one, 1900, pp. 269–77; and Edmund Bray in a letter dated April 12, 1872, to H. H. Bancroft (Bancroft Library, Univ. of Calif., Berkeley).

Some of the narratives of 1844 and earlier years cited in this work resulted from interviews conducted by historian Hubert Howe Bancroft at Pioneer Association reunions in the 1870's. The work of Bancroft and his many assistants in their appreciative gathering in of the rich crop of participant narratives of the overland emigrations remains as an impressive effort in the field of historical documentation and as oral history before the tape recorder.

The interviews selected to help gain a quick view of the emigrations of 1842 and 1843 are those of Sidney W. Moss, Asa Lovejoy, and John Burch McClane. For the year 1844, interviews with Martha Ann Morrison Minto and John Minto were helpful. The letter to Bancroft from Willard H. Rees and the lengthy interview of William Shaw provided valuable information. All these are in the Bancroft collection at the Bancroft Library.

In his interview with Bancroft on June 18, 1878, Sidney W. Moss spoke briefly about Jason Lee, and about the meeting near Champoeg in the summer of 1843 where was "formed a provisional government [which] adopted the statutes of Iowa as our statutes."

Moss's comments about Lansford Hastings are worth noting. Hastings, according to Moss, was "a dark complexioned man with dark hair and dark eyes . . . who thought a great deal of himself and he was arbitrary. I did not like him. We started together from Fort Smith [for the train's rendezvous at Independence] and I had a full opportunity of noting his character. He had ability and could manage the men, and he was a very fair lawyer, pretty well read . . ."

Moss called "Billy Gray's" history of Oregon (William Henry Gray. *A History of Oregon, 1792–1849: Drawn From Personal Observations and Authentic Information,* Portland: Harrison & Holm, 1870) "one of the most untruthful articles" he had ever seen. Moss also claimed authorship of the book *The Prairie Flower,* explaining that the published version had been changed considerably from his original which "was intended to describe the experiences of our trip here." (Several authors have commented on Moss's claim to authorship, some believing it, others not.)

Asa Lovejoy was also a member of the train of '42. His recollections were published as "Lovejoy's Pioneer Narrative, 1842–48," edited by Henry E. Reed, in *Oreg. Hist. Quarterly,* XXXI, Sept. 1930, pp. 237–60. Long before that, however, he too talked to Bancroft about the White/Hastings train. Lovejoy characterized Hastings as "rather an aspiring sort of man and he worked it so that he got the command [of the train]." Lovejoy also said that the train "had a man with us who had seen the country twenty years before but he could not tell us anything where to go." He did not identify the one of whom he spoke. He did refer to the train's having hired Thomas Fitzpatrick near Ft. Laramie to guide them to Ft. Bridger "where Fitzpatrick had been staying."

Lovejoy stated that the members of the train took precautions against Indian attack by camping in "a circle—we always used to form a coral and set a guard." He referred also to the accidental death of one of their number while the train was on the Sweetwater. The accident occurred when the unfortunate man "took out a yager out of his wagon and it went off and shot him. He died the next day and we buried him." Lovejoy did not name the man. James Clyman apparently was unaware of the burial of this man (if indeed Lovejoy's recollection of the placement of the event was correct) when he remarked that Barnette, whose burial near South Pass he conducted, was "the first white man that ever rested his bones on that stream [the Sweetwater]."

Lovejoy's description of what befell himself and Hasting when they inadvertantly remained behind the train at Independence Rock and became trapped there for an uneasy spell by a large group of Sioux is one of the earliest accounts of emigrants being detained and otherwise physically threatened by Indians. Eventually the two were forced to ride one mount on their return to the emigrant camp and it was in this context that Lovejoy added that Hastings "was a very large man," weighing "two or three hundred pounds."

Among the "Great Migration" of 1843 was John Burch McClane, another with whom Bancroft spoke years later. McClane, who started his westward trek from Philadelphia in 1842, was one of the privileged of history, in his case for the opportunity to closely observe the aura of energy and ambition that apparently characterized Marcus Whitman. He had that advantage when he and Whitman rode ahead of the train from Soda Springs to Ft. Hall, and again when these two, along with Perrin Whitman (nephew of Marcus) and three others were once again out ahead of the emigrants when marking a route from Ft. Hall to the Waiilatpu mission.

McClane was one of many who helped promote the "Whitman saved Oregon" assumption, stating that "I presume it was by his [Whitman's] intercession that we were saved from going to the British Government." The American government, he assumed, "was inclined to give up our country to the British. . . [Daniel] Webster was particularly inclined to it. It was thought almost impossible to get wagons across the mountains, and Whitman said he could show them that it was possible." McClane was by his own admission aboard the first wagon taken through by this 1843 emigration.

The interview which Bancroft conducted with Martha Ann Morrison Minto and her husband on June 16, 1878, at "Room 18, Chemeketa Hotel, Salem" (remembered by others as the "Chemetka") was also attended by Mrs. Bancroft, Rev. J. L. Parrish and "the writer, A. B." (possibly Amos Bowman, one of Bancroft's able assistants). There Mrs. Minto told briefly of her Trail experience, but more of the difficulties of her early life in Oregon.

During the conversation, John Minto and J. L. Parrish pursued a spirited disagreement about who brought in the first sheep to the Valley, the offshoot relative to the emigration of '44 being that neither mentioned Joshua "Sheep" Shaw of the 1844 northsider train who was credited elsewhere as being the first to drive sheep overland from Missouri. Two years earlier, Minto had credited Shaw with that distinction in an article he wrote for the 1876 *Transactions* of the Oregon Pioneer Association.

Historian Bancroft used his numerous oral history interviews with emigrants to compile several weighty volumes of Pacific Northwest and California history. The most useful for the present study is *The Works of Hubert Howe Bancroft: History of Oregon, vol. XXIX (1834–1848) and vol. XXX (1848–1888)*, San Francisco: History Co., 1886, 1888.

Bancroft and "A. B." also took down "William Shaw's Narrative and Life" while they were "at the Pioneer's camp meeting, Salem, Oregon, Friday, June 14, '78." In it this captain of a company of the Gilliam train held forth on the "Mississippi & Columbia River Valley Pioneer Life Compared."

Shaw, who at ninteeen years of age had been "in [Andrew] Jackson's War in 1814 and 1815 against the British," went to Missouri in 1819 about the time those who preceded him there "came out of their forts." Shaw was "a man that wanted to live with my character unspotted" and so he took the precautions he did when, a few miles west of the crossing of the Missouri River at "Chapels Ferry," he was put in charge of seeing to Mr. Bishop's burial and to the delivery of the goods of the deceased to the Indian agent nearby.

Shaw can be thanked for having given some statistical information: forty-five wagons in his company; "about" eighty wagons in the train and "about" five hundred people. Shaw confirmed that Henry Sager had "requested me on his death bed to take his family to Oregon and I told him I would do the best I could." A son of Shaw "wrote a journal and he lost it at Fort Boise. I do not know how it was done. He had every circumstance taken down, everything done out, hunting, everything seen and done." Thus another record of '44 was lost.

Bancroft's assistant "A. B." described Captain Shaw as "Stature about five feet seven inches. Not full bodied. Hale and vigorous walk. Face shaven. Full head of hair [at eighty-three years of age] Features well cut . . . a merry expression and manner, and a distinct voice."

Two letters by Willard Hall Rees, his of September 18, 1879, to H. H. Bancroft; and another to John Minto dated October 23, 1874, are in the Bancroft Library, and depict select instances while Rees was with the Gilliam train and later.

One of the most unfortunate might-have-been's of record keeping during the '44 emigration was that of Rees, the first secretary of the Oregon Pioneer Association. Rees was obviously capable of writing as detailed, revealing and otherwise intelligent a narrative as any and his letter to Minto told of his service as adjutant of the Gilliam train. One duty of that job was the keeping of duplicate "records" listing "the names of heads of families and messes, the number of waggons[sic], work oxen and horses belonging to each, the names of all males above the age of 16yrs who owned neither waggon nor stock but were to travel as helpers with the families and messes by special arrangement, also the number of firearms and amount of ammunition belonging to each family or mess." One copy of the "records" went to Gilliam "which was sent to the *Platt Argus* for publication" (and thence the basis likely for the brief reference in the *Daily Missouri Republican* of May 28, 1844). The other copy was kept by Rees. Soon after reaching Oregon, Rees loaned his copy in August 1845 to Charles Saxton just before Saxton returned East with Dr. Elijah White. Rees later learned from Saxton that the record book was inadvertently packed with Dr. White's effects and was only discovered when that party was "far out on their winding way." Rees, writing to Minto thirty-four years later in 1879, had not seen his record book again.

And not only was Rees' record book lost to him, but Fred Lockley lamented justifiably that although Rees actually did write a lengthy narrative, he refused to have it published during his life time but instead stored it in a trunk only to find it reduced to shreds by mice when later he opened the trunk to look for one of the many Trail-related letters he had collected from other emigrants. Disheartened at seeing the irreparable damage done to his manuscript and the other priceless documents, Rees did not repeat his efforts at rewriting his story. And thus was lost an inestimatable addition to the record for '44.

Lockley reported in "Oregon Emigrants of 1844" (*Wash. Hist. Quarterly*, vol. 18, 1927, pp. 93–102) about his visit to a descendant of Rees who showed him "a few pages of Mr. Rees' manuscripts" of which Lockley then quoted nearly 2,500 words, mostly about Rees' first few weeks on the Trail in '44. Fortunately, Rees included a few comments about the 1844 emigration in his letter to Bancroft in response to the historian's inquiry about "the Canadian settlers" of French Prairie (Marion County) Oregon. The letter is preserved in the Bancroft Library.

The Oregon Pioneer Association was responsible for several annual reunions, and for publishing a series of the organization's *Transactions* in which appeared three of the brief narratives cited in this work: "Reminiscences. by T. M. Ramsdell, A Pioneer of 1844," (1897), pp. 108–12; "Mrs. Nancy Dickerson Welch," (1897), pp. 97–103; "Reminiscences of Washington Smith Gilliam," (1903), pp. 202–20 (a similar version appeared in Robert A. Bennett, comp., *We'll All Go Home Again In The Spring; personal accounts and adventures as told by pioneers of the West*. Walla Walla: Pioneer Press Books, 1984, pp 9–12).

"The Occasional Address" in the *Transactions of the Fourth Annual Re-Union of the Oregon Pioneer Association; for 1876.* . . (Salem, Oregon: 1877) was by John Minto and the subject of course was the emigration of 1844, to which was added "The Roll of 1844" of 245 names compiled by "Joseph Watt, William H. Rees and Wm. M. Case."

The memorable and sad story of the Sager family anguish has been told in several versions. One of the best was originally written by Catherine Sager Pringle and edited by Harry M. Majors in the December 1980 issue of *Northwest Discovery: The Journal of Northwest History and Natural History* ("Seven Orphans on the Oregon Trail, 1844," pp. 314–60), which includes many lengthy notes on other source materials and publications.

Lockley's interview with Matilda Jane Sager Delaney was included in *Conversations with Pioneer Women. The Lockley Files*, compiled and edited by Mike Helm (Eugene, OR: Rainy Day Press, 1981, pages 5–11). Another reputable Sager family source is Erwin N. Thompson's *Shallow Grave at Waiilatpu: The Sagers West* (Oreg. Hist. Soc., 1969).

The "Reminiscences of Mrs. Frank Collins, nee Martha Elizabeth Gilliam," edited by Fred Lockley, appeared in *Quarterly of Oreg. Hist. Soc.*, vol. 17, Dec. 1916, pp. 358–72.

Other, earlier, narratives cited in this work include those of Joseph Williams and Thomas J. Farnham which appeared in *To the Rockies and Oregon in 1839–1842*, edited by LeRoy R. Hafen and Ann W. Hafen (Glendale, CA: The Arthur H. Clark Co., 1955); Joel Palmer, *Journal of Travels Over The Rocky Mountains, to the Mouth of the Columbia River; made during the years 1845 and 1846* . . ., Cincinnati: J. A. & U. P. James, 1847); Overton Johnson and Wm. H. Winter, *Route Across the Rocky Mountains, with a Description of Oregon and California*. . . (Lafayette, IN: John B. Semans, 1846); Samuel Parker, *Journal of an Exploring Tour Beyond the Rocky Mountains, under the Direction of the A.B.C.F.M. Performed In the Years 1835, '36, and '37, Containing A Description of the Geography, Geology, Climate, and Productions; and the Numbers, Manners, and Customs of the Natives. With a Map of Oregon Territory*, (Minneapolis: Ross & Haines, 1967, a reprint of the 1838 edition); P. L. Edwards, *Sketch of the Oregon Territory or, Emigrants' Guide*, (Liberty, MO: Herald Office, 1842).

The reports of Fremont's explorations used in this study were contained in *Report of the Exploring Expedition to the Rocky Mountains in the Year 1842, and to Oregon and North California in the Years 1843–'44, By Brevet Captain J. C. Fremont. . .* (Wash., D. C.: Gales and Seaton, 1845). As for Fremont's cartographic contributions, Donald Jackson and Mary Lee Spence, in their *The Expeditions of John Charles Fremont, Map Portfolio* (Urbana, IL: Univ. of Ill. Press, 1970) have provided a reprint work of inestimatable value. Contained therein, in addition to a brief introductory pamphlet of sixteen pages, are five maps (number four comprised of seven separate sections) dating from 1843 to 1848 and representing the work also of Fremont mentor Joseph Nicolas Nicollet and of course of surveyor and cartographer Charles Preuss.

Among the most significant reference publications about the Oregon and California Trails is that which describes in detail one long segment: Historian Merrill Mattes' *The Great Platte River Road: The Covered Wagon Mainline Via Fort Kearny To Fort Laramie* (Nebr. State Hist. Soc. Pubns., Vol. XXV, 1969). This work not only provides the definitive history of the Trail along the Platte River in Nebraska and eastern Wyoming, but also sets forth much essential information about numerous Trail related subjects. The text is also enlivened by copious quotes from emigrant narratives—eye-witness comments appear on nearly on every page of this important book.

Mattes, a key figure in the restoration of Ft. Laramie, has also published numerous articles and books about the emigrations thereby rescuing from obscurity many personages and places of significance. Among his many articles and other publications, one in particular was of special value to the present study: "The Council Bluffs Road" in *Overland Journal* (of the Oreg. and Calif. Trail Assn.), vol. 3, no. 4, Fall 1885, pp. 30–42. The *1985* article first appeared in *Nebraska History*, vol. 65, no. 2, 1984, pp. 179–94. This segment of the Trail, the "northside" route, is the least well known and appreciated of the Great Platte River Road. Though used by the Mormons during their treks west, the northern route has too often been associated almost exclusively with the Mormons who were probably outnumbered ten or twenty to one if one looks at all the traffic on this route up to 1866.

Mattes has more recently compiled yet another major work, *Platte River Road Narratives* (Urbana: Univ. of Ill. Press, 1988), the encyclopedic annotated bibliography of overland trail narratives. The inclusive dates are 1812–1866 for the over 2,000 entries gleaned from some 100 repositories. Mattes has provided not only identification, but descriptive summaries and evaluations of the narratives.

Aubrey Haines' *Historic Sites Along the Oregon Trail* (Gerald, MO: Patrice Press, 1981) identifies hundreds of sites along the length of the Trail and even names the U.S. Geological Survey maps on which each can be found. The book also contains several maps of the Trail in six segments, seventeen maps of select vicinities of special importance, and a bibliography of 411 titles.

Another present-day Trails guide of note is Gregory M. Franzwa's *The Oregon Trail Revisited* (Gerald, MO: Patrice Press, 1972, 1983.). Both Haines and Franzwa benefited from an association with Trail savant Paul C. Henderson (as have many others). Franzwa's Trail guide is well known for detailing each mile of the Trail (and its many variants) from the Missouri River to the Willamette Valley. Also useful to the study of the Trail is Franzwa's *Maps of the Oregon Trail*, a looseleaf collection of topographical and other maps on which the Trails are marked.

Perhaps the most impressive, and trustworthy, global view of the emigrations from the Missouri River to the Pacific is John D. Unruh Jr.'s *The Plains Across: The Overland Emigrants and the Trans-Mississippi West, 1840–1860* (Urbana: Univ. of Ill. Press, 1979). Unruh presented an enlightening view of many vital aspects of trail history and he too allowed participants of the emigrations to speak for themselves often in his text. The hardcover edition of *The Plains Across* included an extensive bibliography; unfortunately, the 1982 paperback edition does not.

Index

Abernethy, George: 238-39
Abolitionism: 223
Afro-Americans: 42, 151, 176
Ague: 98ff.
Alderman, Isaac? Wesley?: 171, 229
Ale (OR): 249
American Board for Foreign Missions: 34, 43, 137
American Falls: 175
American Fur Company: 20, 42
Applegate, Jesse: 44, 47
Asabill, Elizabeth: 214
Ash Hollow (NE): 163, 164, 165, 166
Ashley, William H: 132, 136, 146
Astor, John Jacob: 33, 132
Astoria: 42, 244

Baker, Thomas A: 149
Bakersfield (CA): 148
Baldock Slough (OR): 182
Bancroft, Mrs. Hubert Howe: 244
Bancroft, Hubert Howe: 31, 39, 54, 66, 75, 121, 126, 144, 172, 175, 191, 243, 244, 247, 248
Baptist Missionary Magazine: 81
Baptists: 108
Barlow, Samuel Kimbrough: 186
Barlow Road: 186
Barnette, Mr. ("J. M."?): 110ff., 137, 170, 171, 212, 219, 232
"Batonne, Joe" (at Ft. Platte): 232
Bear River: 205
Beckworth, James P: 140
Bellevue (NE): 201, 223, 224
Bent's Fort: 37, 43, 141
Bidwell-Bartleson wagon train (1841): 38, 222
Bidwell, John: 38
Big Blue River: 90-91, 107, 159, 198
Big Spring (NE): 165
Births to emigrants: 100, 109, 158, 213
Bishop, Mr: 67, 97, 106-07
"Bisnette" (Bissonette, Joseph): 232

Bissonette, Joseph: 40, 232
Black (Big) Vermillion River (KS): 89, 107, 157, 158; "Burr Oak Creek," 159
Bloomington Herald, The (IA): 46
Blue Mountains: 182, 183, 187, 236, 237
Boats: Mackinaw, 141, 168; Columbia R., 189, 190; canoe, 191; schooner, 191; flatboats on Platte R., 201
Boise River: 180, 181, 182
Bonneville, Benjamin L. E.: 54
Bowman, Mrs. William: 100
Bradford Mill (OR): 250
Bray, Edmund: 28, 63, 92, 120, 121, 130, 144, 172
Bridger, James: 36, 52
"Bridgers & Vasqueses trading house" (Ft. Bridger): 171
Brown's Hole (WY): 37, 49, 106, 195
Browning, Mr: 107
Buffalo: 161, 169, 203ff.
"Buffalo pemmican": 176
Bunton, Nellie: 214
Burnett, Peter H: 43, 71, 175, 182
"Burnett's Trace" (KS): 156, 157
Burnt River: 181, 183, 184
"Burr Oak Creek" (KS): 159
Bush, George Washington: 176
Butter Creek (OR): 194

California, emigrants to: 16, 28, 38, 41, 46, 47, 49, 120, 121, 137ff., 144, 174, 248
California gold fields: 244, 248
California gold rush (1849-53): 15, 16, 17, 132
"California Road": 19
"Callapoola" (schooner): 191
Camp, Charles: 232
Camp (corral), description: 160-61
Cape Horn (on Columbia River): 194
Caples' Landing (MO): 57, 67
Caples, Joe: 191
Carson, Kit: 31